what **love** does and why it **matters**

Romance, Relationships, and 1 Corinthians 13

■ ■ ■

Cameron Lee

FULLER INSTITUTE FOR
RELATIONSHIP EDUCATION
Pasadena, California

FULLER

INSTITUTE FOR
RELATIONSHIP EDUCATION

Published by the Fuller Institute for Relationship Education
Fuller Theological Seminary, Pasadena, CA

Cover design: Randa K. Lee

ISBN-10: 069293331X
ISBN-13: 978-0692933312

contents

read me first

On love, everybody is a flailing expert and nobody is original.[1]

Maybe I'm crazy.

So many books, poems, songs, and learned essays have been written about love. It's been analyzed and rhapsodized again and again. Do we really need another book?

I believe we do.

Here's what you need to know about the crazy person writing this book. I wear many hats. As a seminary professor, I teach courses on marriage and family life, and most of my students are training to be therapists. As a minister, I teach a weekly Bible class, preach, and officiate weddings. As a family life educator, I run workshops for couples and parents. I've been a dad myself for over three decades and married to the same wonderful woman for nearly four. These experiences come together in the conviction that we could all use a better understanding of what the Bible means by love.

When couples invite me to perform their wedding ceremonies, I ask if there are particular passages from the Bible that they'd like to have read. The most frequent answer by far is the so-called "love chapter," the poetic description of love found in 1 Corinthians 13:[2]

> Love is patient, love is kind, it isn't jealous, it doesn't brag, it isn't arrogant, it isn't rude, it doesn't seek its own advantage, it isn't irritable, it doesn't keep a record of complaints, it isn't happy with injustice, but it is happy with the truth. Love puts up with all things, trusts in all things, hopes for all things, endures all things. Love never fails. (1 Cor 13:4-8a)

Over the years, I've come to center every wedding sermon on that text, whether the couple requests it or not. I solemnly remind them of God's incredible, patient love for them, and spell out the practical implications of what that means for how they love each other.

Unfortunately, I'm not sure how much of the sermon they actually hear.

That's understandable. For months, they've been obsessed with wedding planning. Secure the venue. Recruit the minister. Negotiate (argue?) with parents over the guest list. Get the invitations out. Find the perfect wedding dress. Choose your colors. Deal with the awkwardness of who's in the wedding party and who isn't. Plan the reception. Figure out the seating. Handle family drama.

By the time the couple gets to the ceremony, they're ready to be done. They're focused on each other, listening only for those final words: "I now pronounce you husband and wife."

I get it. A wedding ceremony isn't a classroom, and I don't expect them to listen the same way as they would for a final exam. But the romantic afterglow of the wedding soon fades. The bride and groom have to get down to the business of being married, for better or for worse. It would be a pity if Paul's words were lost in the shuffle.

Many people, of course, have noticed how often those words find their way into weddings. That includes Robert Polhemus, an English literature scholar. But he's critical of the practice:

> In many wedding ceremonies nowadays...brides and grooms opt to have read Paul's famous "hymn to love"... The biblical context, however, contradicts the modern translation and interpretation. Paul, in this very epistle, denigrates marriage and subordinates it to celibacy as the preferable condition. The "love" that he extols...is not the kind of ideal erotic love that a contemporary audience witnessing a marriage now projects onto a man and woman; it is rather a specifically spiritual Christian love of, by, for, and through Almighty God. The modern performance of the Pauline text usurps the sacred love in Scripture and transmutes it into the requited love of mating people.[3]

I agree with much of what he says. Though the love Paul describes is not of the romantic variety, his words get filtered through the romantic ideals associated with the wedding ceremony and with marriage itself. The crowning statement that "love never fails," for example, may be heard as a vague hope that the warm feelings of the day will last forever. Clearly, that's not what Paul is saying.

But I disagree with Polhemus as well. Paul doesn't "denigrate" marriage. Instead, he holds up the ideal that all Christians should be fully devoted to God, whatever their marital status. And I'm leery of the idea that Paul is teaching a "specifically spiritual" kind of love. Indeed, one of the problems he's dealing with is that some of the believers in the city of Corinth are all too eager to spiritualize *everything*. Their theology is lopsided, their behavior follows, and relationships in the church have suffered (including marriages).

Paul isn't writing about some esoteric kind of spirituality. He is teaching a way of thinking and being that applies to our relationships in very down-to-earth ways.

Nor is he writing about romance or marriage. He's a pastor solving problems in a confused congregation. The Corinthians are supposed to be brothers and sisters in Christ, a family whose life together demonstrates the truth of the gospel. But they're a proud, self-centered lot, who tend to care more about themselves than about each other.

Paul has to show them a better way, a higher way (1 Cor 12:31). And in our own churches and relationships, we have a lot to learn from what he tells them, whether we're getting married or not.

■ ■ ■

It's easy to find plaques, posters, and wall art adorned with verses from 1 Corinthians 13. I have one of these knick-knacks myself; it's in the shape of a cross, with the single word "love" standing out in bold, flowing script. Many inspirational and practical books about relationships also quote from 1 Corinthians 13. It's harder, however, to find books written for a broad reading audience that focus on Paul's love chapter and draw intently upon both biblical scholarship and the psychology of relationships. That's the reason for this book.

I have preached, taught, and blogged extensively about Paul's letters to the Corinthians because I believe we need to grapple with what Paul says. But I also believe that we won't understand him rightly unless we first grapple with what he was trying to teach the *Corinthians*, in the context of that church and those relationships. Only then will we be properly prepared to ask how Paul's teaching about love applies to our relationships today.

I've learned from experience that this is not, in fact, the way many Christians think about the love chapter. Much well-meaning reflection on 1 Corinthians 13 ends up sentimentalizing Paul's teaching, as if it had been written for a Hallmark card.

Jesus calls those who follow him to love one another (John 15:12). Again, it's easy to soften or sentimentalize the commandment. But Jesus isn't just telling us to be nice to each other (though a little niceness wouldn't hurt). He's setting out our vocation as Christians. Jesus embodied the Father's love, and as his disciples, we too are called to be living examples of God's loving character, through the power of the Holy Spirit.

Hopefully, we know ourselves to be broken people in a broken world. Love may be God's very nature (e.g., 1 John 4:8), but it isn't ours. Before we look at what Paul teaches in 1 Corinthians 13, therefore, I want to set the stage by looking at some of the challenges to understanding and embodying love: our language is inadequate, our emotions are fickle, and our imaginations have been shaped by what I call a "culture of romance."

We don't come to the subject of love as blank slates. Rather, we come to our relationships with a history of personal experience and cultural conditioning—and the same was true of the Corinthians. If we are to embody what Paul teaches about love, we'd do well to examine the assumptions that we already inhabit.

Thus, in chapter 1 we'll look at the rich but sometimes confusing variety of ways that we use the word "love." Feeling a need for clarity, we might turn to the Greek word *agape* to define for us the distinctive biblical difference between Christian love and other forms. But the reality is more complicated. When we speak of "love" we are naming something that words can't quite capture. Moreover, to speak of "Christian love" is not to name something entirely distinct from how love is understood more generally. It is, rather, to name our calling: to embody in our day-to-day relationships the love of God as demonstrated in the life and death of Jesus Christ.

Again, that embodiment comes with its challenges. Much of what we mean by "love" is shaped by personal history and cultural values, including what we've learned about romantic relationships. In chapter 2, we'll examine a crucial aspect of that personal history: the emotional dimension of love. We can commit to love as a conscious act of will, but it would be naïve to ignore the unconscious influence of emotional experience.

We then turn to an exploration of the stories and images of love in popular media. We both enjoy and are shaped by our culture's tales of romance. Nothing wrong with that. But have you ever noticed how often the characters in those stories do unloving things in the name of love? We root for those characters, so we look the other way and chalk it all up to the madness of romantic obsession. If we want to know what Paul means by love, however, that attitude won't do.

In chapter 3, therefore, we'll take a closer look at the genre of romantic comedy, from the novels of Jane Austen to Pixar Studios' *WALL-E*. Chapter 4 tackles the subject of fantasy and fairy tale, from Spider Man to the Disney Princesses. Other pop culture expressions, of course, could be used. The point of both chapters is to encourage us to reflect on the lessons of love we've already learned from our culture, and how these might affect the way we read and hear Paul.

Chapter 5 offers a transitional meditation on suffering and the love of God. With the apostle John, Christians affirm that "God is love" (1 John 4:8). How can we love others as Paul directs unless we first believe that God loves us? But it's hard to hold onto that belief when we're in the midst of personal pain. In this chapter, we remember Paul himself as a man who suffered greatly for the gospel and yet was not ashamed to preach a message of love. We then use Jesus' parable of the Prodigal Son to immerse ourselves again in the extravagant mercy of a loving Father.

With chapter 6 we launch into the direct study and application of

1 Corinthians 13. I suggest that Paul's words should be understood against the background of his larger argument about spiritual gifts, and offer a diagram illustrating the structure of the love chapter itself. In essence, Paul answers the Corinthians' concerns about spiritual gifts by giving them a vision of love that will enable them to recognize what's wrong with their behavior toward each other.

The remaining chapters focus specifically on the famous verses we read earlier, in which Paul uses sixteen different verbs to describe what true love does or doesn't do.[4] This is no abstract philosophy of love—it's his pastoral response to the Corinthians' problematic and unloving behavior.

We'll examine Paul's descriptors in order, two or three at a time, with chapter titles suggesting positively what loving Christians do. Those who love remember the patience and kindness of God toward them (chapter 7), repent of their rivalries (chapter 8), consider the well-being of others by "looking out for number two" (chapter 9), get off the merry-go-round of anger and resentment (chapter 10), and rejoice in the gospel (chapter 11). The study concludes with chapter 12, entitled "Love Story," in which we contemplate Paul's claim that love "never fails."

My approach to the subject, of course, is shaped by the kinds of experiences I mentioned at the outset. Much of my professional life is directly or indirectly devoted to helping couples and families succeed in their relationships. Many of the examples I give will therefore be directed toward the home. But again, Paul isn't writing a marriage manual; he's trying to redirect a troubled church. I will therefore also apply what we learn about love to congregations and the Christian life in general.

I've kept the more academic details to a minimum by putting explanations, citations, and references in extensive endnotes at the back of the book. Each chapter also ends with a brief section entitled "Talk or Think About It," in which I've included questions you can use for further personal reflection or group discussion. I hope you'll take advantage of the questions; they should help the content of each chapter come alive in a more personal way.

A note on group discussion. Some of the questions are designed just to get people talking and telling stories. Some are designed to go deeper, and will require some vulnerability to answer. If you're going to discuss these in a group setting, please remember to keep the group a safe place to explore new ideas. For example, give the person who is speaking your full respect and attention, and listen with curiosity. Keep what's said in the group confidential. And make space for others—don't hog the conversation!

Many people have given graciously of their time to respond to earlier drafts of the manuscript. As always, my wife Suha has been my initial sounding board, patiently listening and commenting as I read each chapter to her aloud. Indeed, the production of the book has been something of a family affair. My son Jonathan, a literature scholar, gave me helpful feedback on my use of Jane Austen in chapter 3; my daughter Randa, a photographer and graphic artist, designed the cover of the book.

Still others caught the typos I missed, and helped me know when I needed to be more clear. My thanks and appreciation, therefore, to the following friends and colleagues (in alphabetical order): Brandon Bathauer, Joseph Choe, Maggie Dalzell, Erika Knuth, Andrew McKeown, Kirsten Schmedes, and Nadia Siswanto. Thea Block not only read the manuscript closely, but also suggested ideas for some of the discussion questions used in the book. To all: your honest and constructive feedback has made the final result better than I could have by myself.

As I think of those to whom I owe a debt of gratitude, I remember the couples whose weddings I've officiated. What would I want them to know about love? What would it take for them to live out the promises they made to one another, in the sight of God, on their wedding day?

This book is dedicated to those couples. It's my way of continuing the conversation, and saying thank you for the privilege of being part of their special day. Here's what I wish I could have said, if only we had had the time.

what **love** does and why it **matters**

1

words can never be enough

What happened the first time you told someone, "I love you"?

I don't mean in the breezy way that some friends say it, with light-hearted affection. Nor do I mean the times your parents forced you to say it to Aunt Mildred. I'm talking about the first time you wanted to say, "I'm in love with you, and I hope you feel the same way about me."

Maybe it was an adolescent crush. The first time Andrea (not her real name) said it, she was 12 years old and had her eye on a boy in her French class. But she wasn't one of the cool kids. What could she do?

She had seen enough romance movies to believe the Hollywood storyline. Forget the differences in their backgrounds, in their popularity, in the way they looked and dressed. If she just declared her true feelings, everything would be fine. So she wrote him an anonymous note on bright pink paper, with a pop-up heart that said, "I love you."

Another girl was recruited to deliver the note in math class. But for whatever unknown and unfortunate reason, the other girl gave it to him at lunch, in front of all the other kids. Andrea writes, "Everyone turned to me and stared in complete bewilderment. His face flushed to a deep red—enough embarrassment to split between the two of us. It was never acknowledged again."[1]

That probably wasn't the Hollywood ending for which she had hoped.

"I love you." The words can be exhilarating, terrifying, or

mortifying, either to say or to hear. In romantic relationships, some blurt out the words too soon, wishing they could take them back. Others, in their ambivalence, keep silent until it's too late. No one knows for certain the right moment to say it for the first time; you take the leap and take your chances.

If you get a puppy-eyed look in response, congratulations.

If not, well, it's an opportunity to "define the relationship."

Part of the difficulty is that words are inadequate to convey everything we want to say. None of us come to relationships as blank slates. We say "I love you" out of a complicated mix of personality and personal history, emotion and expectation. Our imaginations are shaped by the stories and values of the cultural contexts in which we live. All of these factors work together to create what philosopher Robert Solomon calls our *love-worlds*, the implicit hopes and dreams we have for love.[2] To be in love is not just to have a feeling toward someone but to want to share an identity with them. You may not have an actual script in front of you. But there are roles to play, and you intuitively know if the other person isn't getting it right.

Thus, when you say "I love you," you want the other to say the same thing back, mean it, and mean the same thing you mean. If you get the wrong response, it feels more significant than just a flubbed line; it can feel like rejection or a catastrophic failure of hope.

How can three little words be so significant? And how can two people say the same words and mean something so different? It's because the words point beyond themselves to entire love-worlds which have yet to be completely mapped. Indeed, even the single word "love" points beyond itself to something that language can't quite contain. Consider, for example, the opening lines of the well-known sonnet by Elizabeth Barrett Browning:

How do I love thee? Let me count the ways.
I love thee to the depth and breadth and height
My soul can reach, when feeling out of sight
For the ends of Being and ideal Grace.[3]

"Let me count the ways." Browning doesn't list the qualities of her beloved, but meditates on the ways of love itself.[4] Few, I think, would accuse Browning of not getting it right. But no poet or philosopher will ever get it all. Human language may be a wondrous thing, but language has its limits. All the love sonnets in the world, taken together with all the learned discourses and psychological studies, can't capture all that we mean by "love."

The wonder of language also gives us these words of the apostle John: "God is love" (1 John 4:8). Without language, we couldn't have such an astonishing statement. There would be no Bible and no theology, no books or sermons to help us understand God. But we don't worship words; we worship the God to whom the words imperfectly and humbly point. Neither love nor the God who is love can ever be completely captured in language.

I will not, therefore, attempt to define love. The dictionary that sits next to my desk already gives eleven definitions for the noun, plus another six for the verb. I have no intention of adding to the list, nor of choosing my two or three favorites. Philosophers and scientists have their own reasons for wanting more precision (and as I'll argue in chapter 2, not always to a good end). But I doubt that such scholarly work will do much to change the fact that people actually use the word in a multitude of overlapping ways.

That's where we'll begin: with a personal look at the many ways in which we use the word "love." By the end of the chapter, I hope to make a case for the idea that Christians don't need a unique definition of love, not even one based on the supposed distinctions between different words in biblical Greek. When Christians use the word "love," they mean some of the same things that others do, and have some of the same joys and struggles. The real question is not what love is, but what love *does*—specifically, what the love of God in Jesus Christ does to transform all these other expressions of love from the inside out.

■ ■ ■

Let's start with a little thought experiment. I'm going to give you what psychologists call a "sentence completion task." That's a fancy way of saying that I'm going to start a sentence, and I want you to finish it with the first thing that comes to mind. Don't overthink it.

Ready? Then quickly come up with two or three different ways that you would complete this sentence: "I love _____."

Got it? I'll wait.

■ ■ ■

Now let's compare notes. Here are some of my answers:

I love my wife.
I love my children.
I love sushi and fried chicken (not together).

For me, all these statements are true. But surely the word "love" means something different in each case. Think about your own list: what do *you* mean when you say you love something or someone?

When we use the word "love," we're naming a moving target of thoughts, feelings, and behaviors. Sometimes we're trying to describe something deep, lasting, and significant. When I say that I love my wife, for example, I think of what a wonderful person she is and how grateful I am for the decades we've shared together.

Our love, however, has changed over the years. You may know what it's like to be in love with someone in a way that sets your pulse racing. There are times when you can hardly think of anything or anyone else. It was like that when we met in college. We were serious and silly, giddy and confused. We said and did things that, frankly, we're embarrassed to remember. (Don't ask.) Then we married at the ripe old age of twenty-one. Two years later, on our second anniversary, we left our families behind and headed off to graduate school.

Our early years of marriage came with predictable challenges. We had to adjust to the differences in our personalities, make our way through school, and learn the ropes as new parents. We rarely fought openly; we tended to simmer quietly instead. As with many couples, it was easy to think, "If you really loved me, you would ____," filling in the blank with the annoyance of the moment. We knew we loved each other. But there were days we could only have said it as a matter of principle.

In time, we mellowed and gained perspective. Our personality differences haven't gone away. What changed was our ability to not make such an issue of them. In other words, hand in hand, we grew up a bit. Disagreements matter less, because we've been through enough together to know that we can count on each other.

Some couples say they are still madly and romantically in love even after decades of marriage. Honestly, I wouldn't say that myself. Recently, my wife suggested that instead of our taking walks together, I should sometimes walk by myself. That way, I could get more cardiovascular exercise; I could walk faster and get my heart rate up. "But, dear," I said impishly, "my heart already beats faster when we're together." There was a brief pause—then we both burst out laughing. Does that mean we don't love each other? Hardly. But these days, our love is less about passion than the warm feeling of security, trust, and contentment.

I also love my children. They're grown now, but I've loved them since the day they were born, perhaps even before. When my son was still in the womb, my wife would sit in the recliner and I would kneel on the floor to talk to him.

This love also changes as kids grow. At first, as we count their tiny fingers and toes, we're awash in feelings of awe and protectiveness—and terrified by an enormous sense of responsibility. But sooner or later, most of us fall in love with our infants. The magical moment is often baby's first unmistakably social smile, the one that says, "Hey, I know you...Hi!" That's when we get the gratifying feeling of having a relationship with someone who's genuinely glad to see us.

That relationship, of course, has its ups and downs. There's the sweet smell of a freshly bathed baby and the stench of dirty diapers.

There are bedtime snuggles and sleepless nights, heartfelt hugs and temper tantrums. As they grow, children make good decisions and bad decisions. They have triumphs and failures.

What keeps Mom and Dad going? Amongst other things, love. We suffer when someone breaks our child's heart, and when our child breaks ours. But we hang in there anyway. It's all part of what it means to love our kids.

Compared to our love for spouses and children, other uses of the word "love" may seem banal. I say I love sushi (*good* sushi, anyway) and fried chicken. Some might object that this isn't love—perhaps it would be better to say I "really enjoy" these things instead?

But that's not what I mean. Some foods are special because of the associations that go with them, including when we eat them and with whom. For me, sushi is celebration food, to be eaten on vacation or on special occasions like birthdays. Fried chicken is more like comfort food. When I say I love them, I'm not just making a judgment about taste and texture. I'm trying to say something about an entire experience.

And so on. I could easily add to the list. I love Pixar movies. I love watching a good basketball game. I love to write. In everyday English, all of these uses of the word "love" are acceptable. You probably use the word in the same kaleidoscopic way. Love encompasses desire and pleasure, intimacy and satisfaction, aesthetic judgment and feelings of appreciation. The meanings don't fit neatly into any one box.

And the same might be said of how the Bible speaks of love.

■ ■ ■

Here are three more sentences:

I love God.
God loves me.
God is love.

Does the word "love" mean the same in these sentences as in the previous ones? Does it even mean the same across these three?

Say it out loud: "I love God." (Go ahead, try it—no one's around.) Perhaps you say it with warmth and full conviction, perhaps with reserve. Some of us might even feel a pang of guilt or regret: *I know I should love God more than I do...*

"I love God." We could all say the same words, but would we mean the same thing? Consider, for example, these words from the spiritual autobiography of Thérèse of Lisieux, a humble Carmelite nun who lived in 19th-century France:

> Now I wish for only one thing—to love Jesus even unto folly! Love alone attracts me. ...I no longer know how to ask passionately for anything except that the will of God be perfectly accomplished in my soul.[5]

Thérèse only lived to the age of 24. Though she never sought recognition, her example of devotion made her one of the most beloved of all the saints canonized by the Roman Catholic Church. On the morning she took her vows, she wrote a prayer to Jesus which she kept next to her heart:

> Take me, rather than let me stain my soul by the slightest deliberate fault. Let me neither look for nor find anyone but You and You alone. Let all creatures be as nothing to me and me as nothing to them. Let no earthly things disturb my peace. O Jesus, I ask only for peace—peace and above all LOVE that is without measure or limits. May I die as a martyr for You. Give me martyrdom of soul or body. Ah! rather give me both! Enable me to fulfill all my duties perfectly and let me be ignored, trodden underfoot, and forgotten like a grain of sand. To You, my Beloved, I offer myself so that You may fulfill in me Your holy Will without a single creature placing any obstacle in the way.[6]

How many of us would be able to claim that we love Jesus with that kind of single-minded surrender? I confess that I cannot. I suspect that most of us would say the same.

What about God's love for us? What does it even mean to say that God "loves"? Theologians through the ages have worried that we might speak of God's love in ways that would short-change his perfection and holiness. Their concern is understandable. If we can't even get our language straight about human love, how could we possibly speak meaningfully of God's love?

The primary biblical question, however, isn't whether and in what way God's love resembles ours, but whether ours resembles God's.[7] Again, the Bible not only claims that God loves us, but that God *is* love:

Dear friends, let's love each other, because love is from God, and everyone who loves is born from God and knows God. The person who doesn't love does not know God, because God is love. This is how the love of God is revealed to us: God has sent his only Son into the world so that we can live through him. This is love: it is not that we loved God but that he loved us and sent his Son as the sacrifice that deals with our sins. (1 John 4:7-10)

What does the apostle John mean when he says that God is love? Here again, language will fail us. But at the very least, we can read John as driving a theological stake into the ground. Whatever we mean by "love," God is the real deal. Human love has its root and reference point in what God has revealed of the divine nature, most particularly through the life and ministry of Jesus.

Some of us are so used to hearing about God's love that it no longer evokes the proper awe or astonishment. When we were children, for example, it was easy to take our parents' love for granted. Later, we may even have betrayed their care and kindness. Hopefully, they still loved us even then. They would have sacrificed just about anything for us to be happy and whole.

Is something similar true in our relationship to God? Do we take God's love for granted?

The analogy from our earthly parents to God, of course, is imperfect. As Marianne Meye-Thompson points out:

> Mom may be the most loving person you have known. She may have shown you what mature, self-giving, genuine love is like. But no matter how full, rich and steadfast her love, the statement "Mom is loving," can never be changed into "Mom is love." For love does not characterize her as it characterizes God.[8]

Only God is love. Only God's love as revealed to us in Jesus can be the ultimate standard. God loves because God is love. To say "I love God" should be a response to that fact, however imperfect our love may be.

Moreover, an honest profession of love has implications for how we see and respond to others:

> We love because God first loved us. If anyone says, I love God, and hates a brother or sister, he is a liar, because the person who doesn't love a brother or sister who can be seen can't love God, who can't be seen. This commandment we have from him: Those who claim to love God ought to love their brother and sister also. (1 John 4:19-21)

Jesus taught that the fulfillment of the entire law of Moses came down to two commandments: love God with your entire being, and love your neighbor (Matt 22:37-40). But if the truth be told, we don't love God as Thérèse did, and our love for others is often lukewarm at best. As John suggests, our inconsistency with the first commandment is the reason for our difficulty with the second.

Love God. Love your neighbor. The words are simple enough. We proclaim God's love on Sunday morning. We sing its praises. And then we emerge from our sanctuaries into a world of competing concepts of love. Does what we say and sing inside the church matter when we're outside?

Everybody wants "true love." But many would say they've never experienced it. Some despair of ever finding it. And it's in such a world that we are called as Christians to embody what we believe about love in the give and take of everyday life.

I don't believe that the Bible teaches one thing about love while the world teaches something entirely different. Such an oversimplification would make it more difficult to connect our faith to how we live and love. Like it or not, we are creatures whose thoughts, feelings, perceptions, and expectations are shaped by the cultures we inhabit and create. It's part of our God-given nature. When we say we love, we do so against a complex background of culture and personal history, of stories, myths, and relationships.

The story of a God who is love, and who demonstrates that love through the cross of Jesus, must enter into those stories. It must open them up from the inside, until at last our imaginations turn inside out: instead of understanding God as a character (albeit an important one!) in our life stories, we begin to see ourselves as characters in God's story. That's what God's love can and must do.

But that doesn't mean that we need a separate conceptual box for a specifically Christian love, distinct from everything else we mean by the word—not even if the box is labeled in Greek.

■ ■ ■

Okay, quick quiz. In the Bible, what's the Greek word that specifically means "Christian love"?

The answer may surprise you: there isn't one.

Again, in English, the single word "love" is used in a rich variety of ways. By contrast, the Greeks had at least four words for love—*storge, philia, eros,* and *agape*—which makes it easier to speak of love with more nuance.[9] *Storge,* for example, refers to something like family affection, while *philia* generally refers to the love between true friends. *Eros*—from which we get the English word "erotic"—is a kind of desire, or as C. S. Lewis once put it, "the kind of love which lovers are 'in.'"[10]   This word is absent from the New Testament. *Agape*, by contrast, is used so often that some people sometimes take it to mean "Christian love."

In secular literature, *eros* gets the lion's share of attention; romance is the reason people buy books about love. Often, *agape* gets barely a mention. But the situation is reversed in Christian literature. *Agape* is the star, and *eros* is demoted to second-class status or worse.

Christians, of course, don't own the word *agape* and never have. Today, for example, secular philosophers often use *agape* to mean a general, benevolent love toward all of humankind, in contrast with *eros,* a romantic love whose desire is focused on one particular individual.[11] Researchers and theorists have also created typologies of love, in which *agape* becomes one way people approach romance. Here, for example, is an excerpt from psychologist John Alan Lee's work on "love-styles":

> A familiar ideology, agape is the love-style urged on us by the Christian religion. It also happens to be—at least in my research—the least common love-style actually practiced in adult partnering relationships. Few of us are on the side of the angels when looking for a partner. Agape is selfless, giving, altruistic love. The lover considers it a duty to love, even when no loving feelings are present. ...Ironically, the most agapic expressions of love in our society may come from persons who practice celibacy and have neither lover nor mate. ...The agapic lover feels an intense duty to care affectionately for the beloved, and the beloved is defined as anyone in need of such care. Thus, the agapic lover in a relationship is likely to see the partner as only one of the many people in need.[12]

Christians might applaud the emphasis on selflessness, altruism, and duty. And it's fine to note that some people approach romance with a sense of moral obligation. Lee (no relation) can call that *agape* if he likes. But does Christianity really "urge a love-style" on anybody? Instead of boxing in the biblical teaching by binding it to our questions about romantic relationships, we should be ready to have a biblical understanding burst the boundaries of our romantic ideals.

Some of how Christians understand the difference between *eros* and *agape* can be traced back to Anders Nygren, a Swedish theologian who in 1953 published an enormous volume on the subject.[13] Nygren wanted to keep *eros* and *agape* in separate boxes, and claimed that this was what the Bible taught. To him, *eros*, the love based on desire and need, was clearly inferior to the unselfish and undeserved *agape* of God. Later writers, following his distinction, commonly referred to the two as *need-love* and *gift-love*, respectively.[14]

But does the distinction work? Can biblical references to love be divided so neatly into these linguistic boxes? On the one hand, I won't deny that God's love is superior to any of our faltering affections. On the other hand, however, I've always admired the honesty of C. S. Lewis, who confessed to the kind of high-minded snobbery that the distinction invites:

> "God is love," says St. John. When I first tried to write this book I thought that his maxim would provide me with a very plain highroad through the whole subject. I thought I should be able to say that human loves deserved to be called loves at all just so far as they resembled that Love which is God. The first distinction I made was therefore between what I called Gift-Love and Need-love. ...There was no doubt which was more like Love Himself. Divine Love is Gift-love. ...And what, on the other hand, can be less like anything we believe of God's life than Need-love? ...I was looking forward to writing some fairly easy panegyrics on the first sort of love and disparagements of the second. ...But I would not now say...that if we mean only this craving we are mistaking for love something that is not love at all. I cannot now deny the name *love* to Need-love. ...The reality is more complicated than I supposed.[15]

That includes the reality of the biblical Greek. In 1 John 4, for example, the word *agape* is used to refer to God's love for us, our love for God, and our love for one another as believers. At first glance, that would seem to support the idea that *agape* refers to a specifically Christian kind of love.

But earlier in the same letter, John writes: "Don't *love* the world or the things in the world. If anyone *loves* the world, the *love* of the Father is not in them" (1 John 2:15). The word "love" appears three times in that sentence, and each time, it's *agape*—despite the fact that the first two instances describe an inappropriate, worldly kind of love. Similarly, *agape* is used in John 3:16 to describe the saving love of God—but just a few verses later (vs. 19), the love that evildoers have for the darkness.

Or consider Jesus' criticism of the Pharisees: "They *love* to sit in places of honor at the banquets and in the synagogues" (Matt 23:6). It sounds like Jesus is describing selfish desire, so we might expect the word *eros*. But Matthew uses *philia*. And to make things even more confusing, the parallel passage in Luke says, "How terrible for you Pharisees! You *love* the most prominent seats in the synagogues and respectful greetings in the marketplaces" (Luke 11:43). Luke's word is neither *eros* nor *philia*, but *agape*.

In other words, the Bible doesn't support the kind of clean distinction between *agape* and erotic desire that Nygren wants.[16] Here's one more striking example. In Genesis 34, we read the story of a man named Shechem who sees Jacob's daughter Dinah and falls head over heels for her. The text says, "He *loved* the young woman and tried to win her heart" (Gen 34:3). That sounds romantic enough. But Shechem had taken Dinah by force and raped her, prompting a bloody revenge by her brothers (34:13-31). And disturbingly, the Greek translation of the Hebrew text describes Shechem's love as *agape*.[17]

It's not that all of the Greek words for love are completely interchangeable or mean the same thing. But each has multiple meanings and uses, and the words overlap. Arguing that a Bible verse is pointing to a special kind of love simply because the word *agape* is being used is, in the words of one scholar, "linguistic nonsense."[18] Indeed, the word was already in wide use before the New Testament was written, suggesting that the biblical authors weren't selecting a special word, but the "normal" one.[19]

What, then, becomes of the attempt to base a biblical understanding of love on some distinct definition of the word *agape*? Gary Badcock puts it this way:

> the New Testament usage, on the whole, simply does not support the notion of an utterly distinctive concept of "gift love," as opposed to "need love"... [I]t is difficult to sustain the idea that agape as divine love and Christian love is to be totally distinguished from other forms of human love.[20]

Of course, there's some wiggle room in Badcock's word, "totally." Careful study of the meaning of Greek words is still profitable, as I hope later chapters in this book will demonstrate. Some distinctions are both possible and useful.

But the Bible's depiction of love is richly diverse, and that includes its depiction of God's love for us. Thus, we shouldn't confine a Christian understanding of love to a box labeled "agape," especially if the word is too narrowly defined. That would risk reading that narrow meaning back into biblical texts that are describing something different. Just think of the strange and forced interpretations we would get by trying to understand Shechem's desire for Dinah as altruistic or benevolent.

God is love, and Jesus was God in the flesh (John 1:14). Love permeates the whole of the gospel story, not just where the word "love" appears. Jesus welcomed sinners to the dinner table, showed compassion to the sick, embraced children, and put up night and day with twelve unruly and thick-headed men, one of whom conspired to have him killed. Moreover, the cross itself was the supreme demonstration of God's love (John 15:12; Rom 5:8). If we looked up all the verses in the Bible containing the word "love," our search wouldn't necessarily take us to any of these passages. But surely they demonstrate the meaning and embodiment of God's love.

Thus, whether in English or Greek, the word "love" has many meanings, pointing to an experience that virtually everyone knows but no one can completely define. Even biblical uses of the word *agape* can't be neatly separated from such things as romantic desire and family affection.

What, then, do we mean by "Christian love"?

To be honest, I'm a little wary of the phrase. It makes "Christian love" sound like a separate option on a menu of ethical choices. If you read 1 Corinthians 13, much of what Paul says about love simply sounds like good advice. Be kind. Don't be selfish. Don't be rude. Who could argue with that? In short, it doesn't sound specifically *Christian.*

And it doesn't have to.

Again, Paul isn't giving the disorderly Corinthians a list of dos and don'ts that only Christians would appreciate. Instead, he wants them to understand his instructions against the background of the gospel story of which they are a part. *My beloved,* he seems to say, *don't you understand what God has done for you in Jesus? Don't you know that God is making you into someone new, including being one body in Christ? Then why are you still acting this way?*

Looking for a unique definition of a distinctly Christian love sometimes gets things the wrong way around. What Christians do in the name of love may look a lot like what others do. What makes love specifically Christian is not some uniquely altruistic quality of action. It's grateful wonder at the good news of the love of God as revealed to us in and through Jesus. It's the empowering presence of the Spirit of Christ in us. It's the desire to keep discovering who we are in Christ—and who we are becoming. It's having our imaginations transformed by the Spirit when we think of and respond to others, especially those whom we would rather keep at arm's length.

As Christians, in other words, we love because God first loved us. No truly Christian understanding of love can ever be separated from the story of what God has done in Jesus Christ and continues to do through his Spirit. So if we need a name for Christian love, perhaps it should simply be this: *Jesus*. As Phil Ryken has written:

> Whenever we talk about love, we always have to go back to Jesus. The love in the Love Chapter is really his love. …We will never learn how to love by working it up from our own hearts but only by having more of Jesus in our lives.[21]

Paul understood himself as called to follow the example of Christ in all that he did, and he urged the Corinthians to do the same (1 Cor 11:1). If we're honest with ourselves, we have to admit that we can be as clueless—and as loveless—as the Corinthians.

And when we recognize that, we're ready to learn from Paul.

■ ■ ■

The word "love" thus points to a reality for which human language—even Greek!—will always be inadequate. Christian love is not a particular species of love to be set alongside others in a typology. Nor do Christians, overall, feel different feelings than non-Christians. To be sure, the gospel may evoke love in new situations, but the emotional experience of what we call love will still be the same.

To speak of Christian love is to name our calling. We must live in a way that declares the good news of a great gift: in and through Christ, the God who is love has literally loved us to death. That same God now calls and empowers us to live in that love, here, now, in the midst of all the messiness of human relationships.

As I write these words, it's Christmas morning. The house is quiet. I'm prayerfully reminded that at Christmas, we celebrate the fact that the Son of God took on our human nature. As the old hymn says, "Love came down at Christmas":

> Love came down at Christmas,
> Love all lovely, Love divine;
> Love was born at Christmas,

Star and angels gave the sign.

Worship we the God-head,
Love incarnate, Love divine,
Worship we our Jesus,
But wherewith for sacred sign?

Love shall be our token;
Love be yours and love be mine;
Love to God and others,
Love for plea and gift and sign.[22]

Love came to us at Christmas, to live in a mortal body like ours: Jesus was divine love "incarnate." In the Christian doctrine of the Incarnation, the church affirms that Jesus Christ was "of one substance" with God the Father but also a flesh-and-blood human being.[23] One implication of Jesus' humanity is that he wrestled with real relationships in the real world. He knew what it meant to live amongst family and friends. He knew how it felt to love and care for them. To depend on them. To argue with them. To be hurt by them. He knew joy and sorrow, desire and disappointment. Like us, Jesus experienced the ups and downs of what it means to be human.

Unlike us, however, his love for God and neighbor was wholehearted. He even loved his enemies—and he called us to do the same (Matt 5:43-48). That's the "sacred sign" to which the hymn calls us: how we love God and others points back to the truth of divine love incarnate.

We are called to be living, breathing signs of God's love, to love not only our family and friends, but also our enemies. And part of the challenge is that even those closest to us often feel like enemies. The people whom we love the most can be the ones who push our buttons the hardest and make us crazy.

That's life. Relationships are an indispensable part of human existence—and they are laden with feeling. As we'll discuss in the next chapter, if we're going to embody what the Bible teaches about love, we'll have to do so amidst the swirl of everyday human emotions.

talk or think about it

1.   If you haven't done so already, try the exercise described at the beginning of the chapter. As quickly and spontaneously as possible, come up with two to three ways you would complete the sentence, "I love..." As a group, discuss what "love" means in each sentence.

2.   What does it mean to you personally to say that you "love God"? And what does it mean to you to say that God loves you? If people in the group give somewhat different answers, what do you make of the similarities and differences?

3.   What, if anything, have you been taught about the meaning of the Greek word *agape*? What difference does it make to you to know that the word has a variety of uses in Scripture?

4.   I have argued that "Christian love" cannot be entirely distinct from other meanings and expressions of love. It is not a "kind" of love, but the declaration that we are called to live out the truth of the gospel of God's love in all of our relationships, including our so-called "romantic" ones. Describe some practical consequences this might have for your own relationships.

2

love and emotion

Mooning over our first crush. Falling head over heels in love. Finding and marrying our soul mate. All of this is part of the language and mythology of romantic love that shapes our experiences and expectations. Maybe you remember a time when you were so much in love that you could hardly do anything except daydream about the object of your affection. If not, it's a safe bet that you know someone who has.

Or maybe you were smitten with a person you'd just met. The French have a term for it: *coup de foudre*, the "lightning bolt." Romantic love can happen, as they say, "at first sight," like a bolt out of the blue, in the most unexpected of places and with the most unexpected of people.

We see it in the movies all the time. *That Touch of Mink*, a 1962 romantic comedy starring Cary Grant and Doris Day, is a classic example.[1]   Grant plays a wealthy businessman whose limousine accidentally drenches Day's dress with dirty rainwater as it speeds by. She's furious, and marches into his office to give him a piece of her mind. But when she sees him for the first time, dreamy music begins to play, and the camera goes soft-focus. She gets one look at that famous cleft chin, and *bam!* She's in love, and soon finds herself jetting around the world as his mistress.

The thunderbolt. Love at first sight. It just happens. We can't explain it, and it makes us act in strange and unpredictable ways.

Is this just a Hollywood fiction? Some research suggests that it isn't.

In 1979, psychologist Dorothy Tennov published her research on love at first sight, using stories told by hundreds of people from different walks of life.[2] Not everyone she interviewed, of course, reported being hit by the thunderbolt. Indeed, some who didn't—together with Tennov's critics—had a hard time believing that anyone could be so muddle-headed.

But there was no denying that romantic lightning did strike at least some people, like this college student, a young man majoring in mathematics:

> I looked up from my books and there was Marilyn. It was an immediate reaction—on both parts, or so it seemed at the time. I would say that within a week—less than that, within three days—my whole world had been transformed. It had a new center, and that center was Marilyn.[3]

What sparked the attraction? No one knows for certain. Romantic passion can be ignited by a variety of subtle cues.[4] We notice each other. We exchange glances. We begin to fall. And the euphoria of newfound love can color our whole existence, as it did for this young woman:

> Problems, troubles, inconveniences of living that would normally have occupied my thoughts became unimportant. I looked at them over a huge gulf of sheer happiness. ...My delight in simply existing eclipsed everything else, and I literally could scarcely feel the ground as I walked. ...Colors seemed more brilliant. ...I glowed and the world glowed back at me. ...No one was an enemy anymore! My affection included the universe. I loved every single creature. A fly landed on my desk, I hadn't the heart to brush it away.[5]

"Wow," you might say. "She's got it bad." But people in this state really do begin to see the world differently. Thoughts of the other intrude throughout the day. The beloved almost glows with positive qualities while negative qualities are downplayed. Lovers look diligently for signs of being loved back; a simple smile or a kind word can leave them walking on air. But other behaviors may be taken as signs of rejection, leading to feelings of emptiness and heartache.[6]

When Tennov began her study, romantic love wasn't considered a legitimate topic for scientific investigation. Researchers were content to let the poets deal with it. Her work, however, was embraced by readers who finally found their own experiences validated in print. Others remained skeptical, even though they grudgingly accepted the stories as true.

There will always be something a little disturbing about the idea of falling so helplessly and irrationally in love. As one author describes it:

Romantic love, it seems, is a panoply of intense emotions, roller-coastering from high to low, hinged to the pendulum of a single being whose whims command you to the detriment of everything around you—including work, family, and friends.[7]

That sounds more like love-sickness than love. And to be sure, some romantic obsessions do grow to pathological proportions. (We've seen *that* in the movies, too.) But many of you reading this book, or others close to you, have experienced the passion Tennov describes.

We just don't talk about it at church. We're too spiritual for that. Aren't we?

Passion is part of the embodied existence with which we have been endowed by God. In this chapter, therefore, we explore the world of emotion. From a biblical perspective, of course, love is more than emotion—but the role of emotion in love cannot be denied. Unfortunately, Christians through the ages have tried to bypass the messiness and inconstancy of our emotions by making the commandment to love a test of willpower. But any concept of love that fails to acknowledge the role of emotion will be out of touch with our lived experience.

■ ■ ■

Decades of research have made it abundantly clear: emotions play an important but often invisible role in our lives. As Sue Johnson has written: "Emotion apprises us that something vital to our welfare is occurring. ...Our feelings guide us in issues large and small; they tell us what we want, what our preferences are, and what we need."[8] Emotions operate more quickly and spontaneously than conscious thought to evaluate what's happening in our physical and social environment. In a sense, our emotions are constantly asking, "Is it good? Bad? Dangerous? And what should I do about it?"[9]

Thus, contrary to the common idea that reason and emotion are enemies, emotions are actually "intelligent" in the sense that they help us navigate the world.[10] They learn from experience what's safe and what isn't, then work in the background to nudge (or shove!) us in the right direction.[11]

Some emotional responses, in fact, seem to be automatic. Think about what happens when you feel something crawling on you. You don't stop to rationally assess the situation. Instead, your body reacts and you start swatting at yourself without thinking. The reaction may be a false alarm—there's no spider. But at the level of our neurology, the working principle is "better safe than sorry": when survival may be at stake, it's better to overreact than not to react at all.[12]

As neuroscientist Antonio Damasio has shown, emotions like fear and anxiety work like a silent alarm system.[13] Imagine you've been invited to his laboratory to play the following game. There are four decks of cards face down on the table in front of you. You draw cards one at a time from any deck you choose, and turn them face up. Each card tells you that you've won or lost so many dollars of play money, and your goal is to win as much as you can.

You're not told, of course, that the game is rigged. Two of the decks are "good." Draw from these, and your winnings will slowly pile up. The other decks are "bad." They tempt you with bigger payoffs, but also punish you with big losses. That way lies failure.

If you're like most participants, you learn quickly which decks are bad and start avoiding them. But you may not be consciously aware of doing so. What's happening is that the repeated experience of being punished by the bad decks is registering in your silent alarm system and warning you away.

Participants with specific types of brain damage, however, keep losing the game. Even if they can tell the experimenter which decks are bad, they can't stay away from them. They're tempted by the higher reward, and lack the silent warning needed to overcome the temptation.[14]

Many people speak of reason and emotion as if they were at odds with each other. Emotion is treated as a bothersome reality that gets in the way of right thinking. And it's true that strong emotion can overwhelm our ability to think calmly and clearly.

But Damasio's research (and numerous studies like it) demonstrates that the relationship between emotion and reason is more complicated than we usually realize. Put simply, if our emotions aren't doing their job properly, our decisions may be irrational. Our emotions help guide us in invisible ways even when our conscious, rational minds are unable to make sense of what's happening.

Here's a classic example. In 1911, a Swiss psychiatrist named Édouard Claparède was visiting a female patient who suffered from a severe memory disorder. He had spoken with her many times, and always greeted her with a handshake. But she couldn't remember their interactions. He had to reintroduce himself each time they met.

On one occasion, he purposely hid a pin between his fingers. When he shook hands with the patient, the pin pricked her and she withdrew in pain. The next time they met, she refused to take his hand. She was unable to explain why, because she had no conscious memory of the pinprick. But she retained an unconscious memory of it—an emotional memory—and this was enough to make her shy away.[15]

Today, Claparède's little experiment would be considered unethical. But it helped lay the basis for how we understand human memory. Think: where did you go on your last vacation? What was the name of your sixth grade teacher? Memories like these are *explicit* and conscious. Much of our emotional life, however, operates in an unconscious and *implicit* way. Through emotional memory, past experiences can influence present behavior in ways we don't notice.

This has important implications for how we live out our ideals of love. There are times in our close relationships when we have to make deliberate decisions about what to do next. But most of the time, we just respond without thinking. And like it or not, much of how we act, think, and feel in those relationships is shaped implicitly by past emotional experience. That's how we're wired. Emotions are part of our built-in security system that learns, adapts, and then predisposes us to act in ways that help us get what we need.

Thus, we may hold conscious ideals of love, even biblical ones. But putting those ideals into practice requires coming to terms with a sometimes inconvenient reality: how we love others relies in part on things happening below the surface of our awareness. That's because our first and perhaps most influential lessons in love were learned before we could even say the word.

■ ■ ■

I was boarding the last leg of a flight home from Chicago, having been away on business. I took my seat next to a young mother and the adorable one-year-old she had seated on her lap. Out of the blue, the mother apologized for her daughter. "I'm sorry," she said wearily. "But I just wanted to let you know that she's probably going to get cranky, and when she cries, she's loud. *Really* loud."

The young woman, it turns out, was the mother of three. It was the first time Mom and baby had been separated for so long from Dad and the boys. And it was their third flight of the day.

A little crankiness, in other words, was to be expected.

I flashed back to when our kids were young. It had been difficult to travel. I remembered how it felt to have others look at us with eyes that said, "What's the matter with you people? Why can't you control your kid?" The mom had already had that embarrassing experience on an earlier flight, and was working overtime to keep the baby from touching or bothering me in any way.

I'm an introvert by nature, so I settled in to finish reading the book I had brought with me. But out of the corner of my eye, I could see the little girl watching me. I put the book down, and decided for all of our sakes that it was time to play.

Playing with a baby is a bit like dancing together—but mostly, it works best when you follow their lead. At her age, children tend to be wary of strangers, so I had to watch her responses carefully to avoid scaring her off. I waited for her to look my way, then turned (not too suddenly!) and smiled at her. She gave me the briefest flicker of a smile back, then buried her face in Mom's shoulder. That's baby-speak for, "Thank you, Mr. Whatever-Your-Name-Is, but that's enough eye contact for now."

I turned away and waited. From the corner of my eye I could see her peeking out at me, so I turned and smiled once more. I added a facial expression of mock surprise, and talked to her softly in that high-pitched exaggerated voice that adults reserve for children and pets.

And soon, we were playing together. She'd point to something in a magazine, then I'd point to something else. She'd make funny noises and I'd imitate her; then I would make a noise and she'd imitate me. Everything became a game. Put the sandal in the cup. Put the cup in another cup. Take it out and put it in again. And again. And again.

Kids don't need iPads to keep them entertained when they have a real live person to play with. There was no crying and no crankiness. The flight passed quickly, and everyone was happy.

Even me.

That kind of play illustrates what little children need from the big people in their lives. They need adults who will tune in to them, dance with them, and follow their lead. Through such interaction with their caretakers, they are learning about the world, about people, about themselves.

That learning begins well before a child is able to speak. Babies can't say, "I'm tired." But attentive adults notice the signs and act accordingly. Babies can't say, "Mom, I'm hungry," or "Dad, I'm scared." But they are capable of remembering—implicitly—how adults responded to them when they cried from hunger or fear, or signaled a readiness to play. Were they ignored? Yelled at? Did their parents come anxiously rushing to their aid, only to "fix" the wrong problem? Or did Mom and Dad quickly, calmly, and accurately read their signals and respond appropriately?

These, in effect, are a child's first lessons in love. Parents whose responses are consistently in tune with their baby's emotional states are laying a solid foundation for their emotional development.[16]

Babies and parents communicate in a hundred implicit, wordless ways. For example, consider the results of a well-known experiment known as the "visual cliff."[17] A baby is placed at one end of a flat surface, which is part transparent Plexiglas. Mom is at the other end. It's perfectly safe for the baby to crawl to her. Looking through the Plexiglas, however, he can see what looks like a four-foot drop. Thus, the baby is confused: the situation looks dangerous, but the surface feels solid. What will he do?

> A typical baby crawls to the edge of the cliff, sees the possible precipice, and then looks at his mother—and makes his assessment of the cliff's lethality by reading her expression. If she radiates calm, he continues crawling, but if he finds alarm on her face, the baby stops in his tracks and cries.[18]

Faced with uncertainty, the baby automatically looks to Mom (or Dad, as the case may be). He doesn't take his mother's facial expression as a neutral piece of information to be weighed in some kind of rational balance. He doesn't make a conscious decision about how to feel. Rather, through their wordless connection, her emotions become his.[19] If she shows fear, that emotion determines how he perceives the world—and he cries because he suddenly finds himself perched on the edge of a dangerous cliff.

This implicit connection between babies and their parents doesn't just happen in the psychologist's laboratory. As children climb down from their parents' laps and begin exploring their world, they look for guidance. And they find it in their parents' faces: children rely upon their parents' emotional cues to anticipate what's safe and what isn't.

There's much more to development, in other words, than mere physical survival. It's obvious that babies need big people to feed, clothe, and shelter them. But they also need strong, stable, and consistent connections with loving and attentive adults if they are to thrive emotionally. They need adults who will patiently and accurately decipher their squeaks and squawks and do what's needed. Without this, they will be hampered in their ability to trust others and to manage their emotions. In other words, it will be more difficult for them to learn to love well. As psychiatrist Norman Doidge has written:

> Children are needy and typically develop passionate attachments to their parents. If the parent is warm, gentle, and reliable, the child will frequently develop a taste for that kind of relationship later on; if the parent is disengaged, cool, distant, self-involved, angry, ambivalent, or erratic, the child may seek out an adult mate who has similar tendencies… [E]arly patterns of relating and attaching to others, if problematic, can get "wired" into our brains in childhood and repeated in adulthood.[20]

Not that Doidge believes for a moment that what happens to us in childhood determines our destiny, in love or anything else. Quite the contrary. Doidge is an enthusiastic advocate for the principle of *neuroplasticity*, an idea that has been demonstrated so many times in so many ways that it's taken as an incontrovertible fact by neuroscientists.

The brain learns from experience, such that early relationship patterns can get "wired" in. But neuroplasticity means that the brain is still capable of learning, changing, and adapting throughout life—of "rewiring" itself—making possible the most miraculous of recoveries from the most traumatic of injuries. Change may not come easily. But it is possible. And sometimes, the biggest barrier is not that we can't change, but that we *think* we can't.

We need to recognize the ways in which we bring what we've learned in past relationships into our present ones, without even knowing it. Researchers have shown time and time again that we can be driven by emotions we don't even know we're having. When experimenters subtly manipulate people's emotions in the lab, their perceptions, judgments, and behaviors shift accordingly. We're just not the coolly rational people some of us would like to believe.

But does that mean that we're incapable of reason? Even in matters of love? Hardly. It has become almost fashionable to use neuroscience to show all the ways in which reason fails. The irony, however, is that one must assume the proper operation of reason for one to understand the science in the first place.

The explosion of neuroscience in recent decades has given us tremendous new insight into the biology of emotion. But morally speaking, I believe it's short-sighted to narrow the definition of love to emotion and its underlying biology. The following is a case in point.

■ ■ ■

Barbara Fredrickson is a social psychologist. Her pioneering research on positive emotion has contributed enormously to our understanding of human happiness. She argues that states like joy and gratitude are not only enjoyable but good for us. When you're in the grip of positive emotion, you see the world differently. You notice creative possibilities that you might otherwise miss. And when you intentionally cultivate these emotions, you put yourself on an upward spiral of benefits.[21]

Fredrickson wants to cut through the tangle of competing understandings of love. You may have learned to think of love as desire, loyalty, or trust. But these things, Fredrickson insists, are just part of the social context. As a scientist, she wants to redefine love more simply as a momentary bodily experience she calls *positivity resonance*. From the body's point of view, love "springs up anytime two or more people connect over a shared positive emotion."[22] And such experiences of resonance are marked by specific biochemical changes.

Think about a time when you've shared a moment of real

connection with someone else. What was happening below the surface? As you responded unconsciously to fleeting expressions on your partner's face—a slight raising of the eyebrows, the beginnings of a smile—your brains literally synchronized. You both experienced the same emotion and felt understood. There was a surge of hormones that promoted feelings of calmness, trust, and cooperation.[23] And the more you connect like this, Frederickson argues, the more you'll experience benefits in other areas of your life. Ultimately, her hope is that understanding these benefits will help you cultivate the conditions needed for it to happen.

As suggested earlier, our bodies, and the emotions that come with them, are a gift of creation. We are inescapably biological creatures. Work like Fredrickson's may indeed help us learn how to foster healthier and more loving connections.

But here's the million-dollar question: why should our body get the last word? Restricting the definition of love to biological terms may be more scientifically precise. That's good for researchers. But is anything important lost when we do this? I believe there is. Consider, for example, the following passage from Fredrickson's book:

> Positivity resonance is not exclusive, not something to be reserved for your soul mate, your inner circle, your kin, or your loved ones. Positivity resonance is not lasting. Positivity resonance is not unconditional. It doesn't emerge no matter what, regardless of conditions. It obeys preconditions. Yet once you understand those preconditions, you can find positivity resonance countless times each day.

That makes sense. Positive emotions can be shared with many different people. The conditions need to be right, but if we want it, we can do something about it.

But I have to confess to a little sleight-of-hand. Those aren't Fredrickson's exact words. Where I've written "positivity resonance" above, she actually has the word "love." And while I believe my rewording accurately represents her view, it shifts the meaning and impact of the paragraph. Here's the original quote, with emphasis added. Try reading it out loud:

> *Love*, as your body defines it, is not exclusive, not something
> to be reserved for your soul mate, your inner circle, your kin,
> or your so-called *loved ones*. ...*Love*, as you'll see, is not
> lasting. ...And perhaps most challenging of all, *love* is not
> unconditional. It doesn't emerge no matter what, regardless
> of conditions. ...It obeys preconditions. Yet once you
> understand those preconditions, you can find *love* countless
> times each day.[24]

If love is nothing but positivity resonance, the two paragraphs should
be equivalent. But does the second reading leave you with a different
impression? Why? *Love* is neither exclusive, nor lasting, nor
unconditional, Fredrickson says. She knows that such a claim will
shock many if not most of her readers. And that's the point. She says
it that way to jolt us out of our preconceptions and clear a space for
her cleaner, more precise redefinition of love.

But again, what are the consequences of redefining love in this
way? Listen to Fredrickson muse about how her new understanding
of love has changed the way she looks at her own marriage:

> What does it mean, then, to say that I love my husband, Jeff?
> It used to mean that eighteen plus years ago, I fell in love with
> him. So much so that I abandoned my crusty attitude toward
> marriage and chose to dive right in. I used to uphold love as
> that constant, steady force that defines my relationship with
> Jeff. Of course that constant, steady force still exists between
> us. Yet...I now see that steady force, not as love per se, but as
> the bond he and I share, and the commitments we two have
> made to each other, to be loyal and trusting to the end. ...If I
> take my body's perspective on love seriously, it means that
> right now—at this very moment in which I'm crafting this
> sentence—I do not love my husband. Our positivity
> resonance, after all, only lasts as long as we two are engaged
> with each other. Bonds last. Love doesn't.[25]

I appreciate that Fredrickson wants to shake us out of our complacency. Being married for eighteen years is no guarantee that a husband and wife still love each other; it's too easy to take love for granted. If love (as positivity resonance) is a momentary state that's good for us and everyone around us, we need to be more intentional about making it happen.

Fine. But I believe that Fredrickson sacrifices too much of what is typically intended by the statement, "I love my husband." Sometimes it does indeed mean, "He's here in the room with me, and I'm feeling warm and connected." But it can also mean, "Even though he's not here, I feel happy because I'm thinking about him." Or even: "We have a lot of history together, and I'm committed to him, even though he's driving me nuts." There is, in other words, a moral dimension to saying "I love you" that's obscured when we reduce love to biology. And that becomes even more important in marriages where moments of shared positive emotion are few and far between.

To be fair, Fredrickson still believes that commitment, loyalty, and trust are important in marriage. She simply moves them to another box called the "bond." That leaves her free to say that love is just the experience of positivity resonance and nothing else—forcing her to admit that she can't love her husband if he's not in the room.

I value Fredrickson's scientific contribution, and others like it, to a fully embodied understanding of love, particularly one with practical implications for how we should live. But though the science of positivity adds to our understanding of loving relationships, there is no intrinsically scientific reason for reducing love to positivity. From a biblical perspective, her biologically-centered vision is too narrow. Making positivity the be-all and end-all of love changes things. As she says later in the book,

> Thinking of love purely as the romance or commitment that you share with one special person—as it appears most on earth do—surely limits the health and happiness you derive from micro-moments of positivity resonance. ...Think of the old-school view of love as pouring a thick layer of cement over a garden that has been planted with a thousand flower

bulbs. Although any single flower might still push its way through cracks in the cement and bloom nevertheless, the odds are severely stacked against it.[26]

It's a compelling image: the stodgy, old-school approach to love smothers what otherwise might be a lush and beautiful flowerbed. Sow the seeds of positivity instead, and reap health and happiness for you and your loved ones. Surely no reasonable person would want to argue against that!

Don't worry: I have no intention of painting some grumpy, gloomy portrait of love that goes stomping about people's flowerbeds. I want people to be healthier and happier, too.

But love, according to the Bible, is not something we do to make us happy. Paul pairs love and joy together as expressions of the life of the Spirit (e.g., Gal 5:22), but that's not because he thinks of the first as the pathway to the second. When he says that love "never fails" and commands the Corinthians to "pursue love" (1 Cor 13:8; 14:1), he's not talking about cultivating temporary biological states. And when the apostle John insists that "love is from God," and even more importantly, that "God is love" (1 John 4:7-8), he isn't counseling people to be more happy but more holy.

In short, as Christians we are taught to love not because it's good for us but because it's good, period. We aim to be more loving because we aim to be more like the God we love and worship, in ways that are concretely embodied in real-world relationships. It's one thing to say that we should love because it's better for us. But it's another to say that sometimes we must love because it's the right and godly thing to do. The question is not just about what we feel or want to feel, but what kind of world we want to create by our actions.

■ ■ ■

I've emphasized our emotions in this chapter because I'm concerned that some Christians are overly suspicious of them. Emotions are portrayed as a volatile and undependable guide for the Christian life, and believers are advised to be something like a devout version of the ever-logical Mr. Spock of *Star Trek* fame.

You may, for example, have heard this from the pulpit: "Love is not a feeling, but a decision." Maybe you've even said it yourself.

I understand what's meant. To love as Christ loved entails sacrificial obedience. And sometimes, that means doing the loving thing even when we don't feel like it. That's the "decision" part: in faith, we deliberately decide to act lovingly toward people who at that moment feel more like enemies.

But to make love a matter of the head rather than the heart is problematic. First, the shock value of the statement, "Love is not a feeling," depends in part on taking exactly the opposite for granted: there *are* feelings involved in what we normally call love. To deny this creates unnecessary distance between biblical wisdom and our everyday experiences of love.

Second, the idea risks relegating reason and emotion to separate boxes. This make little sense psychologically, for as we saw earlier, the reasoning by which we make decisions often relies upon the proper operation of our emotions in the background. If we deny the role of emotion, we're more likely to delude ourselves into believing that we're only doing what cool, dispassionate reason demands. As Benjamin Franklin wryly observed, "So convenient a thing it is to be a reasonable creature, since it enables one to find or make a reason for everything one has a mind to do."[27] And again, what one has a "mind" to do is in part quietly shaped by our emotions.

Moreover, separating reason and emotion makes little sense biblically. Unlike many writers and thinkers of the modern West, the biblical writers didn't consider reason and emotion to be two separate and distinct faculties.[28] As philosopher Phillip Cary observes:

[I]n the Bible, you feel and think in the same place. ...[T]he New Testament never contrasts heart and mind, as if they were rivals or enemies, and it regularly speaks of the thoughts of our *hearts*, just like the Old Testament. And just like the rest of the Bible, it never once speaks of thoughts being in our *heads*.[29]

Of course, if some prefer head to heart in their understanding of faith and love, others have the opposite preference. Many Christians are suspicious of anything that sounds too heady or intellectual and prefer to follow their hearts.[30]   Their unspoken motto is, "Just believe!"—in other words, don't overthink the faith, or you'll get confused.   But either way, whether one prefers head or heart, the mistake is in artificially separating the two. Reason and emotion need each other. Neither is to be denied.

Third, the Bible is shot through with strong emotion. We may want to idealize love by scrubbing it clean of its messier or more embarrassing emotional aspects. But what will we do, then, with all the other emotions on display in Scripture?   There are positive emotions like joy and delight, but also negative ones, like jealousy and anger—and God is described as expressing all of these. Consider, for example, this passage from Hosea, describing the love of God for his people:

When Israel was a child, I loved him,
and out of Egypt I called my son.
The more I called them,
the further they went from me;
they kept sacrificing to the Baals,
and they burned incense to idols.
Yet it was I who taught Ephraim to walk;
I took them up in my arms,
but they did not know that I healed them.
I led them with bands of human kindness,
with cords of love.
I treated them like those
who lift infants to their cheeks;
I bent down to them and fed them. ...
How can I give you up, Ephraim?
How can I hand you over, Israel?
How can I make you like Admah?
How can I treat you like Zeboiim?
My heart winces within me;

> my compassion grows warm and tender.
> I won't act on the heat of my anger;
> I won't return to destroy Ephraim;
> for I am God and not a human being,
> the holy one in your midst;
> I won't come in harsh judgment. (Hos 11:1-4, 8-9)

Here, God is a loving and attentive parent agonizing over the fate of a rebellious adopted son. Israel's continuous idolatry is deserving of divine wrath and judgment—but God relents of his anger, choosing compassion instead. And why? Precisely because God is God. As Elizabeth Achtemeier writes:

> God's holiness is his divinity, that which distinguishes him as God. And because he is holy he is inexhaustible love (cf. 1 John 4:8, 16). That is the nature, the divinity of God, which he cannot set aside, even in the face of Israel's total faithlessness and refusal to return his love. God will not give up his people Israel, whom he has adopted as a beloved son, precisely because he is a God who is love.[31]

We should take care, of course, not to ascribe emotions to God in exactly the same way we would to fallible human beings. Many of the gods in the religions of the ancient world acted like petty dictators or bickering children—in other words, like people with more power than they know what to do with.

By contrast, the emotions of the God of the Bible, such as love and wrath, are presented as expressions of his holiness. That last point is crucial. Love and wrath aren't competing qualities in a God who is holy in all his ways.[32] And if we hold onto that premise of holiness, then we don't have to worry that emotions somehow make God less God:

> God's emotions are always in line with his holiness and moral character. God's emotions are always correct, righteous and moral because God is always correct, righteous and moral.

Further, human emotions are part of man being made in the image of God.[33]

Thus, on both biblical and psychological grounds, we must learn to acknowledge and appreciate the positive role emotions play in our lives—even (counterintuitively, perhaps!) in the way we reason and make decisions. Emotions may be messy and difficult to manage. But emotions in themselves aren't the problem: sin is. Think, for example, of the words of Paul: "Be angry without sinning" (Eph 4:26). We can sin in our anger, but anger itself is not sin.

It's not a question of whether we should have emotions, therefore, but whether our emotions are godly. We will inevitably get angry—but will we be angry in the right way and for the right reasons? Emotions are part of our nature, but can be expressed in ways that are either more faithful or less.[34]

And so it is with love.

Let me state the obvious: Christians experience the same range of human emotions as anyone else. Their perceptions, attitudes, and behaviors are influenced by their past relationships, just like everyone else. People can fall in love to the point of giddiness whether they believe in Jesus or not. When Christians fall in love, they have the same hormones and neurochemicals coursing through their bodies. And when Christians come together in relationships, whether of the romantic or churchly variety, their personal histories and emotional tendencies are in play.

Emotional experience will necessarily be part of any realistic understanding of love. But that doesn't mean that love must be entirely defined by emotion. Nor must emotion itself be defined by biology. Robert Solomon, for example, acknowledges that emotions have a neurological basis, but insists on a broader understanding. Emotions are "strategies for getting along in the world": they involve judgments and decisions, and are oriented toward a goal.[35] When you're angry, you make a judgment that someone's done you wrong. And far from being just a momentary feeling, your anger may harden into an ongoing habit of how you see and respond to that person, perhaps even the whole world.[36]

Something similar can be said about the emotions involved in love. Emotions are rooted in our physiology and early experience, and there may be some truth to the idea of the thunderbolt. But love isn't something that simply happens to you. It involves a series of decisions, made with the intention of building a shared identity—a love-world—with someone you've chosen to be with. And the more consistently we make such decisions with that vision in mind, the more our emotions will fall in line.

If Robert Solomon is right, then our feelings, expectations, and decisions regarding love are all shaped, often implicitly, by the stories we value most, the stories we want to live. What are those stories, and where do they come from? We'll explore that in the next two chapters.

talk or think about it

1. Have you ever had the experience of falling in love, maybe even at first sight? What was it like?

2. Think about your early relationship with your parents, and the relationship you saw between them (if applicable). How do you think these experiences shaped the way you express or receive love today? How would your answers differ from others', particularly others who are close to you?

3. Many people treat emotion and reason as opposites, even as enemies. Some go further, and want to prioritize "head over heart" or "heart over head." How have you seen these tendencies expressed in the church? What would be the problem with going to the extreme in either direction?

4. Emotions have a normal and expectable role to play in how we perceive and respond to others, in how we reason and make decisions about the world. Emotional factors will also play a role in our struggles to love others as God would have us do. Think of someone toward whom you believe God would have you be more loving. What emotions seem to get in your way?

5. At the same time, I've suggested that when it comes to love, "the question is not just about what we feel or want to feel, but what kind of world we want to create by our actions." Discuss the implications of this quote, and why it might still be important to know what we actually feel.

making sense of our sensibilities

Here's a movie title that I would never have imagined on my own: *Pride and Prejudice and Zombies.*[1] It's based on an earlier novel of the same name, an improbable but creative mash-up of horror fiction with Jane Austen's romantic classic.

We might have seen this coming. It's been over 200 years since the publication of *Pride and Prejudice,* but the story's popularity hasn't waned. A whole slew of authors have tried their hand at variations to the original plot. Each tries to ask and answer the question, "What if...?"—including, apparently, "What if Regency-era England had been plagued by legions of the undead?"

Answer: heroine Elizabeth Bennet and her sisters would have been sent to a Shaolin temple to learn martial arts, the better to defend the quiet life of the English countryside.

Obviously.

At best, the whole thing is a supremely silly idea. At worst, to the purists among the Austen faithful, it's an act of sacrilege.

But to tweak the old saying, imitation and adaptation may be the sincerest (and the most profitable) form of flattery. Amazingly, Austen's novel continues to survive the treatment. She was a keen and witty critic of the romantic norms of her day, and there's a certain timelessness to her observations that still translates across the centuries.

In the spirit of adaptation, therefore, I've borrowed the title of this chapter from her first published novel, *Sense and Sensibility.* The novel contrasts two ways of approaching love and romance, as embodied in the lives of the Dashwood sisters. Elinor is calm and level-headed, so much so that her younger sister Marianne and even her mother accuse her of being unfeeling. She represents the "sense" of Austen's title. Marianne, however, represents "sensibility." She's the one to obey her passions and plunge headlong into romance.

Pause and ask yourself: why should people get married? What's the number one reason? In much of today's world, the answer is plain: romantic love. One of the major goals in life is to find and marry your "true love," your "soul mate," or at the very least, your best friend. And weddings are often more romantic rituals than religious ones. After officiating one ceremony, I overheard one of the guests grumble, "I didn't know this was going to be a *religious* wedding."

The romantic way of thinking about marriage, however, isn't universal. Nor was it always the case even in Western culture. Not that romance is a modern invention. But people didn't expect to marry primarily for love. Marriage was supposed to serve the common good. The idea that one *must* marry for love and companionship, some historians insist, is a product of the western emphasis on individual happiness.[2]

In her novels, Austen explores and critiques the relationship between love, marriage, and money. Beneath her humor is a deep dissatisfaction with the way things are. In her world, it was risky for a woman to turn down a proposal of marriage from a man of means or social standing. Never mind whether she actually loved him. Hopefully, that would come in time. If not...well, she still had to avoid scandalizing the neighbors.

In *Sense and Sensibility*, both Elinor and Marianne are in love. Elinor loves the quiet and unremarkable Edward Ferrars, but carefully wraps her feelings in well-mannered and reserved behavior. Marianne loves the dashing John Willoughby, and expresses her feelings openly.

What neither of them know is that both men harbor secrets. Edward cannot court Elinor, because he's engaged to Lucy Steele, a woman he doesn't love. Willoughby, for his part, had seduced a teenage girl and abandoned her when she became pregnant. His aunt has therefore disinherited him. Though he loves Marianne, he has decided to marry another woman for her money. Both sisters are heartbroken when they discover the truth. Elinor manages to maintain her composure, while Marianne, with characteristic drama, nearly dies of grief.

The story ends happily with a double wedding. Edward is threatened with disinheritance unless he breaks his engagement to Lucy. As a matter of gentlemanly honor, he refuses to renege on his promise. The inheritance therefore passes to his younger brother, whom the ever-scheming Lucy marries instead. Edward is thus freed to marry Elinor, and her longsuffering is vindicated. Marianne marries Colonel Brandon, a man whom she had originally thought too old and stuffy. Cured of her obsession with Willoughby, she discovers a more modest yet genuine love.

Though Austen seems to prefer Elinor's good "sense," it's worth noting that Elinor's poise doesn't save her from suffering. It's only Lucy's fickleness and greed that make it possible for Elinor to marry Edward. And for many readers, Marianne's passion makes her the more sympathetic character.

Thus, Austen doesn't simplistically reject emotion in favor of reason and respectability, but seems to ask us to consider the relationship between the two. For the story to work, both sisters must fall deeply in love.[3] The question is what they will do with the emotion they feel. Each sister is independently minded in her own way. Each must make a string of moral decisions in answer to the implied question, "What should I do?"[4] But in making such decisions, they follow different moral codes and different visions of love and romance.

Put differently: each sister imagines herself as part of a different story of love—a different love-world—and acts accordingly. Marianne imagines what we would consider the more typically "romantic" story. She wants to be swept off her feet and follows her passion, even at the risk of offending polite society. Following her romantic dreams leads to disaster and nearly to death. But she is still a favored character for readers who hope that her kind of true love will win in the end.

Elinor envisions a different kind of relationship. As ethicist Karen Stohr argues, she is the wiser and more mature of the two sisters. She keeps a tight rein on her emotions because she is always aware of how her behavior will affect others. With her strong moral center, Elinor can only fall in love with and marry a man whom she admires for his goodness.[5]

As Austen's novel illustrates, therefore, stories are one of the most important ways we make sense of our sensibilities. As we saw in chapter 2, our experience of love may involve strong emotions. But we must still make sense of our emotions in a way that guides our behavior and expectations. Stories—many of them supplied by our shared culture—help us to interpret what is happening now and to imagine future possibilities. The question is whether we're aware of the stories that shape us. Are they the stories we want? And do we choose them, or do they choose us?

Austen's novels still capture our imaginations because we still fret over questions of love and marriage. The complexity of her characters, of course, sometimes gets lost in the profit-driven world of romantic fiction and movie-making. One critic has even lamented the "harlequinization" of her novels—the stripping down of plot and character to the formulaic stereotypes of Harlequin romances.[6]

In today's media-saturated world, movies may be the most popular source of romantic stories. They draw us in emotionally, shaping how we imagine romance. But the story can't just indulge a screenwriter's whims. To some extent, it has to conform to the expectations audiences already have.

In this chapter, we go to the movies. In particular, we'll look at the genre of romantic comedy, or "rom-com" as it is commonly known. By examining how such films tell love stories, we learn some of the culturally prescribed ways to think about our own relationships.

Why do we believe in love at first sight or the idea that romantic soul mates will be brought together by destiny? We didn't learn it from the Bible. But we will find these ideas and others in the movies.

Not all movies about love, of course, end well. Some characters are selfish and manipulative, and pay the price in romantic failure.

But few people in love, I think, aspire to live out these stories in their own lives. Romantic comedies offer a far more hopeful prospect.

Romantic comedies are often funny, but technically, that's not what makes them "comedy." Take *Silver Linings Playbook*, one of the most commercially and critically successful films of recent years, as a case in point.[7] The main characters, Pat (Bradley Cooper) and Tiffany (Jennifer Lawrence), are not likeable people. They're explosive, vulgar, and tormented. Their initial moment of bonding happens over how much they hate taking their psychiatric medication.

What makes this a comedy is the shape of the story, the sure movement toward a feel-good ending. Pat and Tiffany stumble badly through life. They wrestle with personal demons and their families are nutty. But they're pursuing their happiness. You want them to find their silver lining. You root for them to discover what you, the audience, already know or suspect—that they are each other's one true love.

Thus, though details vary, romantic comedies share a fairly predictable plotline. Boy meets girl, often in the context of uncertainty or heartbreak: unrequited love, a failed or failing relationship, loneliness, loss. The two characters may not be openly attracted to each other at first, but there are hints of possibility. Some conflict or obstacle threatens to keep them apart, and the odds are stacked against them. Yet by the end of the story the two come together, sometimes in marriage, sometimes just for a long, lingering kiss, as gleefully satirized in *The Princess Bride*.[8] In our minds, we may even supply the implied fairy tale ending: the couple will live happily ever after.[9] Love conquers all, and it must do so by the final scene.

Not all romantic movies, of course, end the way we might expect. Consider *La La Land*, writer/director Damien Chazelle's homage to the classic movie musical.[10] Mia (Emma Stone) and Sebastian (Ryan Gosling) fall in love and share a frustrating on-again, off-again romance. Though they proclaim their love for each other, by the end of the film, Mia has married another man, and both she and Sebastian are left wondering what might have been if they had been able to work out their differences. No happily-ever-after there.

Notice, however, that the dramatic punch of the ending relies on taking us by surprise; we *expect* Mia and Sebastian to get together. As much as Chazelle loves the old MGM song-and-dance romances, his message is: *Enjoy the stories, but don't forget that they're Hollywood fictions. Don't mistake them for reality.*

I agree. But I have to admit that I was disappointed by the ending. Oh, well. I guess I must *like* living in la-la land.

We know the formula. We know what to expect. If the story doesn't have a happy ending, we may feel cheated. Just ask Pat in *Silver Linings Playbook*, who reads a Hemingway novel and then furiously chucks it through the window. Why? Because the heroine dies instead of getting her happily-ever-after.

◼ ◼ ◼

When it comes to love, our imaginations can be captured by novels, movies, and fairy tales. Indeed, several websites now make it possible to star in our own romantic fiction.[11] Pick from their selection of pre-written novels, give them some information about yourself, pay your fee (it's not cheap)—and *presto!* In a matter of days, a steamy novel will arrive at your doorstep, with your picture on the cover and your name on nearly every page.

Unless we're out of touch with reality, though, we don't really expect these exotic adventures to happen to us in real life. Nor do we literally expect to be the characters we see on the screen. The influence of these stories comes is usually subtler. In popular romantic fiction, certain ideas and plot elements show up again and again. These create an implicit and sometimes unrecognized sense of how romantic stories are *supposed* to go—including our own.

Love at first sight is one of those ideas. As we saw in the last chapter, this happens to real people. But could it be that the folks in Dorothy Tennov's research told their stories that way because they already "knew" how such stories are supposed to be told?

Think, for example, about what it means to give your "testimony" in church. Everybody knows that there's a right way to tell the story. It has to follow what I call the "Amazing Grace trajectory": the story begins with being lost and ends in being found. A person can't get up and say, "I was raised as a Christian from birth by godly parents. I grew up in a loving Christian community. I stayed strong in my faith throughout high school and college. I've always loved Jesus, and I know I always will." It might all be true, and we should be happy to hear stories like that. But it wouldn't count as a proper testimony, because it doesn't follow the pattern of being rescued out of darkness and into light.

I'm not saying that the men and women whom Tennov interviewed lied. But ask someone for their love story, and they'll tell it in a form they've learned is appropriate. One sociologist, for example, presented people with a story of two strangers who meet on a train, make eye contact, and marry two days later. The people dismissed such behavior as impetuous and irresponsible. Ironically, however, when the same people were asked to recount their own fondest memories of romance, they always told stories of falling in love at first sight.[12]

Tennov herself noticed how the stories she was told rivaled "the *grands amours* of fiction."[13] Why the similarity? It's a chicken-and-egg question. On the one hand, writers of romantic fiction deal with experiences already familiar to us as readers. On the other, we as readers also learn to interpret our lives through such tales. Movies don't invent romance. But they make emotionally compelling stories available to a mass market, and these influence how we make sense of our own experiences of love.

Not every story begins with love at first sight. There are other plot conventions. Whether it's a major theme or only implied, for example, many stories of love involve some sense of destiny. Love not only triumphs over adversity, it brings together the most unlikely, mismatched couples.[14] In *That Touch of Mink*, Doris Day's character is unemployed, and has quaint, small-town values, while Cary Grant's character is a worldly millionaire. In *The Lady Eve*, a con artist (Barbara Stanwyck) falls for her rich but naive mark (Henry Fonda). In *Sabrina*, the ruthless executive (Humphrey Bogart or Harrison Ford) falls for the chauffeur's daughter (Audrey Hepburn or Julia Ormond). In *Notting Hill*, the world-famous American movie star

(Julia Roberts) falls for the owner of a floundering London bookstore (Hugh Grant). In *Love Actually*, the Prime Minister (Hugh Grant again) falls for a much younger member of his household staff (Martine McCutcheon).[15]

There's nothing new in this notion of romantic fate, though the stories don't always end well. Shakespeare's most famous lovers were "star-cross'd": Romeo was fated to love Juliet, despite the war between their families. Tristan loved Isolde, despite the war between their kingdoms. Lancelot loved Guinevere, despite the fact that she was married to Arthur, his king.

The heart will have its way. In tragedy or comedy, romance isn't just about loving *because*, but loving *nevertheless*. True love breaks boundaries.

Today, the idea of romantic destiny often goes like this: somewhere out there is The One, Mr. or Ms. Right, your soul mate. And when you find that person, you have to be with him or her, no matter what.

Even if you're already engaged or married to someone else.

Consider *Serendipity*, a film whose script openly flaunts the idea of destiny and dares you to disbelieve.[16] Jonathan (John Cusack) and Sara (Kate Beckinsale) are Christmas shopping at Bloomingdale's—he for his girlfriend, she for her boyfriend. They meet over the last pair of black cashmere gloves, then spend some time chatting in her favorite café, named Serendipity. But she won't give her last name or phone number to Jonathan, because she has faith in destiny. If the two of them are meant to be together, she insists, they will be.

Sara sets up two ways for fate to give them a sign. She has Jonathan write his name and number on the back of a five-dollar bill, and promptly spends the bill without looking at it. Then she shows Jonathan the book she's reading, tells him that her name and number are written in it, and sells it at a used bookstore the next day. If, somehow, the bill comes back to her or the book to him, they'll know that fate has intervened. They separate, each carrying a single glove.

Fast forward a few years. Both are engaged to other people. But neither can let go of the nagging suspicion that they're missing their romantic destiny. They begin to search for each other, with the help of their best friends. When Sara and her best friend Eve (Molly Shannon) fail to find Jonathan, they reluctantly call off the search. Eve gently chides her friend: "It's a wonderful thought—the idea that all of life, that every single event, is all part of some master plan designed to lead us to our universal soul mate. But if that's really true, then what's the point of living? Or making decisions?"

Sara resigns herself to the truth. She knows Eve is right. Indeed, as a therapist-in-training, Sara herself had warned one of her clients about the danger of believing in a soul mate, of thinking that the universe has one and only one person with whom you could be truly happy. By going home, Eve insists, Sara isn't "giving up," she's "growing up."

But then, of course—spoiler alert!—fate finally has its way. Sitting on the plane just before takeoff, Sara finds Jonathan's five-dollar bill. And elsewhere, Jonathan receives Sara's book as a gift. From his bride-to-be.

In the end, if you get caught up in the story at all, you want Sara to call off her engagement to her self-absorbed fiancé. You want Jonathan to call off his wedding. With everything that's happened, they must be soul mates. They were meant for each other. And when they reunite—when the two cashmere gloves come together again as a pair—it just feels right.

Serendipity practically pummels you with the theme of romantic destiny. The screenplay piles up coincidences and near misses to the point of absurdity, walking the line between comedy and farce.[17] It's as if the writers are giving us a conspiratorial wink and saying, "We know it's all a bit silly. But who cares? Just go with it. Enjoy the feeling."

The notion of destiny isn't usually so obvious. Typically, it functions more subtly as a background assumption. In *Notting Hill*, for example, Hugh Grant plays William, a man who has twice been unlucky in love. His best friends are a happily married couple. Trying to make sense of what he believes is another inevitable heartbreak, he tells them, "I think you've forgotten what an unusual situation you two have. To find someone you actually love, who'll love you, I mean, the chances are always miniscule."

Listen to his language. "To find someone." "The chances." William makes true love sound like winning the lottery; everyone wants to play, but few actually win. And he says this to a couple in which the wife is confined to a wheelchair and unable to have children because of an accident. There is nothing in his words about commitment, sacrifice, or devotion—only chance. The implied hope is that one day he too will be as lucky as they.[18]

You know he will. The script requires it.

▦ ▦ ▦

The idea that such stories shape our imaginations has become so commonplace that there are even rom-coms about the influence of other rom-coms.

Exhibit One. The theme of romantic destiny once again takes center stage in *Sleepless in Seattle*.[19] Sam (Tom Hanks) is recently widowed. Annie (Meg Ryan) hears him talking about his loss on a call-in radio talk show, and begins to wonder if they're meant to be together. She compulsively stalks him from afar, only occasionally wondering if she's crazy to do so. "What if this man is my destiny, and I never meet him?" she asks her friend Becky (Rosie O'Donnell).

The added wrinkle is that Annie and Becky are enamored of the 1957 romantic classic *An Affair to Remember*.[20] They've watched it so many times they've memorized the dialogue. In that movie, Cary Grant and Deborah Kerr are thwarted from meeting at the Empire State Building as planned. Annie begins to imagine that her life will complete that unfinished rendezvous. Fate speaks to her through coincidences that she interprets as signs. And on Valentine's Day, she breaks her engagement with her fiancé and runs off to the Empire State Building without knowing if Sam will be there.

Becky's criticism of Annie's behavior nicely sums up the theme: "That's your problem. You don't want to be in love. You want to be in love in a movie."

And apparently, she's not the only one. Consider Exhibit Two. Movie musicals are frequently romantic comedies with...well, music. *Hello, Dolly!* is one of my personal favorites.[21] Dolly Levi (Barbra

Streisand) is a professional matchmaker, hired by Horace Vandergelder (Walter Matthau), one of the richest citizens in the town of Yonkers, to find him a suitable wife. But Dolly has designs on marrying Horace herself. Her madcap, meddling scheme is the movie's main story line. Is she marrying for love? In a sense, yes. But Dolly is a widow. Her expectations are down-to-earth and very practical.

Not so with the movie's B story-line. Cornelius Hackl (Michael Crawford) is pushing thirty and has "never kissed a girl," stuck in a dead-end job as a clerk at Vandergelder's Hay and Feed store. As part of her plan, Dolly sends Cornelius off to New York, to meet and court Irene Molloy (Marianne McAndrew), the woman Horace thinks he's marrying.

Cornelius and Irene are an improbable match. He's an underpaid nobody pretending to be someone he's not; she's a social sophisticate who owns her own business. The only thing they share in common is a desire for adventure. All in the course of a single pandemonium-filled evening, they hold hands, kiss, and fall in love.

And, of course, they sing about it. Their theme song, "It Only Takes a Moment," teaches that true love happens in an instant and lasts a lifetime.

To be fair, their entire romance is played with a touch of satire. The writers seem to poke fun at the romantic conventions. But the song and the story pop up again nearly forty years later, without the satire, driving the romantic arc of another, very different movie.

Pixar Studios' animated feature *WALL-E* is a science-fiction adventure story set in a bleak vision of the future.[22] Centuries ago, humans left a toxic, garbage-strewn Earth to live the lazy life on an enormous spaceship. Oblivious to the planet their ancestors called home, what remains of the human race must return to repopulate the Earth.

To me, however, that's the B story line. The other side of *WALL-E* is pure romantic comedy.

The music of *Hello, Dolly!* weaves through the film from the opening scene. WALL-E, a trash-compacting robot left behind to clean up Earth, has found an old videotape of *Dolly* and plays it every day. He acts out the dance routines. He hums the songs. In particular, he's fascinated by "It Only Takes a Moment," watching Cornelius and Irene hold hands and wondering what it might be like.

When another robot named EVE arrives, he's smitten.[23] She's sleek and sophisticated, while WALL-E is the robotic equivalent of the working-class yokel from Yonkers. EVE is out of his league, but he loves her nevertheless, and longs to hold her hand. Eventually, of course, the two come together. They share a zap of a first "kiss" and dance together in space. The hand-holding theme runs through the entire movie, right down to the end credits. In the climactic scene, in fact, a distraught EVE hums, "It Only Takes a Moment," while holding WALL-E's hand.

Hello, WALL-E! Romantic comedy isn't just for grown-ups.

And Exhibit Three helps to reinforce that point.

Love Actually has been billed as "the ultimate romantic comedy," boasting an all-star cast playing out multiple interwoven vignettes. The movie deserves its R-rating and, unlike *WALL-E*, is not suitable for children. But one of the vignettes shows how movies might shape the romantic imaginations of even the youngest of viewers.

Daniel (Liam Neeson) is a grieving widower left to raise his young stepson Sam (Thomas Brodie-Sangster) by himself. Not surprisingly, the boy has been sullen and withdrawn. When Daniel works up the courage to ask what's wrong, however, the answer surprises him: at school, Sam has a crush on Joanna (Olivia Olson), who doesn't seem to know he's alive. Relieved, Daniel laughs and admits he feared something worse. The boy fires back, "Worse than the total agony of being in love?"

Daniel takes on the task of mentoring the boy in romance. Together, they watch *Titanic*, and the mismatched romance between Kate Winslet and Leonardo DiCaprio.[24] Later, when Sam is discouraged about his crush, Daniel tries to put things in perspective: "I'm sure she's unique and extraordinary, but general wisdom is that in the end there isn't just one person for each of us." But Sam wants nothing of this wisdom. "There was for Kate and Leo," he answers matter-of-factly. "There was for you. And there is for me. She's the one."

Daniel passively accepts that verdict. And when their plan to get Joanna's attention seems to fail, he tells Sam, "You've seen the films, kiddo. It ain't over till it's over." In the end, even young Sam has to play out the romantic plot conventions. Schooled by the movies, Sam suddenly decides he must declare his true feelings to Joanna. There's the stereotypical frantic drive to the airport to catch her before she boards her plane. Sam makes a mad dash for Joanna's gate, dodging obstacles, with airport security hot on his heels. He catches Joanna just before she disappears around a corner, and tells her how he feels. She rewards him with a kiss (on the cheek!), and Sam returns to Daniel through the security gate, leaping into his arms in jubilation.

It's instructive that when the characters in these stories seem to be too caught up in their obsessions, someone is recruited to play the voice of reason. In *Serendipity*, it's Jonathan and Sara's best friends. In *Sleepless*, it's Annie's best friend. In *Love Actually*, it's stepdad Daniel. And their counsel is often wise. But never mind. The advice is ignored, the advisors give in, and romantic destiny wins again, to everyone's delight.[25]

I guess it's never too early to learn how love is supposed to work, or to have what we already know about romance reinforced. And the entertainment industry is always standing by, ready to help.

▓ ▓ ▓

To be sure that you don't take me for a cranky old cynic, let me declare my true feelings: I enjoy romantic comedies. Though part of me still leans toward action flicks, there's nothing quite like the snappy dialogue and screwball humor of the old black-and-white gems from the 1930s and 40s.[26]

We've heard the arguments that media violence—not only movies, but games that are almost cinematic in quality—represent a wider culture of violence that shapes the attitudes of youth and adults alike. Some researchers consider the matter settled, arguing that exposure to media violence has both short- and long-term negative effects on youth.[27]

But if there's a culture of violence, there's also a culture of

romance, a set of shared values and expectations that are more caught
than taught as people consume popular media and negotiate the twists
and turns of romantic relationships.[28]   Take popular music as an
example. Some songs are worshipful in the way they present love and
romance, while others lament betrayal and broken promises. As the
main character in the movie *High Fidelity* muses about his own
heartbreak:

> What came first? The music or the misery? People worry
> about kids playing with guns or watching violent videos...
> Nobody worries about kids listening to thousands—literally
> *thousands*—of songs about heartbreak, rejection, pain, misery
> and loss. Did I listen to pop music because I was miserable, or
> was I miserable because I listened to pop music?[29]

The answer to that last question is, "Yes." It's both/and. The music
we listen to can affect our moods.[30]   Indeed, imagine watching a
movie without a soundtrack. Emotionally, the experience would be
more flat, because we're used to having music cue our emotions as we
watch. It swells majestically to celebrate triumph, or darkly warns us
when danger lurks behind the next door.

But it's also true that we choose music to match or modify our
moods, to regulate our emotions.[31]   Think about the music you
listened to as a teenager, when your feelings were often unpredictable
and intense. There were songs you listened to over and over.
Sometimes you needed them to pick you up. Other times you needed
music to help you express your anger at the world. And some songs,
music and lyrics, probably shaped your romantic sensibilities.

Lisa Bevere writes of a time her son was utterly captivated by a
love song performed by a Christian group. He played it again and
again. When he invited Mom to listen, she wisely agreed. He wanted
her to hear what he heard, to be moved as he was moved. But she was
troubled instead:

> Out of the corner of my eye, I noted that my son knew each
> word, tone, and inflection of the song. He'd obviously studied

it, and as he sang along with such heartfelt tenderness, I found myself becoming slightly uncomfortable. The song proclaimed the power of the artist's undying love and his promise to lay down his life for the object of his love. It was a young man's pledge of his soul in love to a young girl. But something just didn't ring true for me; I have lived long enough to know however noble these sentiments are when they're sung, the follow-through is rare.[32]

We don't just want to be in love. We want to be in love in a movie. Or a song.

Or for that matter, a commercial.

Romance is big business, and advertisers are happy to tell us what we need to buy to get it right. Every year, as Valentine's Day nears, video streaming services promote their stock of rom-coms. Local merchants put flowers and candy at the front of the store. Restaurants offer specials and gear up for extra business. Jewelry advertisements show us handsome men giving diamonds to beautiful women. The women gasp and look at their men with grateful adoration, or with the unspoken promise of a romantic evening to come.

Commercials don't just sell us products. They sell us dreams. "This is what love is supposed to be like," they whisper, accompanied by images that hint at a romantic Utopia.[33] "This is what you're aspiring to. And if you want *that*, you need to buy *this*."

I guarantee that you will never see a jewelry commercial in which the woman, holding some glittering bauble, looks up and says, "But I don't want diamonds. I want you to love me." Instead, we're supposed to accept the myth that diamonds *are* love—a myth that largely owes its existence to a marketing campaign by diamond manufacturer De Beers.[34] It's now expected that a marriage proposal should be accompanied by a diamond or some other precious stone.

As the slogan for Kay Jewelers reminds us, "Every kiss begins with Kay." It's frightening to think what the world would be like if that were really true.

Again, please don't misunderstand. I am not anti-romance. I

know what it means to be light-headed with infatuation. When my wife and I were dating, we spent hours on the phone and wrote each other love notes. We exchanged goofy tokens of affection and saved every one. We're not like that anymore, but I remember those days fondly. And I know young men who have gone to heroic lengths to propose marriage in ways that would rival anything coming out of Hollywood. Loving couples cherish such memories, and rightly so.

None of this, however, happens in a vacuum. Relationships play out against the backdrop of values we've absorbed from the world around us.

Consumer culture continually reinforces the idea that we need to buy certain things to express our love and to make ourselves more attractive. I doubt that anyone truly believes that the right shampoo or mouthwash is going to land them the person of their dreams. Some advertisers even exaggerate the sales pitch, as if to let us in on the joke: *Hey, look at this loser—he uses our deodorant, and suddenly beautiful women are throwing themselves at his feet!* We laugh, and feel superior.

It's hard, however, to resist the underlying message that life is in fact about having the dream. We see boy and girl come together in love, and it feels good.

But do they really live happily ever after?

Sometimes, as I sit at the end of a romantic comedy watching the credits roll by, I feel torn. In *Silver Linings Playbook*, Pat and Tiffany declare their love to each other and kiss. I enjoy the happy ending. But then what? I can't help thinking, *These people are going to need some serious therapy.* At some point, the honeymoon will be over. They will awaken from the dream and into reality.

▥ ▥ ▥

Art imitates life; life imitates art. Movies are part of our shared pop-culture heritage. So are novels, music, and advertising. Together they represent a culture of romance that weaves through our hopes and expectations, even our perceptions of what's normal.

The enduring popularity of Jane Austen's work is a testimony not only to her prose but her insight, her ability to matter-of-factly lay open the thoughts and feelings of those who struggled with her society's romantic norms. She was both a child of her time and its critic. We can learn not only from the stories she told, but the way that she told them. We can look at our own culture of romance, and ask where we find it wanting—particularly when it comes to making sense of our own experience.

Romantic comedy is a good place to begin. Which films are your favorites (or do you refuse to watch them altogether)? Which character or characters do you identify with most closely, and why? How does their story relate to your own?[35] Exploring such questions may give you insight into your own taken-for-granted romantic ideals.

We needn't simply thrust such ideals aside. There's nothing intrinsically wrong with believing in love at first sight. But we can and should be curious: when do our romantic ideals become burdensome, as when we wait and wait for a destiny—a soul mate!— that never comes? And might there be a more biblical alternative?

The unspoken contract Hollywood makes with its viewers is: *Watch the movie, enjoy the ending, and don't ask questions—in exchange we'll give you a couple of hours of entertainment.*[36] But it's not merely entertainment. Romantic fiction lends order and meaning to our emotional experience. It helps us make sense of our sensibilities. As we'll see in the next chapter, however, in real life we don't always get the fairy tale ending.

talk or think about it

1. Discuss your answers to the questions on the previous page. Do you watch rom-coms, and if so, which are your favorites? What do you enjoy about these movies? Which characters do you identify with, and why? (If you don't watch rom-coms, say why, and listen with care and curiosity to what others say.) Alternatively, what do you *dislike* most about one or more of the rom-coms you've seen?

2. Even those who don't read romantic fiction or watch rom-coms have been exposed to other messages of the romance culture, through music and advertising. Think of the lyrics of the songs you know about relationships, or commercials showing couples together. What messages do they convey? How might these messages shape our expectations about love?

3. How do any of these messages and expectations relate to the way you would tell the story—or would *want* to tell the story—of your own most important relationships? Alternatively, how have such messages or expectations made your own relationships more difficult, uncertain, or confusing?

4

happily ever after...?

I was in our local Target store, sent on a mission by my wife: find wrapping paper for a shower gift for relatives who were having a baby girl. Husbands in my situation worry that when they get home, their wives will roll their eyes and say, "I can't believe you chose *that*." But I was determined to do my best.

I already knew where to find the greeting cards. And there, just behind them, was the gift wrap display. My eye was drawn immediately to the bright pink rolls of paper adorned with the Disney Princesses. Snow White, Cinderella, Ariel and the rest were all dressed in flowing gowns, as if on their way to the ball. "Love to sparkle!" the paper declared in silvery script, amongst the swirls and tiaras.

There was no gift wrap for baby showers, and I knew the parents were big Disney fans. Maybe the Princess paper was the best choice? I picked a roll off the rack and stared at it for a good long while. Then I put it back. To me, it screamed of stereotypes and felt too crassly commercial. I looked at every other possible option. But in the end, I gave in, and went with pink and princesses.

Not long ago, those characters could not have been found gracing the same piece of gift wrap, nor anything else. It began in the year 2000, when a newly-hired marketing executive attended a *Disney on Ice* show. Finding himself surrounded by little girls in homemade princess costumes, he had a light-bulb moment: how had they missed this marketing opportunity? Soon after, the "Disney Princess" brand was born and became a staggering success. Thousands upon thousands of DP items now generate billions of dollars in revenue, feeding what seems to be an insatiable demand.[1]

The princesses even have their own website, where visitors can learn more about their favorite characters and movies. They can even get advice for "Turning Yourself into a Disney Princess." Here's how that blog post begins:

> So you love the Disney princesses. We understand that because we love them too. Maybe you love them so much that you want to emulate them in your everyday life. That's cool with us; they're strong, independent ladies. ...But remember: being you is the best thing you can ever be. So take the below as guidelines while knowing that the most important way to be like a princess, is to just do you. Okay? Okay.[2]

Some of the advice offered is good. Who could object to suggestions like, "Practice kindness," "Be open to new experiences, even if they scare you," and "Know your worth...you are not a prize to be won"? Not surprisingly, though, there's also a fairy tale emphasis on following your heart and chasing your dreams. What kind of dreams? They don't say. But visitors can take quizzes like, "Who's your Disney soul mate based on your zodiac sign?" and "How many of these Disney guys would you date?"[3] The latter quiz begins with the introduction, "Disney guys, they're pretty great. Have you even considered how dateable they are? Now's your chance."

That's not the dream I'd want for my daughter.

■ ■ ■

Fantasy and fairy tale: it's part of growing up. Kids learn quickly that the phrase "Once upon a time" beckons them to other worlds. Whether they pretend to be pirates or princesses, children grow through imaginative play, and fairy tales are often part of the process.

The stories present problems of good and evil in a way young children can easily grasp. They show heroes and heroines who triumph through persistence and good character. A particular story may become a child's personal favorite, because it helps them cope with unnamed emotions and fears.[4] Children learn that things don't have to be as they are now. Fairness and justice are possible.[5] Cinderella *can* go to the ball.

And like the comedies described in chapter 3, fairy tales are part of our culture of romance.

I've always enjoyed Disney movies. My sister and I grew up with them. Back then, if you wanted to see a movie, you had to go to a theater or watch whatever was being shown on network television. In our family, the theater was a rare treat. But we knew the Disney classics from watching *The Wonderful World of Color* on TV. Uncle Walt would even introduce the movies personally.

I did not, of course, grow up dreaming of being Cinderella. My fantasy world was populated with comic book superheroes. Occasionally, I would drape my bathrobe over my shoulders as a cape and jump off the furniture. I read Marvel Comics almost exclusively. I wanted to be Spider Man: a freewheeling, web-slinging teenager who wisecracked his way through his battles with evil. And I pretended my G. I. Joe was Captain America, using a little red plastic dish as a shield.

But that's not to say I had no early education in love and romance. I never thought of being Cinderella, but I knew all about Prince Charming and white knights rescuing damsels in distress. And comic books weren't only about stylized, super-powered violence. The genius of Marvel Comics was their feet-of-clay characters, who struggled with the whole range of human emotions.[6] Captain America, for example, was forever reliving memories of the war, filled with remorse over the fallen comrades he couldn't save, including his teenage sidekick, Bucky.

And no one had a more complicated love life than Spider Man.

His romantic storyline made a lasting impression on me. Peter Parker is Spider Man's alter ego. Gwen Stacy, the daughter of a police captain, is his true love. During an epic urban rooftop battle between

Spider Man and his nemesis Doctor Octopus, an avalanche of rubble is sent tumbling to the street below. Captain Stacy valiantly pushes a toddler out of harm's way, and is crushed by the falling debris. Spidey tries to rush him to a hospital, but it's too late. The captain dies in Peter's arms, calling him by name: he knows Peter's true identity but has never revealed his secret—not even to his own daughter. With his last breath, he assures Peter of Gwen's love, and asks him to take care of her.

This is the classic superhero dilemma: can you ever take off the mask and have a normal life? Gwen loves Peter. But now she also blames Spider Man for her father's death. For love's sake, Peter decides that Gwen must never know the truth. And in a later move that rocked the comic book world, Gwen dies of whiplash when Spidey tries to save her from a fall.

Poor Peter is cursed with the "Parker luck." His wisecracking superhero persona is a way of coping with a life that overflows with contradictions and personal problems. He accidentally killed his girlfriend, his best friend is a supervillain, and his boss hates Spider Man. His actions are constantly misunderstood: some think he's a hero, but others, a monster. Every day, he dons the suit and risks his life. But when he takes off the suit, he's a nobody who can't make ends meet.

The comic book view of life and love, in other words, is often a tragic one. If you are blessed with power, you must use it for the good of humanity, even at the cost of great sacrifice. It's a lonely calling.

Superheroes often wonder why they should keep going. Some even go to therapy. To keep their loved ones safe from bad guys, they have to hide their super-identities—meaning that the people they care most about may never know them for who they are. Apparently, you can't save the world and have love too.

The immense popularity of superhero movies attests to the continuing power of comic book characters to capture our collective imagination. And whether we recognize it or not, these action-packed films teach us lessons about love. Here's one more example.

When Hollywood finally got around to making a big screen version of *Wonder Woman*, both moviegoers and critics alike praised its heroine for being powerful and yet sensitive and caring.[7] In the voice-over narration at the end of the film, she even describes the moral lesson she's learned from her adventures: "only love can truly save the world." It's a nice sentiment. But what does it mean? In the script, it's her sudden rage over her lost love that makes her powerful enough to kill her enemy—Ares, the god of war. Love, it seems, can overcome war with superior violence.

That's how love saves the world?

In what follows, I've chosen to focus on princess stories. They illustrate nicely what was said in the previous chapter: we make sense of our lives through story, particularly when it comes to love and romance. The Disney princesses in particular are a prime example of what happens when the old tales are repackaged for mass consumption.

But don't worry, Disney fans. I'm not going to suggest that princess stories will single-handedly ruin our children for life. It's just that fairy tales are part of our collective imagination, and they're everywhere. It's worth asking how such stories might mold impressionable minds on matters of love and romance—whether it's our children's minds or our own.

■ ■ ■

Contrary to the website description quoted earlier, the Disney princesses weren't always "strong, independent ladies." The earliest ones—Snow White, Cinderella, and Sleeping Beauty—were "Walt's princesses."[8] Each needed to be rescued by a handsome prince who would bring true love.

Much has changed since then. The princesses who came after Walt Disney died were less passive and more capable. And princes? They're not so charming anymore. They need to be transformed by a woman's love, and must learn through adversity to be more humble and caring.[9] Newer offerings like *Frozen* and *Maleficent* even engage in a bit of bait-and-switch, playing up the fairy tale expectation that true love's kiss will come to the rescue—and then knocking it sideways.[10]

Yet some of the old stereotypes keep sneaking in the back door. Consider, for example, *The Princess and the Frog*, in which audiences were treated with great fanfare to Tiana (Anika Noni Rose), Disney's first African-American princess.[11] As children, Tiana and her friend Charlotte (Jennifer Cody) were read the story of *The Frog Prince.* Charlotte would swoon with delight while Tiana declared that she would never do anything so disgusting as to kiss a frog.   Charlotte grows up to be a rich, spoiled southern belle. She always gets her way and dreams of marrying a prince. Tiana grows up to be a hard-working waitress. She's trying to save enough money to start the restaurant she and her father had always dreamed of opening.

Enter Prince Naveen (Bruno Campos) of Moldovia, a young man as self-centered and spoiled as Charlotte but without the money. He and his valet Lawrence (Peter Bartlett) encounter a voodoo witch doctor (Keith David) who turns Naveen into a frog, and makes Lawrence look like the prince in order to marry Charlotte and steal her father's fortune.

Naveen meets Tiana at a masquerade ball. He's a frog; she's dressed as a princess. Knowing the fairy tale, he confidently promises to reward her if she will but kiss him and turn him back into a prince. Thinking of her restaurant, Tiana overcomes her disgust, kisses Naveen—and promptly turns into a frog herself.

What follows is a fairly standard romantic storyline (just greener and slimier). Boy and girl dislike each other but are forced to work together. They grow closer through their adventures and eventually fall in love.

Tiana, however, isn't one of Walt's helpless princesses. At the beginning of the film, she works long hours to fulfill her dream. She fights back against the racism and prejudice that stand in her way. Later, as a frog, she's more resourceful than the clueless Naveen. And as one scholar has noted appreciatively, she's the first Disney princess whose happy ending isn't romance or marriage: it's opening her restaurant.[12]

Agreed. But we shouldn't ignore the fact that in the closing minutes of the film, Tiana willingly gives up her dream when she becomes convinced that she and Naveen are fated to remain frogs for the rest of their lives. They return to the swamp, and marry. Then—and only then—comes the magical moment. When they kiss, they become human again (because they're married now, so she really is a princess, and when the frog kisses a princess...well, you get the idea), and work together to make the restaurant a reality. True love's kiss, in other words, may not be the dream itself, but the dream is impossible without it.

Maybe the old French saying has it right: the more things change, the more they remain the same.[13]

◼ ◼ ◼

Some mothers who indulge their daughters' pleas for princess products are perfectly aware of the old damsel in distress stereotype—and hate it. When journalist Peggy Orenstein asked moms what they thought about the tales that inspired the products they buy, one mother replied, "Oh, I don't let the actual *story* in the house. Just the *costumes.* Eleanor doesn't know the stories." Another mother agreed. "Those stories are horrible. Every single one is the same: it's about romance, love, and being rescued by the prince. I *will* protect my daughter from that."[14]

But is that really possible? Can children play with the toys and be sheltered from the stories? Some of the moms Orenstein interviewed knew that their daughters were still getting the stories from other kids. And Orenstein herself argues that parents can't keep children completely away from cultural messages about romance and sexuality. Even the fairy tales themselves warn against locking children away in a castle tower.

Yet it's helpful to remember that none of these influences are as simple and straightforward as getting hit by a bus. True, kids engaged in pretend-play know the fairy tales inside and out, and will sometimes police each other: "No! That's not how you're supposed to do it!" But as one researcher found, if kids in a classroom are given the chance to tell the story their own way, even Sleeping Beauty may awake and slay her own dragons without a prince's help.[15]

There will always be parts of fairy tales that we don't like. But such stories have a firm grip on the imaginations of children around the world. That's not necessarily a bad thing. As suggested earlier, fairy tales can help kids deal with the harsh realities of the present. One psychologist, who uses superhero stories in his work with children, tells of an adopted child who struggled to make sense of how his parents could have loved him and at the same time given him away. The story of Superman, who had to journey from Krypton to Earth to find a new family, was his favorite. It gave meaning and hope to his own unfolding story.[16]

Here's another example of coping through story. Six-year-old Timmy was a leukemia patient who had already undergone one painful spinal tap and was scheduled for another. He waited with tears in his eyes for the moment the nurse would come and the procedure would begin. His mother had her own fears and was of no help in calming her son.

G. Frank Lawlis was the psychologist assigned to the case. He had tried teaching Timmy to handle the pain through relaxation techniques, to no avail. So he tried a different tack.

He asked Timmy if he'd like to hear a story about another boy like himself, and Timmy agreed. "Once upon a time," Lawlis began. He spun the heroic tale of "Big T," a boy who had to show his neighbors how to cope with a disease that threatened their village. Big T even had to have blood taken from his body and mixed with a magic potion, a painful process. But he had traveled far and wide to learn from sages. He knew how to cope courageously with pain through relaxation and controlled breathing. And he taught these skills to others, earning him the praise and respect of the villagers.

Timmy listened with rapt attention. When the story was finished, he sat quietly for a few moments. Then he calmly and confidently went over to comfort his anxious mother.[17] That's one side of the power of story: it can train our imaginations in new and positive directions.

But there's another side. Lawlis also describes an informal study done with twenty young women, ages 15 to 22, from poor inner-city neighborhoods. Each woman was asked to identify a favorite childhood story and tell what the story was about. Then they were asked if they ever thought about the story when they were troubled, and what the story taught them about life. Lawlis reports:

> Sixteen of the twenty interviewees revealed their favorite story was Cinderella. Most of them answered that it was about "people not treating you right." They said that sometimes they remembered it when they were depressed or blue, "because it shows how unfair the world really is." ...[But] three women answered that, "the only thing the story taught you was that there was not much hope of life getting better because Princes are just make-believe."[18]

We know the story. Unlike Snow White or Sleeping Beauty, Cinderella doesn't lie under a magic curse. Instead, she's tormented by her stepmother and stepsisters, who treat her like a slave. Justice comes in the form of a fairy godmother, who transforms Cinderella's rags into a beautiful gown. Cinderella becomes the belle of the ball; the prince falls in love with her. But she must flee before the fairy godmother's enchantment wears off. In her haste, she loses one of her delicate glass slippers. When the prince searches for the woman whose foot fits the slipper, he and Cinderella are reunited. They marry and live happily ever after.

But what if life keeps telling us that there's no magic, no fairy godmother, and no prince?

The tragedy isn't that the women who were interviewed loved fairy tales. It's understandable that they would have identified with Cinderella; the unfairness of her situation mirrors the injustice of their own. The story might even have given them a glimmer of hope that things could be better. But bitter experience has taught them that their prince will never come, or worse, that "Princes are just make-believe." Sadly, instead of trading the whole Cinderella premise for a more fitting and hopeful story, these women find themselves stuck with a fairy tale robbed of its happy ending.

That's not a dream. It's a nightmare.

How much of our own disappointment with love comes because we can't let go of the fairy tale? Or more subtly, might we even be unaware of the extent to which the hope of a romantic happily-ever-after has a hold on our imagination?

Perhaps this is mostly a phenomenon of American culture. But the fantasy and fairy tale impulse crosses international lines, and in today's global economy, that's a marketing opportunity. The values of American popular culture come pre-packaged with every export, from movies to fast-food franchises. I expect the world's imagination to become increasingly Disney-like.[19]

After all, it's already happened in the church.

■ ■ ■

Whether we want to admit it or not, many Christians suffer the same kind of disappointment already described, the disillusionment of having one's romantic hopes dashed. Leslie Ludy, thinking back on her days of dating and breakup, writes:

> I longed to be loved and cherished. I had dreamed of a perfect love story ever since I was a five-year-old girl watching Cinderella. But somewhere in the midst of the endless cycle of one temporary romance after the next, my dreams had shattered right along with the broken and fragmented pieces of my heart. Yes, I was still young. But even so, I'd already begun to give up on the idea of ever finding real love.
>
> Growing up in church, I had listened carefully to the instructions given by my youth group leaders and tried to follow the Christian rules of dating to the letter. But those rules failed to protect me from a broken heart and shattered life. And as I observed my Christian friends, I saw we were all following the same pattern: an endless cycle of shallow and cheap romances that never lasted and left us emotionally bleeding and insecure.[20]

Youth group kids are often taught "rules of dating" that boil down to behavioral limits. "Don't have sex before you get married" is the first and greatest commandment. But youth who are hungry for love, affection, and the esteem of their peers need more than just a list of don'ts. Rules by themselves encourage a shallow legalism that leaves matters of the heart untouched.

Nor are youth who pledge to wait until marriage immune to trouble. Some jump into ill-advised marriages just to keep the no-sex-before-marriage rule. Many more struggle to figure out how far they can go without crossing the line, rationalizing away all kinds of questionable activity.

Donna Freitas has written poignantly about the different attitudes toward sexuality on American college campuses.[21] At the Catholic and religiously unaffiliated schools she studied, students found themselves in the midst of a "hookup" culture of the kind of casual sex that would have made Doris Day blush. Expectations beyond the moment were intentionally vague or non-existent. Many students ridiculed the outdated religious teachings of their youth, if they had a religious tradition at all. Students at these colleges simply took the hookup culture for granted. But that doesn't mean they liked it. They just weren't sure how else to handle the social pressure to conform.

Freitas tells the story of Tom, one of the "alpha males" who set the sexual standard at his nonreligious university, the kind of young man that "parents hope their daughters will avoid."[22] He spoke degradingly about women, declared that having a steady girlfriend would be too much work, and even scoffed at the idea of hanging out with a woman during the day.

Yet at one point in the interview, Tom turned wistful, reminiscing about the woman with whom he fell "totally in love" in his very first week at college.[23] The relationship lasted over a year. But her other activities eventually crowded him out of her life. Tom was the one who pleaded for more time together, who waited for the phone call that never came. When at last she broke up with him for good, he was devastated.

Did he want another relationship like that? Freitas asked. Yes, he replied. But he had been searching for a year and a half with no success. So he contented himself with a string of hookups that he would brag about the next day.

What about evangelical students? According to Freitas, they have some of the same hopes and values as students at other colleges. For example, their spirituality is important to them, they have sexual desires, and romantic fulfillment is a top priority. And like other students, they struggle to hold all these things together.[24]

What's different is that the hookup culture may be replaced with a so-called "culture of purity" in which sexual abstinence before marriage is supposed to be the norm. The operative phrase, of course, is "supposed to be." Students who are sexually active or even just struggling with their thoughts and feelings must hide it from friends, or from the adults who could give them guidance. And for the women in particular, there's often a "Ring by spring!" pressure to get engaged before graduation. The burden of that expectation complicates relationships. If a young man and woman spend time together, just the two of them, the gossip mill begins to churn.

Don't misunderstand: I believe that it's right, good, and biblical to reserve sex for marriage. In that way, I affirm the purity movement and grieve the way that sex has become little more than a form of commitment-free recreation. But to me, the romantic expectations of the purity culture can sound too much like a Christianized version of waiting for Prince Charming:

> God has a husband already picked out for her. One day, God will reveal to this man what wife he is to marry, at which point the man will start a chaste courtship. In the meantime, she is to wait patiently, submissive to God's will. Her only real job is to guard herself from missteps that could derail this romantic ideal—like dating the wrong guy.[25]

As far as I can tell, this religiously revised soul mate idea isn't biblical.[26] That's not to say that God can't reveal to a man whom he should marry (though one might ask why the woman isn't copied on the memo). God told the prophet Hosea, for example, to take Gomer as his wife (Hos 1:2-9). But the story hardly qualifies as a tale of romance.[27] God also told Joseph to take Mary as his wife (Matt 1:18-20). But that was after they were already betrothed, and God had to intervene when Joseph found Mary inexplicably pregnant.

Again, I support the encouragement to be chaste, patient, and obedient to God's will—provided that the advice is given to men and women alike. One would hope that anyone who is consistently and prayerfully seeking God would make wiser decisions about relationships.

But some of the romantic ideals Freitas describes sound like an attempt to put a pious shine on secular ideas. The fulfillment of romantic hopes and dreams is taken as a measure of God's blessing or one's faithfulness. This encourages desperation in some and arrogance in others. Freitas writes of one student who married while still in college and wore that fact like a badge of superiority:

> Emily lived the fairy tale and was now embarked on a happily ever after with Prince Charming. And she isn't just proud of this accomplishment; she is smug. She knows that the overwhelming majority of her peers "fail" as princesses; most girls don't get the fairy tale. And while female classmates are deep into what is popularly known on campus as "the senior scramble"—the mad dash to find a husband by graduation— Emily can sit back, relax, and just watch. And she does.[28]

Not getting a ring by spring is thus one way to fail in the purity culture. Being sexually active is another. Women who cross the forbidden line may be perceived as damaged goods. They may even struggle to believe in the possibility of redemption, because it's assumed that those who "fail in this quest for purity...forfeit the Christian fairy tale."[29]

Standards surrounding sexuality have changed in recent decades. There's no question of that. But our fundamental longings, the things we want from our relationships, are still the same. We want to be heard and understood. We want to be valued, appreciated, and cherished. As Kerry Cronin has written about the college students she's taught and interviewed:

I find that what really concerns young adults—what really scares them, what fascinates them, what moves them—are not really questions of sex but rather questions of intimacy. In the midst of their ubiquitous posting and twittering and snapchatting, despite their seemingly constant connecting through all modes of social media, the students I meet speak overwhelmingly about feeling quite disconnected, lonely, and fundamentally *not known* by others. ... What haunts them most is not ever being seen, or recognized, or loved by anyone beyond their own family circles. In worse cases, their fear is not mattering to anyone even within those most important first circles. In the very worst cases, there is the darkness of feeling that you do not matter even to God, that you are not held by God.[30]

Ultimately, as Cronin suggests, it's not simply about popularity, or romance, or even sex—not even for the alpha males like Tom, whom we met earlier. As I suggested in chapter 2, it's about the longing to be known and loved for who you are. And in that way, college students are pretty much the same as everyone else.

Shared stories trickle down through layer after social layer. Cinderella stories—and there have been many variations throughout history—are read to children or translated into other pop-culture expressions. The ideas of the damsel in distress and the handsome prince show up again and again, even in the way Christians talk about love and romance.

And these stories in turn get embodied in the social life of many Christian college campuses. Students quickly pick up the rules of their school's romance culture. What do other students talk about? What *can't* be talked about? What's "normal" or expected in the area of relationships? Which students are held up as the winners or losers? And in the midst of all of this, each student has to come to terms with more deeply personal questions of identity and acceptance. *What do I have to do to fit in? What if I don't want to fit in? Is it okay to be me? And who am I, anyway?*

As if navigating the academic system wasn't challenging enough, students have to find their way through a relational minefield too. Parents and pastors hope that youth have been grounded solidly in their moral convictions before going off to college, so that they can avoid doing things they may later regret. We've given them the rules. But what stories of love have we knowingly or unknowingly packed with their pillowcases and toothbrushes?

▓ ▓ ▓

Our imaginations are shaped by the stories of our culture, including novels, movies, fairy tales, and more. In this, we might identify with the grandson in *The Princess Bride*.[31] The boy (Fred Savage) is sick in bed, playing video games. His grandfather (Peter Falk) comes to read him a book, a swashbuckling story of adventure and romance passed down for generations from father to son. The grandson is skeptical at first, asking with suspicion, "Is this a *kissing* book?"

But soon, he's swept along with the tale and begins to care about what happens to the characters. Even though he's never heard the book before, he knows how the story is supposed to go. The evil prince must be defeated. The hero has to survive, so he can rescue and be reunited with his true love. And the boy gets upset when the story seems to take a wrong turn.

From the time we begin playing pretend as children, we strive to make sense of our lives. Through the stories we hear and the stories we tell, we weave a continuous thread that runs from our remembered past through the present and into the future.[32]

> [S]tories do not simply report past events. Stories project possible futures, and those projections affect what comes to be, although this will rarely be the future projected by the story. Stories do not just have plots. Stories work to *emplot* lives: they offer a plot that makes some particular future not only plausible but also compelling.[33]

That includes, of course, the stories and images that form the background of what we expect a love relationship to be. We already know, at some level, how the story is supposed to go.

Moreover, as one theory of love suggests, we "fall in love with people whose stories are the same as or similar to our own, but whose roles in these stories are complementary to ours."[34] Every Cinderella needs a Prince Charming for there to be a happy ending. Every white knight needs a damsel to rescue and a dragon to slay. Superheroes need someone to come home to after a hard day of saving the world. In countless films, including westerns and even musicals like *Guys and Dolls* or *The Music Man*, there is the role of the gunslinger, rogue, or con-man and the role of the loyal, virtuous woman who sees beneath the rough exterior and redeems him by loving him anyway.[35] The examples go on and on.

But such stories don't have to be of the Hollywood variety. Perhaps we imagine that love means working side by side with someone on a common interest. If so, we'll need to find someone who shares that passion. Or maybe our ideal of love is to be a sacrificial caregiver. If so, we'll need to find someone who would cherish receiving our care. If our ideals are mismatched, the result may be disappointment and conflict.[36]

The point again is that we don't come to relationships as blank slates. We have ideals and expectations of which we may not even be aware. Early relationships with Mom and Dad—and even *between* Mom and Dad—influence our developing stories too, by coloring them with an emotional tone.[37] If we've been loved deeply and cared for consistently, our stories will be hopeful and positive.

But if we've been consistently hurt, our stories will be more tragic. Expecting to be hurt again, we'll be more cautious and defensive, seeing negative motives where there may be none. Not all of the stories we construct to make sense of our lives, therefore, are positive ones. We don't all expect to live happily ever after. And even those who hope for the fairy tale ending don't always get it.

Still, we never outgrow our fascination with or our need for story. We explain our behavior to ourselves and others with story: "When I was a kid..." We wrestle with the events of our day through story: "You'll never believe what happened to me today..." Others tell us their story, and we connect with them through a story of our own: "You know, that happened to *me* once..." And whether we recognize it or not, story shapes our moral sense of how the world should be and what goals we should pursue. As philosopher Alasdair MacIntyre has said, "I can only answer the question 'What am I to do?' if I can answer the prior question 'Of what story or stories do I find myself a part?'"[38]

We live in a world awash in love stories: the ones we see and hear through the media, the ones we witness in childhood, the ones we continually revise as we pick our way through relationships. Some stories promise too much, others too little. And happily-ever-after isn't the only storyline that comes out of Hollywood. As one script puts it, the best we might be able to hope for is "messily-ever-after."[39]

But to some extent, our problems of love are problems of story. We expect unhappy endings, or happy endings that never seem to come. We think we *have* the happy ending, only to stumble over an unexpected twist in the plot.

As Christians, we supposedly put our faith in The Greatest Story Ever Told. What does that faith mean? We read the gospels, and believe that they describe real events of human history. Jesus was born. He walked the earth. He died on a Roman cross. He was raised from the dead.

But there's a difference between believing in a story's historical claims and living inside the story itself.[40] The book of Acts, for example, isn't the tale of a group of people who attended one of Jesus' lectures and decided to start a social movement. It continues what the gospels begin. The kingdom that Jesus jump-started became a living reality embodied by his followers, who were empowered by the very Spirit of Jesus himself.[41] And the story isn't finished yet.

Many years ago, as I was preparing to take the pulpit, a friend asked what I would be preaching on. I gave him my title: "The Twenty-Ninth Chapter of Acts." But before I could explain, he gave me a quizzical look and asked, "You're going to preach on the whole chapter?"

The book of Acts, of course, only has twenty-eight chapters (at least in my Bible). Luke begins the tale with the risen Jesus' parting words to his disciples, followed by the giving of the Holy Spirit at Pentecost and the birth of the church, with particular emphasis on the apostle Paul's mission to the Gentiles. The drama twists and turns as we follow Paul on his journeys, as the gospel is sometimes received, sometimes rejected. The story ends on a positive note, with Paul freely preaching the gospel in Rome: "Unhindered and with complete confidence, he continued to preach God's kingdom and to teach about the Lord Jesus Christ" (Acts 28:31).

That's how Luke's written account ends. But the story behind the account goes on, and we are part of it. Every Christian living today is a distant beneficiary not only of what Jesus did on the cross, but of the missionary work of Paul and the other apostles. In that sense, our lives are part of the twenty-ninth chapter of Acts.

It's a long chapter indeed. The drama continues to weave through the centuries and into every corner of the world, and we are characters in it. But if we can understand ourselves that way, then the question is this: will we play our parts well and faithfully? Will any of this make a difference to the stories of love we tell and embody?

Let me tell one more princess story, one that I hope will point us in the right direction.

■ ■ ■

The late Audrey Hepburn's first major screen role, for which she received an Academy Award, was as young, sheltered Princess Ann in *Roman Holiday*.[42] She's been taught how to carry herself with regal bearing, but privately chafes under the burden. In Rome on a goodwill tour, Ann throws a royal tantrum. The doctor sedates her and leaves her to rest. Alone in her room, she seizes the opportunity to escape out the window.

Soon, she's overcome by the sedative and falls asleep by a curb, where she's found by Joe Bradley (Gregory Peck), an American reporter coming home from a poker game. At first, he doesn't know who she is, assumes she's drunk, and lets her sleep it off in his apartment. He discovers the truth the next morning. Yet he pretends not to know, taking advantage of the situation to get an exclusive story on the runaway princess. He doesn't tell Ann that he's a reporter. And Ann lies to him too, pretending to be a truant schoolgirl so she can have her one day of freedom.

You can probably guess what happens next. The two enjoy Rome together. They laugh, dance, and even find themselves in the middle of a brawl, while Joe's friend Irving (Eddie Albert) secretly catches it all on film. Eventually Joe and the princess kiss. Without intending to, they fall in love.

How must the movie end?

How would we want it to end?

Roman Holiday is usually considered a romantic comedy, yet it may be more of a coming-of-age story. The young princess has had her romantic fling. But she knows her duty. She can't run away with the man she loves. Soberly, sacrificially, she returns to the embassy and embraces her royal role, refusing to be treated like a child any longer.

Joe and Irving attend Ann's press conference the next day. They secretly reassure her that there will be no sensational headlines, no scandalous pictures. The two lovers' last contact is a formal handshake as she greets the reporters individually. Then, with a fleeting expression of regret, the princess beams a smile to her public, turns, and walks away.

Joe and Ann still love each other. You sense that they always will. But the boy doesn't get the girl nor vice versa. Both understand that Ann's destiny is to be the princess. Her love for Joe cannot replace her love for the kingdom. And for love's sake, Joe must also embrace her destiny.

■ ■ ■

Does that ending seem disappointing? The question is whether we can believe that Ann's devotion to her kingdom can or should trump her romantic feelings for Joe. If we can accept that she loves the kingdom that much, then the ending seems noble and right. If we can't, we may think her a fool for sacrificing her happiness to the emptiness of mere duty.

Which is the priority for us? Which story captures our imaginations more completely, and figures more prominently in our life goals and decisions? Is it the story of the kingdom, or the story of romance? I'm not suggesting that we must choose between God and all other loves. It's far better to say that a true love of God puts all of our other loves in their proper order.

Perhaps, for example, I want to live one type of love story, with the expectations and roles that go with it. My partner, however, wants to live a different story. Perhaps we even marry. If and when we notice these stories and expectations are different, what happens next? Will it be a contest to see whose love story "wins"?

If so, we may both lose.

The alternative is to make the story of the kingdom the higher priority, and with it, the embodiment of the kind of love it describes.

There's a place for fairy tale. Indeed, as Frederick Buechner once suggested, Scripture has its own fairy tale element.[43] We are children of the king. One day, the king will return to gather those who belong to him and bring them into his kingdom, where they will live happily ever after.

But if that story fails to shape our lives and loves in the here and now, we may need to have our imaginations captured once again by the story of the God who loves, of the God who *is* love.

talk or think about it

1. Who were your favorite fantasy / fairy tale / comic book characters when you were a kid? What did you like about them? What kind of relationships and/or relationship complications did they have?

2. Alternatively, pick a favorite character, and think about what lesson that character's life teaches about relationships. Use that lesson to complete the following sentence, "The moral of the story is..." Tell each other who the character is, then explain and illustrate the "moral" with examples from the character's life.

3. In what ways have you encountered the idea of meeting your "soul mate" (or some similar concept) and living happily ever after? What consequences has the idea had in your life (or the life of others you know), whether positive or negative?

4. Discuss this statement from earlier in the chapter: "To some extent, our problems of love are problems of story." Give examples, if you can, of how two people might approach a relationship together with very different stories of how the relationship should go, and what consequences this has. What would change if we began to understand our personal stories, romance and all, as part of the "twenty-ninth chapter of Acts"?

5

a father's embrace

Before we had kids, I didn't really know what it would mean to be a dad. I had not been close to my own father, nor had he been close to his. Both of them were products of their time and culture, and such things weren't expected of men. To be sure, Dad reliably provided for his family and never did anyone wrong. But I don't remember him taking an active interest in my life, playing with me, or even having a role in my discipline. I have no doubt that he did at least some of these things from time to time. I just have no memory of it, and it feels a bit like a hole in my childhood. I don't blame him for that. If he were alive today, I'm sure he would say that he had loved me in his own way, quietly.

When it came time to raise my own kids, though, I wanted to be a loving, involved father. I just had no model to follow.

Thus, when I first became a Christian, I had no clear concept of God as Father. What could it mean to pray as Jesus taught his disciples to do—to address the God of Israel, the Creator of the universe, as "Father"? Jesus the Son even addressed God the Father as *Abba*, an ancient word which reflects the warmth of their relationship (though it doesn't quite mean "Daddy," no matter what you've heard).[1] And he invited his followers into that same warm intimacy.

Moreover, as Michael Reeves has insisted,

Again and again, the Scriptures equate the terms *God* and *Father*... Since God is, before all things, a Father, and not

> primarily Creator or Ruler, all his ways are beautifully
> fatherly. It is not that this God "does" being Father as a day
> job, only to kick back in the evenings as plain old "God." ...He
> is Father. All the way down.[2]

God is not Father only sometimes, when the mood strikes. He is
Father eternally. Before the dawn of creation, he was already loving
his Son (John 17:24). Thus, when with the apostle John we speak of
the God who *is* love, we speak of the God who is a loving Father.

I'm still learning what all that means. And it helps, I think, that
I've been a father myself. Until we had children, I didn't know—in
some ways, *couldn't* know—how much those tiny little fingers would
wrap themselves around my heart. I didn't know the joy of a good-
morning hug, nor the protective feeling of having a troubled child
melt into your shoulder.

Nor did I know, frankly, how angry I could get when they were
being disobedient or stubborn. Love and wrath. It took becoming a
dad to teach me that the second can sometimes be an expression of the
first. As suggested in chapter 2, we have to be careful not to read
what the Bible describes as the love and wrath of God as nothing but
bigger versions of our own. "Be angry without sinning," Paul
commands (Eph 4:26). The implication is that we may sin in our
anger. But the same is not true of God. Again, John says "God is love"
(1 John 4:8)—not "God is wrath." It is only because of our sin that
wrath becomes a necessary expression of God's essentially loving
nature.

The Bible ascribes emotions to God, and invites us to know God as
Father. What does that mean? As Jesus taught his disciples, our
heavenly Father know our needs, wants to give us good things, and
loves us (e.g., Matt 6:25-34; 7:9-11; John 14:21, 23; 16:27). If we're
rebellious, of course, our Father may discipline us. That sounds
unpleasant. But discipline is the sign that our Father delights in us
and cares about the kind of people we become (Prov 3:11-12; Heb
12:4-11). And as we'll see at the end of this chapter, Jesus paints a
startling, vivid word picture of God as a father who joyously and
tenderly embraces even the most wayward of his children.

Here's the question: do we know, personally, that God the Father loves us? God's love is clearly and repeatedly announced in Scripture. It's the core of what makes the good news good. But is it more than just an intellectual proposition to us, a box we check off on a list of statements we're supposed to believe?

On my very first day of college, two young men shared a gospel tract with me. They told me that God loved me, and that I needed what Jesus had done for me on the cross. They asked if I wanted to pray to accept Jesus as my Savior, and I said yes.

Afterward, they cautioned me that I might not feel any differently. They showed me a little diagram of a train with three cars labeled "fact," "faith," and "feeling." "Fact" was the locomotive pulling the train; "feeling" was the caboose that brought up the rear. Their point was that I needed to believe with my mind what the Scriptures declared as true, regardless of how I felt. God loved me, I had prayed the prayer and therefore was saved. That was that.

In one way, they were right. I knew that I had just done something momentous. But I didn't feel any differently, and my emotions had no direct bearing on the facts. Either Jesus had died for me or he hadn't. Either God loved me or he didn't—again, no matter how I felt.

But our emotions matter, especially when it comes to love. God's love is not a mere fact to be believed, but a gift given for our joy. And that gift is meant to be both cherished and shared. As Jesus prepared to sacrifice his life for the sake of love, he specifically invited his disciples into the loving relationship he had with his Father:

> As the Father loved me, I too have loved you. Remain in my love. If you keep my commandments, you will remain in my love, just as I kept my Father's commandments and remain in his love. I have said these things to you so that my joy will be in you and your joy will be complete. This is my commandment: love each other just as I have loved you. No one has greater love than to give up one's life for one's friends. (John 15:9-13)

Think for a moment about the significance of what Jesus is saying. God as Father loves the Son, eternally, because fatherly love is intrinsic to God's very character and being. And as we see repeatedly in John's gospel, Jesus the Son loves him back. In turn, Jesus also loves his disciples with the Father's love. Such love is willing to make the ultimate sacrifice. Why? So that we might know the joy of sharing in the love between the Father and the Son.

Jesus used a metaphor to make his point. His followers were to "remain" in his love as the branches of a grapevine "remain" in the root and stock that give them life (John 15:1-8). Without this, the branches can produce no fruit. If we are to love one another, if we are to know the meaning of joy, we must remain in the Father's love for the Son and the Son's love for us.[3]

We are deeply loved by God. In response, we are called to love God with all our heart, all our being, all our mind, and all our strength (Mark 12:29; cf. also Deut 6:5; Matt 22:37; Luke 11:27). "All": that doesn't mean to love God four different ways with four different parts of ourselves, but to love God with every bit of who we are, as whole human beings, emotions included.

And we are commanded to embody our love for God in our love for one another. First Corinthians 13 is not some freestanding ethical ideal, nor a set of rules for making people more religious. It's a pastoral vision of what happens when a group of people truly know themselves to have been lovingly embraced by their heavenly Father. To consistently live what Paul teaches about love, then, we must wholeheartedly receive that embrace and all that it means.

But that may be easier said than done. Perhaps we have no experience of loving fatherhood. Or perhaps we find ourselves in the midst of a whirlwind; too many things go wrong too often for us to trust that God is truly loving.

Thus, it may take some imagination for us to connect or reconnect to the idea of God as a loving Father. To that end, I offer a meditation on one of Jesus' parables, retelling the story in a way that I hope makes it easier to grasp personally. But first, we need to clear a little space by dealing briefly with the matter of suffering—including Paul's.

■ ■ ■

"God loves you."

"Jesus loves you."

We hear a lot about God's love. It's the message we want to share with those who are suffering. And if we're going to be the loving people God wants us to be, we'll need to keep a firm grip on that love in the midst of our own suffering.

But suffering has a way of commandeering our thoughts and emotions. We're pulled in opposite directions by trust and doubt. The life of faith is like that. Sometimes, all we can do is reach heavenward in the hope that God is as loving as the Bible insists.

Not everyone believes that God is loving, let alone that God is love. Throughout the centuries, many have pondered what C. S. Lewis aptly called, "the problem of pain."[4] If God is just, loving, and all-powerful, then why is there so much suffering and evil in the world?

Pain and suffering, tragedy and injustice. We take these as facts of life, staples of the daily news. Too often, they complicate your own story, or the story of someone close to you. We live in a world fractured by sin. We suffer the consequences of evil, selfishness, and sheer stupidity, whether ours or someone else's.

But wait: wouldn't a good and loving God want to spare us all of that? If evil persists, or so the argument goes, one of three things must be true. Either God is not loving (and is possibly even mean-spirited), or God is powerless against evil, or God could stop evil but chooses not to, leaving us to wonder why.[5]

The philosophical questions are real, and I have no new answer to give. But it's important to recognize that the Bible itself doesn't shy away from the problem. Suffering isn't minimized or ignored. Instead, it's held in tension with the loving faithfulness of God.

When things go wrong, we need help holding onto our faith. Many find that help in the Psalms. Some of the most emotionally wrenching passages in all of Scripture are found in the so-called psalms of lament, which put the problem of pain boldly and bluntly. Lament psalms complain that things aren't right, and it's up to God to do something about it.[6] Some begin with complaint but end with hopeful anticipation:

> How long will you forget me, LORD? Forever?
> How long will you hide your face from me?
> How long will I be left to my own wits, agony filling my heart? Daily?
> How long will my enemy keep defeating me?
> Look at me! Answer me, LORD my God!
> Restore sight to my eyes!
> Otherwise, I'll sleep the sleep of death, and my enemies will say, "I won!"
> My foes will rejoice over my downfall.
> But I have trusted in your faithful love.
> My heart will rejoice in your salvation.
> Yes, I will sing to the LORD because he has been good to me.
> (Ps 13:1-6)

But others, like Psalm 88, aren't so optimistic. The psalmist cries out for God to hear his prayer, because his "whole being is filled with distress" as he stands "at the very brink of hell" (vss. 1-3). The psalmist *wants* to hope in the God of miracles. But he feels rejected and ignored by God, or worse, persecuted and punished with no relief (vss. 14-17). The song ends on a bleak note of loneliness and despair: "You've made my loved ones and companions distant. My only friend is darkness" (vs. 18).

That's it. That's the end of the psalm.

Have a nice day.

If we want clear or direct answers to the problem of pain, we won't find it here. Texts like this give the lie to all the simplistic platitudes we use to cheer people up. We might even ask, as does Old Testament scholar Walter Brueggemann, "What is a psalm like that doing in our Bible?" He suggests the beginnings of an answer:

> First, life is like that, and these poems intend to speak of all of
> life, not just the good parts. Here, more than anywhere else,

faith faces life as it is. Second, we observe that this psalm is not a psalm of mute depression. It is still speech. It is still addressed. In the bottom of the Pit, Israel still knows it has to do with Yahweh. It cannot be otherwise. ...To be Israel means to address God, even in God's unresponsive absence.[7]

Yes, life is like that. The people of God suffer in a variety of ways, for a variety of reasons. They cry out to God—and not politely.

You would think that if they truly believed God was punishing them, they'd be a bit more careful about their choice of words. But no. Ironically, what sounds like faithless moaning reveals its own kind of faith: *Yahweh is our God, there is no other, and we needn't fear retaliation if we complain honestly.*

We may never fully reconcile our suffering with God's love. But the psalms give us permission to plead our case as passionately as we please. Go ahead: God can take it. And in response, God invites us into his story.

Sometimes, all the people of God can do is cling to the memory of God's past faithfulness. They remember that God is the one who brought the people out of Egypt because he had at last heard their prayers. As God said to Moses:

> I've clearly seen my people oppressed in Egypt. I've heard their cry of injustice because of their slave masters. I know about their pain. I've come down to rescue them from the Egyptians in order to take them out of that land and bring them to a good and broad land, a land that's full of milk and honey... So get going. I'm sending you to Pharaoh to bring my people, the Israelites, out of Egypt. (Exod 3:7-8a, 10)

God calls the Israelites "my people," and later at Mount Sinai "my most precious possession" (Exod 19:5). He loved them, knew their pain, and heard their cry for help. God therefore rescued them out of slavery and into freedom, and eventually brought them into the land of promise.

The story twists and turns through centuries of rebellion, idolatry, and disobedience, while God remains steadfastly, inexplicably faithful throughout. And the story isn't over yet. But we get a sneak peek at the last chapter. God, victorious over death and evil, will make his home among the redeemed and put an end to all their suffering:

> I heard a loud voice from the throne say, "Look! God's dwelling is here with humankind. He will dwell with them, and they will be his peoples. God himself will be with them as their God. He will wipe away every tear from their eyes. Death will be no more. There will be no mourning, crying, or pain anymore, for the former things have passed away." Then the one seated on the throne said, "Look! I'm making all things new." (Rev 21:3-5a)

We shouldn't miss the immediate context of those hope-filled words: "I saw the holy city, New Jerusalem, coming down out of heaven from God, made ready as a bride beautifully dressed for her husband" (Rev 21:2). Added to that is the image of the wedding celebration of the Lamb (Rev 19:7-10)—and the fact that Jesus was fond of describing the kingdom using stories about weddings and banquets (e.g., Matt 22:1-14; 25:1-13), with himself in the lead role as bridegroom.

Why all the talk about weddings?

Because in some sense, from start to finish, from creation all the way through to the final redemption, the biblical narrative is a love story of cosmic proportions. The story the Bible puts in front of us is not simply that (a) God made something nice, (b) we broke it, and (c) God had to go to great lengths to fix it. As Robert Farrar Capon has written with characteristic flair, "It's the oldest story on Earth: Boy meets girl; boy loses girl; boy gets girl! He marries her and takes her home to Daddy. The Word romances creation till he wins her."[8]

To some, that may sound exaggerated or silly. But let's not get things the wrong way around. Clearly, the Bible is not a Harlequin novel nor a Hollywood romantic comedy. That's not to say, however, that our human penchant for romantic storytelling doesn't draw from a much deeper well.

God created the heavens and the earth—but not out of whimsy or boredom. Creation was an act of love, an outward movement of the eternal love between the Father, Son, and Spirit.[9] And to this day God loves what he created.

To fashion a universe that's shot through with freedom and contingency, however, is risky business. It's a terrible policy decision if God is nothing more than a divine CEO or stage manager. But God doesn't just manage, he loves—because God *is* love. And what is love, Capon asks, "if it's not the indulgence of the ultimate risk of giving oneself to another over whom we have no control? ...Why *love* ? Why *risk* at all?"[10]

I don't take Capon to be saying that God is incapable of having control over his creation. But he points to something we already know: love requires that the beloved's response be free from coercion. We can't make people love us, or it wouldn't be love. That freedom in turn entails the risk of rejection, of mockery, of betrayal. Therein lies the deepest of mysteries: that the God of the universe would love at all. It seems like a divinely reckless thing to do.

Until we begin to understand what it means to say that God *is* love.

When it comes to making sense of our lives and loves, all of us engage in a certain amount of imaginative "fiction-making."[11] We are the heroes and heroines of the tales we spin from the stories we've heard and the traditions we've inherited. The question is whether we can hear, in the background of such stories, the echo of something grander and more sacred: the story of a God who loves, risks, and pursues, who not only cares about suffering, but takes that suffering upon himself in order make all things new.[12]

That's the story in which Paul finds himself when he writes about love.

◼ ◼ ◼

In his relationship to the church in Corinth, the apostle Paul had to deal with his own version of the problem of pain. It's there in the background of 1 Corinthians. But it comes out much more forcefully in 2 Corinthians, after a disastrous confrontation that left the relationship in tatters.[13]

In that letter, Paul was obliged to deal with a new threat. Some impressive sounding teachers had come to Corinth. Like many others of that time and culture, they made a living from their rhetoric. Exactly who they were and what they taught is uncertain. But they styled themselves as apostles, making them rivals to Paul. To undermine Paul's authority, they questioned his fitness as an apostle. They pointed to all the hardships Paul suffered in his ministry. They insinuated that a real apostle would show more signs of God's blessing and protection.

To people like the Corinthians, who were accustomed to idol worship, that's a pretty compelling argument.

Think about it. Sometimes, when people suffer, we sympathize and pray. But if they keep having problems, we begin to wonder what's wrong with *them*. Maybe they're harboring some secret sin, or not praying hard enough? Behind this is often the latent assumption that bad things shouldn't happen to faithful people—and that goes double for apostles.

Paul's response is instructive. Instead of minimizing away his suffering, he almost revels in it. If his opponents are going to brag about their qualifications and strengths, Paul will boast instead in his weaknesses (2 Cor 11:30; 12:9).

It's not that Paul has failed in ministry. The very existence of the Corinthian congregation is clear evidence to the contrary, and at times, Paul seems almost dumbfounded that they don't see this. But the competition with his rivals isn't to be won on points. He must get to the root of the matter, and transform how the Corinthians understand suffering itself.

Thus, he makes no secret of his trials and tribulations. Contrasting himself with his rivals, Paul writes, "What I've done goes well beyond what they've done..." And then, counterintuitively, he rattles off a jaw-dropping list of troubles instead of successes. He's been whipped, beaten, stoned, and shipwrecked. He's been in danger everywhere, from everybody, including those he should have been able to trust. He's gone without sleep, food, and warm clothing. And on top of all that, he suffers the stress of being a pastor who has to watch the people he loves fall prey to deceit, as the Corinthians have (2 Cor 11:23-29). It's a strange résumé, one that portrays suffering as part of the job.

But that's not the point of listing his woes. What he wants them to know is that faithful people endure—by the power of God.

Earlier in the letter, Paul writes, "we commend ourselves as ministers of God in every way. We did this with our great *endurance* through problems, disasters, and stressful situations" (2 Cor 6:4).[14] He even describes how God has empowered him to show "genuine love" through all that he suffered (vs. 6). In Christ, Paul comes to see his troubles in a new light: "because when I'm weak, then I'm strong" (2 Cor 12:10).

Paul never forgets the man he was: Saul of Tarsus, zealous persecutor of those who dared to follow the Way (Acts 9:2). He remembers the men and women he threatened and arrested, believing they were following a false messiah. He remembers the face of Stephen, the one who begged God to forgive those who were killing him as Saul stood by, watching with approval (Acts 7:54-8:1). He knows he doesn't deserve to be an apostle. But by the love and grace of God in Christ, Paul embraces his commission as part of the good news: "I am what I am by God's grace, and God's grace hasn't been for nothing" (1 Cor 15:9-10).

Paul gave everything in suffering service for the gospel. He wasn't trying to pay for the evil he had done in the past. Jesus had already accomplished that on the cross, and there was nothing to be added. Rather, he was compelled by the love of Christ, the love that suffered for his sake, the love that made a friend of an enemy.[15]

Thus, Paul doesn't give a philosophical answer to the problem of pain. Instead, he invites the Corinthians into a new way of thinking. Bad things do happen to faithful people. The power of God in the lives of believers is not measured by how much trouble they suffer, but by how they endure. As Paul would later write to the church in Rome, the love of God in Christ sees him through every hardship:

Who will separate us from Christ's love? Will we be separated
by trouble, or distress, or harassment, or famine, or nakedness,
or danger, or sword? As it is written, *We are being put to
death all day long for your sake. We are treated like sheep for
slaughter.* But in all these things we win a sweeping victory
through the one who loved us. I'm convinced that nothing
can separate us from God's love in Christ Jesus our Lord: not
death or life, not angels or rulers, not present things or future
things, not powers or height or depth, or any other thing that
is created. (Rom 8:35-39)

In the midst of troubles so severe that he feared for his life, Paul
experienced the comfort and encouragement of a compassionate God
(2 Cor 1:3-11). Thus, when we read his letters, we should think of
them as written by a man who loved Jesus deeply, with astonished
gratitude.

Are we as certain of God's love as Paul was?

■ ■ ■

I confess: at times, I myself struggle with that question.

It's not that I don't believe God loves me. I do. But I sometimes
find it hard to grasp that truth as deeply or securely as I would wish.

Even where love truly exists, we won't experience it the same way
in every moment. Feelings of love are to be cherished as part of our
relationship to God, but they won't always be present. To know that
God loves us begins with the revelation of that fact in the cross of
Jesus Christ. But more than this, the knowledge and appreciation of
God's love can and should be cultivated.

One of the ways we do this is through our participation in a
community of believers. The Christian life is not a solo endeavor,
because the biblical drama is not merely about the salvation of
individuals. It's about God creating and empowering a people whose
love demonstrates his character.[16] That was the problem in Corinth.
They may have known the fact of God's love, but their day-to-day
relationships with each other were anything but loving.

And whether in community or by ourselves, we can also cultivate a personal appreciation of the Father's love by meditating on what the Bible tells us about the depth and breadth of that love. Where do we begin? Jesus the Son revealed the Father's character in both his life and teaching. If we want to know more about the Father, we can return again and again to the words Jesus spoke, the prayers he prayed, and the stories he spun.

Here, for example, is one of my favorite parables of Jesus, retold.[17]

Once upon a time, there was a man with two sons.

The man was a wealthy Jewish landowner and therefore a pillar of respectability in the village where he lived. The older son was dutiful but dour. The younger, however, was irresponsible, and no longer wished to live under his father's authority.

One morning, the younger son approached his father with an unthinkable request. "Father," he said boldly, "I know that someday I will inherit my rightful portion of your estate. But life is short and there is so much to do and see. Therefore, I beg you, let me have my inheritance now, that I may enjoy it while I am still young."

The father's heart was grieved. What his son was asking was deeply disrespectful, and showed neither love nor loyalty. But he agreed nevertheless, much to his son's delight.

When the older brother heard the news, he scoffed. "Be off with that worthless fellow," he muttered to himself as he returned to his work. The villagers, for their part, were incensed. The young man had to sell off his portion of the inheritance as quickly as possible, then set off for faraway lands.

He indulged his whims and spent his money freely. But whatever his ill-considered plans might have been when he left home, he soon found himself alone and penniless in a strange country. There was also a famine in the land, and he was forced to take the most menial of jobs just to eat. He was a Jewish boy from a respectable family—but found himself working for a Gentile, feeding pigs.

Then one day, he came to his senses. "Why should I suffer

an empty stomach?" he wondered aloud. "I have only to return home and humble myself before my father. I have nothing to lose by begging him to take me back as a hired servant. In time, I may be able to make enough money to redeem my failure. But whatever happens, I can't do any worse than I'm doing now."

So the son began his long journey home. He knew that his father had no reason to forgive him. And if his father didn't treat him as dead, beat him, or drive him away, the neighbors might. But he had no choice. Thus, trying to envision the reunion with his father, he rehearsed his apology again and again: "Father, I have sinned against heaven and against you. I am not worthy to be your son. So please take me back as one of your hired men instead." He trudged along, hoping against hope, murmuring the script of his apology as he went.

The father was standing out in the street. Some of his servants were with him. Every day since his son left, he had looked to the edge of town, watching and waiting. Then, in the distance, a lone figure appeared, the shadow of a young man, his head bent in weariness.

The father recognized him immediately. He had not forgotten what the boy had done. But at the sight of the forlorn figure the father's chest filled with love and compassion. Casting all dignity aside, and in front of the bewildered villagers, he ran up the crowded street to his son, enfolded him in his arms, and kissed him.

No one was more surprised than the son himself. His plan had been to fall on his face and kiss his father's feet in a show of repentance. But he had not expected to find himself wrapped in the arms of a loving father, who ran to him despite the hushed whispers of the startled townspeople. Broken and astonished, the son could only stammer out the first part of his planned apology. Gone was any intention of wheedling his way into his father's good graces. Gone was any suggestion of earning his keep. He was stricken and humbled by his father's love, and the apology was honest: "Father, I have sinned against heaven and against you. I am not worthy to be your son."

But the father was busy giving orders to the servants who

had come running with him. He commanded them to bring the things that would cover the boy's shame and transform the destitute wanderer back into the figure of his beloved son. "Hurry! Bring my best robe and put it on him. Put a ring on his finger. Bring sandals for his feet. Then kill the fattened calf and prepare a feast. For here is my son, home at last. He is neither dead nor lost. He is alive, and I have found him!"

And together they celebrated into the night, loudly and joyously.

This is the first part of what is commonly known as the Parable of the Prodigal Son. But the star of the story is really the father, who acts in ways that would have surprised Jesus' audience. No man of his culture and social standing should run in public. Neither should he take the boy back. But scandalously, he does both.

I have friends who remain heartbroken because they've been estranged from their children for years, even decades. They know what it's like to watch for a lost child to return. They would give anything for the kind of joyous reunion Jesus describes. And if they saw their children on the horizon, trudging home, they would run.

These friends of mine, of course, are fallible and sinful people, as am I. None of us are perfect parents. We all have regrets. Whenever there's conflict between us and our children, we have to wonder to what extent we ourselves are to blame.

Not so the father in Jesus' parable. He has done nothing wrong, while the son is portrayed as impossibly rebellious and disrespectful. As Kenneth Bailey has said, in that cultural context the boy's request to take possession of his inheritance would have been tantamount to saying, "Drop dead."[18] The father is blameless. He has no need to repent. But he is the one who runs. He is the one who reaches out. He is the one who forgives.

Jesus describes the father as "moved with compassion" (Luke 15:20). The Greek word suggests a visceral or gut reaction.[19] In the gospels, the word is used repeatedly to describe Jesus' response to the people who came to him with their needs (e.g., Matt 14:14; 15:32; 20:34). In one instance, Mark tells us that Jesus and the disciples were so busy with the throngs who were coming and going that they couldn't find time to eat. Jesus therefore packed the disciples into a boat to find a quiet place to rest. But news travels quickly. People figured out where they were going, and by the time the boat landed, Jesus found himself once again confronted with a large crowd.

How did he respond? If it had been you, tired and hungry, how would you have responded?

Mark says that when Jesus saw the crowd, "he had compassion on them because they were like sheep without a shepherd" (Mark 6:34).

This is the Jesus who in the gospel of Matthew taught his disciples the Sermon on the Mount (Matt 5-7) and then promptly demonstrated what he meant by the kingdom of heaven. He healed a man with leprosy by touching him, an act that should have resulted in his being contaminated by the leper's uncleanness (Matt 8:1-4). He agreed to heal the servant of a Roman centurion, even though it was forbidden to come under a Gentile's roof (Matt 8:5-13). He freed two men from the demons that possessed them (Matt 8:28-34), forgave a paralyzed man his sins and restored his ability to walk (Matt 9:1-8), healed a woman who had suffered for twelve years with a hemorrhage (Matt 9:20-22), raised a dead little girl back to life (Matt 9:18-19, 23-25), and gave two blind men back their sight (Matt 9:27-31). Matthew summarizes all of this in a way that echoes Mark:

> Jesus traveled among all the cities and villages, teaching in their synagogues, announcing the good news of the kingdom, and healing every disease and every sickness. Now when Jesus saw the crowds, he had compassion for them because they were troubled and helpless, like sheep without a shepherd (Matt 9:35-36).

Good news, healing, compassion. The words go together. The compassionate and loving father Jesus describes in his parable is the same God Jesus embodied in his life and ministry.

Can we believe that God loves us like that, with heartfelt compassion?

Jesus reveals a God who neither begrudges us salvation nor acts with cool detachment. This God is a shepherd who cares for his sheep and knows them each by name. This God is one who touches the untouchable, heals the sick, and raises the dead. This God is a Father who runs to embrace his wayward and lost children.

And this God asks us to respond to his love by loving others in turn.

▪ ▪ ▪

Perhaps we don't identify with the prodigal. We haven't made such a mess of our lives. We haven't been foolish and irresponsible. We haven't run off into the far country.

Maybe, though we might be loath to admit it, we identify more with the Pharisees. Jesus told the story in response to their griping and grumbling about the company he kept: traitorous tax collectors and other obviously sinful people (Luke 15:2). He challenged the Pharisees to imagine a God whose love extends in a scandalous way to those who don't deserve it, a God who seeks lost people and throws a raucous party when one is found.[20]

And just for the grumpy scribes and Pharisees in Jesus' audience, there's another brother in the story (Luke 15:25-32).

As Jesus tells it, the older son was in the field.[21] When he returned home for the evening, he heard loud music and the sounds of celebration coming from the house. What could be happening? Why didn't he know about it?

He called a servant over to ask what was going on. The servant wisely stuck to the facts: *Your father has killed the fattened calf because your brother has returned safely*. A fattened calf would feed a large number of people, and a party was in full swing. The neighbors would probably have disagreed with the father's actions in welcoming his disgraced son home. But by joining the party out of respect for the father, they signaled their acceptance of his decision. The reconciliation between father, son, and village would be complete.

The older son was furious. How could that worthless brother of his be forgiven so easily, so lavishly? He refused to take part in such nonsense. As a dutiful son, he should have gone into the party immediately to greet the guests—they were *his* guests, even if he disagreed with what his father had done. But he put his own peevish anger above his father's honor.

Once again, the father was being publicly shamed. Just as the father could rightly have disciplined the prodigal, so too could he have beaten the older son for such a brazen act of disrespect. Nobody would have blamed him.

But he didn't do that. The father left his guests, once again lowering himself in their eyes by being the one to humbly take the initiative, to go out to his son, to beg him to come in. Still the son refused, disrespectfully spouting a loud litany of complaints, unjustly accusing the father of being a stingy slave-driver and his brother of squandering the family estate on prostitutes.[22]

And still the father responded with patience and kindness: "Son, you are always with me, and everything I have is yours. But we had to celebrate and be glad because this brother of yours was dead and is alive. He was lost and is found" (Luke 15:31-32). He reminded his son that the estate was already his, and asked him to join the celebration as he should.

Jesus leaves the parable unfinished. He doesn't tell us what the older brother did next.

Why? Because it's up to his hearers to finish the parable by their response.

Jesus is asking the scribes and Pharisees to accept that spending time with sinners and seeking their good is the way of God's love. He's inviting them to the party. Bailey summarizes his message to them:

> You are the older son. Costly love was offered the prodigal. Even more costly love is offered to the older son. In spite of your hostility to me and my actions, I love you and urge you to sit and eat with me. When I sit and eat with sinners, we are not celebrating their sin but my costly love. That same costly love is now offered to you. My banquet table is spread. If you accept, then the banquet is an occasion of even greater

joy. I seek not only them but also you! Come! Be reconciled to your brother! Accept the love I offer! I know that you are offended at my table fellowship with sinners. But *do you not understand*, my dear friends, that *if I do not sit and eat with sinners, then I cannot sit and eat with you!*[23]

To the extent that we, like the Pharisees, consider ourselves to be decently spiritual people, that last line is a hard pill to swallow. It's clear why sinners don't deserve to share Jesus' table. But why would *we* be lumped in the same category with *them*? Only prodigals need "costly love." We just need the respect we're due, because we're not prodigals.

Or are we?

In this chapter, we've thought together about the problem of pain, the question of why bad things happen to good people.[24] But for the proud and stingy of heart, the question takes another form: why do good things happen to bad people? Why do prodigals get banquets? The older son could not celebrate the father's grace because he treated love as a zero-sum game: *If my brother wins, I lose. If there's a party, it's being paid for out of my inheritance. It's not fair. I'm the good son! I'm the respectable son! I've obeyed the rules and done everything right. Why isn't anyone throwing a party for me?*

I don't like to think of myself as the prodigal son, even though Paul insists that "All have sinned and fall short of God's glory" (Rom 3:23). Compared to a holy God, I'm a sinner. God is perfect, and I'm not. I'm aware of the many ways in which I fall short of his glory.

But I'm not really that bad of a sinner, am I? I'm certainly not as bad as the prodigal. Nor am I even as bad as those self-righteous scribes and Pharisees. We can't invite *them* to the party—they're so snotty and full of themselves that they'll just ruin everything.

And therein lies the problem. Am I put off, even just a little, by the way Jesus offers costly love to the Pharisees?

If so, then I too am the older son. I am proud and my heart is hard.

I am lost, and need to be found by a loving Father who will speak tenderly to me.

▓ ▓ ▓

The Corinthians have heard and received the gospel Paul preached. The Holy Spirit is active in their midst, in obvious and sometimes stunning ways.

But they're a proud bunch: proud of their spiritual gifts, proud of their knowledge, proud of their sophistication. What's missing in their congregation is love. They are pursuing a kind of spirituality that uses the name of Jesus without embodying the love of Jesus. When they come to Paul, therefore, with questions about the spiritual life, he knows that he must redirect them first. He must ground them in love.

And if we are to learn anything from what Paul tries to teach them, then we too must be grounded in the assurance of the Father's generous, costly, undeserved love.

The invitation is to prodigals and older brothers alike. The party is already in progress. The Father awaits with open arms.

Will we go in?

talk or think about it

1. Do you remember the first time you heard that God loves you? When was it, and what were the circumstances? How did that statement impact you then? What does it mean to you now?

2. How, if at all, have suffering or unwanted circumstances made it more difficult for you to believe that God is love?

3. Think of your relationship to your own earthly father. Does that relationship make it easier or harder for you to imagine God as Father in the way the Bible describes? In what way?

4. What, if anything, is new, surprising, or personally significant to you about the way the Father is portrayed in the parable of the Prodigal Son?

5. Earlier, I described the biblical narrative as "a love story of cosmic proportions." In Jesus' parable, this takes the form of a loving father embracing a wayward son. In what ways can you see yourself as a character in the cosmic story? How might this affect the way you perceive and relate to others?

6

taking the high road

Paul wasn't preaching a wedding sermon.

He wasn't waxing eloquent about romance.

And he certainly wasn't writing love poetry to his girlfriend.

When Paul penned those famous words about love in 1 Corinthians 13, he was writing as a pastor trying to help a fractured congregation find their way.

Over the years, I've spoken with many pastors about the congregations they've served. I've heard stories of both joy and sorrow. Some church relationships were warm and wise, and others downright crazy-making. Some people gave their pastors loving support, and others nearly made them give up on ministry altogether. And all these things could be true of the same congregation.

But few pastors have ever had as mixed-up a congregation as the one Paul founded in the Roman colony of Corinth.

In the previous chapter, I described some of the struggles the members of that church had with Paul himself. Not surprisingly, they also had struggles with each other. Here are some of the issues that seemed to plague them.[1]

- Different members of the church were loyal to different leaders, and this was causing division among the people (1:10-12).
- A man in the congregation was carrying on an incestuous relationship with his stepmother, and some people seemed to think this was just fine (5:1-5).

- One church member was publicly suing another, thereby shaming the church (6:1-6).
- On the one hand, some argued that devotion to the spiritual life meant that what you did with your body didn't matter. They believed they were therefore free to indulge themselves sexually (6:12-17).
- On the other hand, some thought that the spiritual life entailed abstaining from sex—even if you were married. This was, unsurprisingly, causing some tension among couples (7:1-7).
- Various members refused to give up some of their former pagan habits. They argued that it was fine to go to idol temples and eat the meat that was sacrificed there, because pagan idols weren't real gods. They prided themselves in being spiritually mature, but their behavior was wounding the conscience of those who were less sure of themselves (8:1-13; 10:27-30).
- More generally, some believed in a kind of "Christian freedom" that meant "I can do whatever I want, regardless of what other people think" (9:1-23; 10:23-24).
- When coming to the Lord's Supper, the behavior of wealthier members of the church was dishonoring and disenfranchising the poor among them (11:17-22).
- They seemed to be promoting a spiritual pecking order according to who had the gift of tongues and who did not (12:1-31; 14:1-25).[2]
- Some had stopped believing in the resurrection (15:12-34).

Anybody want to volunteer to pastor *that* church?

Perhaps we should give the Corinthians the benefit of the doubt. We live at a very different point in history, and take much for granted that they could not. For example, the church where my wife and I are members is over six miles from our home, even though within a six-mile radius, there are dozens of churches from which we could choose. I have numerous print copies of the Bible on my shelf in different translations, and access to many, many more online. I have hundreds of Christian books on theology, biblical studies, church history, and spirituality. I studied at a Christian institution of higher learning, and have now taught there for over three decades. Hundreds of recorded sermons and podcasts are only a few mouse-clicks away. And I live in a country where many people already know the basics of the gospel, and uttering the statement "I am a Christian" won't get me shot.

By contrast, the Corinthians were recent converts to the faith from a pagan culture. Some of the believers were wealthy aristocrats, while the majority were slaves, or former slaves trying to move up in the world. They lived in an extremely prosperous and metropolitan city in which idol temples were common, church buildings non-existent, and the name of Jesus relatively unknown. They had no Bible; their only "Christian literature" was their correspondence with Paul. As their founding pastor, Paul loved these people like a father (1 Cor 4:14-15; 2 Cor 6:13, 12:14), and he was trying to guide them. But he had to do it from a distance with letters that took a long time to go back and forth.[3] A lot could happen in the meantime. And did.

Nevertheless, they were experiencing a strong movement of the Holy Spirit and trying to make sense of it all. In short, they were a relatively new congregation that had to figure out what it meant to follow Jesus in the midst of a highly pagan society, without the resources of centuries of Christian tradition. They were making it up as they went.

I've heard people lament over the state of the church today, pointing to passages like Acts 2:42-47 and wondering how we lost our way. But the church has always struggled with its call to discipleship. Part of the reason, of course, is our own stubbornness and sin. But we are also products of the cultures (and subcultures) we inhabit. In ways that too often go unnoticed, we embody values, attitudes, and beliefs that conflict with a gospel of love.

That's why I've delayed a direct discussion of 1 Corinthians 13 until now. We stand a better chance of hearing Paul rightly if we are aware of some of the cultural biases through which we filter his words. In the first part of this book, I highlighted some of these biases, particularly those related to the romantic ideals of American popular culture. Do we want to know what Paul meant by "love"? Then we must understand, as best we can, what Paul was saying to the people in Corinth, in their situation, before trying to determine what he might be saying to us.

We'll begin, therefore, with a bird's-eye view of 1 Corinthians 13 as a whole, approaching it from the context of the chapters on either side of it. We'll then take a closer look at chapter 13 itself, and how Paul puts it together. All of this, hopefully, will better prepare us for an even more focused look at love in the chapters to follow.

■ ■ ■

Want to get a sense of what Paul is up to when he writes about love in 1 Corinthians 13? Try this experiment:

- First, read chapter 12, and ask yourself what must be happening in the congregation for Paul to write as he does.
- Then skip chapter 13 and go immediately to chapter 14. Ask yourself how that chapter continues and complements what Paul began in chapter 12.
- When you can make sense of those two chapters together, then ask yourself: why does he need chapter 13 at all? Why sandwich a discussion of love between two chapters on spiritual gifts and the good working order of the church?

Here's one way to reconstruct Paul's reasoning.

As suggested earlier, the Corinthians were a troubled congregation. On the one hand, they had believed the gospel, and the Holy Spirit was alive and well among them. On the other, they were confused, both individually and as a church, about what it meant to follow Jesus in the midst of a pagan empire. They wrote to Pastor Paul with their questions, hoping to get some clarity.

One of their biggest concerns had to do with the gifts of the Holy Spirit, a matter that Paul tackles in chapters 12 and 14. What was the issue? We don't have a copy of what the Corinthians wrote, so we have to guess what was happening on the basis of Paul's responses alone. But we know that this was a contentious congregation, and their questions weren't idle ones. They were trying to resolve the disagreements among them. And one of the disagreements, apparently, was about spiritual gifts.

Paul's strong emphasis on unity in chapter 12 suggests their *lack* of unity on the subject of gifts. Yes, Paul says, there are differences between the members of a congregation in terms of gifts and what today we might call "ministry involvements." But he insists that these differences come from "the same Spirit...the same Lord...the same God" (vss. 4-6).[4] The implication is that there's no division in God, and thus there should be none in the church.

The apostle then illustrates his point with a metaphor: the church is like a body. Indeed, it's the body of Christ (vss. 12-27). Everyone knows that the human body "is a unit and has many parts; and all the parts of the body are one body, even though there are many" (vs. 12). Pressing the metaphor, he mentions feet and hands, ears and eyes, and even our "private parts" (vs. 23). His basic point is that the church as a body is made of many parts with different roles to play, and each part needs the others for the body as a whole to function normally and well.

But there are two harmful attitudes that threaten the organic unity of the church body—attitudes which presumably were dividing the Corinthians themselves. One is that "I'm not part of the body" (vss. 15-16), an attitude that says, "I'm expendable, so I don't really belong." The other attitude is "I don't need you" (vs. 21). That error is the flip side of the first: "You're expendable (but I'm not)."

Imagine how this might play out in a congregation today. In any organization—including churches—people can be distinguished by marks of power and status. Who makes decisions? Who gets listened to, and who gets ignored? Who has a more public role, and who does the grunt work behind the scenes? In other words, who's assigned higher status and why?

There are numerous roles to play in the life of a local church. Someone preaches. Someone sets up chairs. Someone leads worship. Someone hugs babies. And ideally, the roles are filled by those suited to the task at hand. The person in the pulpit needs the proper skill and passion; the person who hugs babies should have a heart for children.

But whether we're aware of it or not, we also assign different social values to the roles. Nobody's jealous of the person who makes the coffee—even though everyone will be upset if the coffee isn't made. In a culture dominated by entertainment media, we admire people in the spotlight more. Those in high-status roles are tempted to think of themselves more highly than they ought (Rom 12:3), while those with less status fade into the background and may be taken for granted.

Some of this is a function of the size of the congregation. Smaller churches tend to have more of an "all hands on deck" mentality. If something needs to be done, everyone pitches in, and people play multiple roles. But as the church grows, so does the talent pool. Perceptions and expectations change. We want everything to be done "professionally." And now, when some task is needed, it's easier for people to look around and think, "Surely someone else will do it, and do it better than I would."[5] People become more like consumers than contributors.

It should be no surprise, then, that some members of a congregation might think, "I'm not important, so I don't really belong," while others think, "I'm important and you're not." Both stances are symptomatic of the same theological problem: not believing that God wants every member of the body to contribute to the life of the church, and therefore assigns a diverse range of gifts and ministries.

Paul insists that "God has placed each one of the parts in the body just like he wanted" (vs. 18; see also vs. 11). Not everyone will have what the world would consider the showier roles and abilities. If we accept God's wisdom in this matter, then there should be no place for arrogance or envy. All the parts of the body should have "mutual concern for each other" (vs. 25).

In other words, they should love and value each other, whatever their gifts may be. Unfortunately, that's still problematic today.

▪ ▪ ▪

It's been many years since it happened, but I can still picture the scene in my mind. I had just finished preaching the last service of the morning. As I came down from the stage, an older gentleman approached me. His whole demeanor was downcast, his shoulders slumped like a man who had carried a heavy burden for years.

I listened as he haltingly shared his story. He had loved Jesus for as long as he could remember, and had tried to follow him faithfully. But he had grown up in a church that taught that true believers, the ones truly blessed by God, would eventually receive the gift of speaking in tongues. Decade after decade he had waited, praying for the gift, trying to hold the feeling of abandonment at bay.

The gift never came.

He was silent for a moment as he finished his story. Then he raised his head and looked me in the eye. "Am I a Christian?" he asked, with both hope and despair in his face.

My heart went out to him. I tried to imagine all those years of feeling spurned, of never having had the sense that he was loved and accepted by the Lord he worshipped and served.

The man was reaching out for reassurance, not some lengthy theological discourse. "Yes," I said to him simply, with as much earnestness as I could muster. "Yes, you are a Christian."

He smiled weakly and nodded. Then he turned and walked away.

Thinking back, I wish I had also said, "And Jesus loves you." That was the question he was really asking, and I should have answered it.

But I never saw him again.

▧ ▧ ▧

That encounter comes to mind whenever I read 1 Corinthians 12 and 14. Apparently, when the Corinthians wrote to Paul, a gap had been forming between the spiritual "haves" and the "have-nots"— quite possibly, between those who had the gift of tongues and those who didn't. The have-nots were left to think they weren't part of the body, and the haves weren't doing anything to persuade them otherwise.

When dealing with problems in churches, Paul's usual strategy is to try to renew the people's vision and understanding first. In chapter 12, therefore, Paul sidles up to the problem by mentioning tongues as one gift among many without making a particular issue of it. His desire is to give them a vision of unity that can help them accept and appreciate their diversity.

In chapter 14, however, he gets straight to the point. In contrast to their over-fondness for the gift of tongues, Paul holds up prophecy as the gift of choice. By "prophecy," Paul doesn't mean fortune-telling or predicting the future. He means bringing a specific and authoritative word from God, as the prophets did in the Old Testament.

Why is prophecy superior? The first and most important reason is that it serves to build up the church as a whole, and not just the individuals within it:

> This is because those who speak in a tongue don't speak to people but to God; no one understands it—they speak mysteries by the Spirit. Those who prophesy speak to people, building them up, and giving them encouragement and comfort. *People who speak in a tongue build up themselves; those who prophesy build up the church.* I wish that all of you spoke in tongues, but I'd rather you could prophesy. Those who prophesy are more important than those who speak in tongues, unless they are able to interpret them so that the church might be built up. (vss. 2-5, emphasis added)

Second, Paul is concerned about the church's witness to unbelievers who might be curious about what goes on in the congregation. If these people walk in on a chaotic scene in which everyone is speaking in tongues, Paul suggests, "will they not say that you are out of your mind?" (vs. 23). But if everyone is prophesying instead, speaking intelligible and convicting words from God, "they will fall down and worship God, exclaiming, 'God is really among you!'" (vs. 25).

How might the congregation respond to Paul's words? On the one hand, some who have the gift of tongues might be tempted to scoff and say that Paul doesn't know personally what he's talking about. For them, he throws down this rhetorical gauntlet:

> I thank God that I speak in tongues more than all of you. But in the church I'd rather speak five words in my right mind than speak thousands of words in a tongue so that I can teach others. (vss. 18-19)

On the other hand, people might begin striving for the gift of prophecy for all the wrong, self-centered reasons, and suppress those who speak in tongues. For that reason, he explicitly instructs them to "try to get the gift of prophecy," but not to "prevent speaking in tongues" (vs. 39). His final word on the matter is that "Everything should be done with dignity and in proper order" (vs. 40).

In summary, then, the Corinthians' newfound spirituality had become a source of individual pride and status that was causing confusion in the church. Some of the Corinthians spoke in tongues or had some kind of special knowledge, and were proud of that fact. Those who didn't were feeling overlooked or left out. Paul responds by giving them the metaphor of the church as the body of Christ, a united whole with different parts serving different functions, all valuable, all necessary. The health of the body as a whole is the top priority; thus, people should be most eager for the gifts (like prophecy) that best serve that end.

If all that makes sense, then we are left with this question: why does Paul need chapter 13? He's given them a grounding metaphor for the unity of the church. He's given them specific instruction on what to do about the problem that was causing disorder among them. Isn't that enough?

Why does he need to talk about love?

Because he's not done shaping the vision they so desperately need.

▓ ▓ ▓

Picture your favorite event at the Olympic Games. At the end of the competition, only three individuals or teams are awarded medals. The winners stand proudly on elevated platforms, waving to the crowds. But gold medalists stand in the place of greatest honor: on the highest platform, with the silver and bronze medalists on either side.

Can you imagine the scene in your mind? Good—because something like that Olympic platform can help us understand what Paul is doing in 1 Corinthians 13.

Paul wasn't writing love poetry, but that's not to say that he wrote in a haphazard or artless way. First Corinthians 13 is neither a random, off-the-cuff musing, nor something Paul dashed off for his Twitter feed. It has a carefully crafted structure which Paul uses to lead the Corinthians from their concerns about spiritual gifts to something more important: the practical embodiment of love in their life together.

Paul's argument can be thought of as a pyramid leading upward from spiritual gifts to love, as represented in the diagram below.[6]

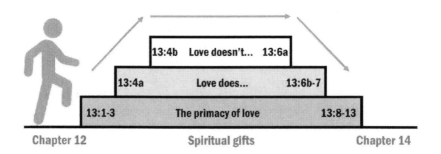

Imagine this diagram as a more complex version of the Olympic medal platform. When the Corinthians raise questions about speaking in tongues, Paul leads them to the left-hand side of the platform, and together they mount the steps. As we've seen, Paul addresses spiritual gifts in chapter 12. The argument will continue on the far side of the platform, in chapter 14.

But at the beginning of chapter 13, Paul "steps up" from spiritual gifts to the primacy of love:

> If I speak in tongues of human beings and of angels but I don't have love, I'm a clanging gong or a clashing cymbal. If I have the gift of prophecy and I know all the mysteries and everything else, and if I have such complete faith that I can move mountains but I don't have love, I'm nothing. If I give away everything that I have and hand over my own body to feel good about what I've done but I don't have love, I receive no benefit whatsoever. (13:1-3)

Notice how he leads with the gift of tongues, the Corinthians' favorite. Later, in chapter 14, Paul will suggest that speaking in tongues sounds like gibberish without an interpreter. Here, the point is even stronger: without love, it's just meaningless noise.

That should get their attention.

He follows with the gift of prophecy, which as we know is *his* favorite. But prophecy, too, comes to nothing without love. Paul goes down the line with other gifts and religious behaviors. Do you have special knowledge or insight about spiritual mysteries? Good for you. Do you have the kind of faith that can move mountains? Terrific. Do you give sacrificially, perhaps even to the extreme of sacrificing your very body?[7] Impressive. But without love, it's all for nothing.

Taking another step up, Paul gives a positive description of the character of true love: "Love is patient, love is kind" (13:4a). As we'll see later, I believe that Paul is specifically pointing to the nature of *God's* love here, to the divine patience and kindness without which we would all be condemned. And having briefly described what true love is like, Paul brings the Corinthians to the summit by giving a negative description of what love is *not* like, the things it doesn't do: "it isn't jealous, it doesn't brag, it isn't arrogant, it isn't rude, it doesn't seek its own advantage, it isn't irritable, it doesn't keep a record of complaints, it isn't happy with injustice" (13:4b-6a).

By putting this negative section at the pinnacle, Paul gives it pride of place. But why emphasize the negative? Simply put: if the positive statements "patient" and "kind" can be said to describe a loving God, then the negative statements describe the *un*-loving Corinthians themselves.   Paul builds on a positive vision of love, but these negative behaviors are where the practical application begins.

In other words, Paul can't answer their questions about spiritual gifts by merely saying, "Gifts are necessary, but prophecy is best, and here are some rules you should follow so things don't get out of hand." The congregation needs more guidance than that before their gifts can be understood and used rightly.   Paul has already tried to give them a vision of unity with the metaphor of being one body in Christ.   Now he needs to give them an even higher vision: the love of God embodied in his people.

That's why the negative statements are at the top of the pyramid. Paul wants the Corinthians to take a good, hard look at themselves. They're vying with each other to be more "spiritual," but in a way that is arrogant, rude, touchy and resentful—hardly a reflection of the God they supposedly serve.   They're not lacking for spiritual gifts. They're just lacking in love.

We'll examine the top two steps—Paul's descriptions of what love does and what love doesn't do—more closely in the remainder of this book.   Meanwhile, Paul still needs to get to some specific instruction about spiritual gifts in chapter 14, so he leads the Corinthians back down the steps on the right-hand side.   Thus, from his pointed teaching of what love doesn't do, Paul returns to what love does: "it is happy with the truth. Love puts up with all things, trusts in all things, hopes for all things, endures all things" (13:6b-7).

And from there, he steps down again to the primacy of love over spiritual gifts by themselves:

> Love never fails. As for prophecies, they will be brought to an end. As for tongues, they will stop. As for knowledge, it will be brought to an end. We know in part and we prophesy in part; but when the perfect comes, what is partial will be brought to an end. (13:8-10)

This time, Paul only mentions three gifts: prophecy, tongues, and knowledge. He doesn't need to name any others, because prophecy is at the top of Paul's list of preferred gifts, and the other two at the top of the Corinthians' list (e.g., 1 Cor 1:5-7). If he can make his point with these, the rest will follow.

Note that Paul has nothing bad to say about these or any other gifts; they are all legitimate expressions of the Spirit. And yet, they are only of temporary importance. A new day is coming, a day in which all the piecemeal imperfection of the present world will give way to perfection. That day will mark the end of prophecy, the end of speaking in tongues, and the end of special spiritual knowledge.

But not of love.

To help make his point, Paul brings in another metaphor: "When I was a child, I used to speak like a child, reason like a child, think like a child. But now that I have become a man, I've put an end to childish things" (13:11). It's possible that Paul is speaking autobiographically here, suggesting that he was once as immature in the faith as the Corinthians now seem to be. He has, after all, used the metaphor of childhood in the letter before. In chapter 3, he called them "babies in Christ" who weren't yet ready for solid food, and who showed their lack of spiritual maturity by their jealous infighting (3:1-4). If that's his meaning here, the message is, "Grow out of it," and he uses himself as an example to tone down the harshness of the criticism.[8]

Certainly, the Corinthians have a lot of growing up to do. Paul, however, may be making a different point. Childhood is one time of life, adulthood another. What might be considered appropriate for a boy is inappropriate for a man. Similarly, spiritual gifts may be valuable for the present age, but not for the age to come. In other words, he isn't calling them childish to shame them into submission.[9] He's trying to widen the horizon of their imagination. *This life is not all there is*, he seems to say. *This life is imperfect, incomplete. Spiritual gifts are good and valuable for now. But the day is coming when they'll no longer be relevant. That's the day we long for. That's the day we live for.*

He brings in yet another metaphor: "Now we see a reflection in a mirror; then we will see face-to-face. Now I know partially, but then I will know completely in the same way that I have been completely known" (1 Cor 13:12).[10] Here again we have the contrast between now and then, imperfect and perfect, partial and complete. We think we see. We think we know. And we live under the illusion that what we see and know is all there is. *But no*, Paul insists, *there's more. And it would be silly to prefer what is partial to what is complete.*

I occasionally have to travel for professional or ministry reasons. When my children were small, I tried to keep my travels to a minimum, so as not to sacrifice those early years for the sake of my career. And I found myself missing them when I was away. I always packed a framed family photo in my suitcase, which I would then set up on the nightstand in my hotel room. Sometimes, I'd even say goodnight to those tiny faces before going to sleep.

But when at last I would return home, I didn't keep looking at the picture.[11] I had the real thing to hug and kiss. Why settle for less?

What we think we know about God today is nothing compared to what we will know when we see God "face to face." We will know God as God knows us: directly, without the need for special insight, the experience of speaking in tongues, or words of prophecy. Such spiritual gifts will be a distant memory, as will all the things we thought we needed to get ahead in this life.

But love will neither be forgotten nor cease to exist.

Paul ends the chapter on a resounding note: "Now faith, hope, and love remain—these three things—and the greatest of these is love" (13:13). These three qualities, known as the *theological* or *cardinal virtues*, can be found together elsewhere in Paul's letters (e.g., Rom 5:1-5). In the early days of the church, they may have functioned like a pithy reminder of the essence of the Christian life.

Why is love the greatest of the three? Because faith and hope each have their own kind of incompleteness. For now, they are the necessary condition of the Christian life; we simply cannot see all that God is doing, nor do we enjoy the final fulfillment of God's promises. But love expresses the very being of the eternal God. There's no time in which it's irrelevant, no place in which it's unneeded. In the eternal plan of God, love has no sunset clause.

N. T. Wright sums up nicely:

Paul sees all of life within the framework of God's future...which has burst into the present in the person of

Jesus of Nazareth... Love is the way of life in the new world to which, by grace, we are bound. We need to learn it here and now. It is the grammar of the language we shall speak there. The more progress we make in it here, the better we shall be equipped.

Paul places these abiding certainties over against the things which the Corinthians were priding themselves on. Prophecy? Who will need it in the world to come? Tongues? Why would we need to speak them in the world where everyone understands everyone else at once? Special knowledge? We shall all know everything we can know and need to know. These are things that belong to the country we live in at the moment. Love is God's river, flowing on into the future, across the border into the country where there is no pride, no jostling for position, no contention among God's people. We are invited to step into that river here and now, and let it take us where it's going.[12]

That's the vision the Corinthians need. That's the vision we need.

▦ ▦ ▦

Members of a congregation may have different gifts and different ministries, but they are one body in Christ, formed by one Spirit, by the will and design of the one God. Paul doesn't want the Corinthians to stop pursuing or practicing spiritual gifts. They just need to keep everything in perspective, a perspective defined by the primacy of love.

Paul ends chapter 12 and transitions to his discussion of love with these words: "And yet I will show you the most excellent way" (1 Cor 12:31b). In Scripture, the metaphor of a road or way can stand for a particular way of life, an ethical path one follows in harmony with God's will or against it (see, e.g., Ps 1:6; Matt 7:13-14). But Kenneth Bailey believes that the translation "most excellent" misses some of Paul's meaning. He argues that Paul, thinking of the mountainous areas surrounding Corinth and the narrow roads across them, was "comparing the way of love to a stiff climb over a mountain pass."[13] The journey is strenuous. But it's the only one worth taking.

The Corinthians were an ambitious folk, and Paul needed to redirect their energy. Their way of pursuing spirituality was self-centered and divisive. Any direction he tried to give them could be co-opted and twisted by their superior I-know-more-than-you-do mentality. He had to show them a "higher way."[14] Only in love could the church fulfill its calling to be one body in Christ.

It's important to note, however, that Paul's comparison of the church to a human body is more than just clever rhetoric. If his only point is to teach the principle of unity in diversity, then we would be free to choose a different metaphor. The church, for example, could be compared to a smoothly functioning automobile engine: "The crankshaft cannot say to the cylinders, 'I don't need you.'"

But could we then say that the church is "the engine of Christ" without losing something of Paul's meaning? The crucial missing element would be the idea of embodiment. To call Christians the body of Christ is not merely to say that they should cooperate with each other, but to suggest that their very vocation is to embody the life of Christ by the power of the Spirit. Again, to quote Wright:

> [For Paul] to choose the image of a human body to express what those who belong to the Messiah have now become, and how they are to live, is deep with significance. The church is to be the place where, together, we learn how to be God's genuinely human beings, worshipping God and serving him by reflecting his image in the world.[15]

Ultimately, that's the best reason for wanting to understand what Paul teaches about love. Love is not a self-improvement program we undertake for individual reasons. It's a matter of our discipleship, of fulfilling our shared calling to embody God's loving, gracious character in our relationships to one another.

I would hope, of course, that following the way of love would lead to greater happiness and contentment in our relationships, including in our marriages, families, and churches. Love is God's way, and there is ample biblical precedent for believing that God's way is the way of blessing.[16]

But the biblical concept of blessing is not the same as the modern concept of happiness.[17] What blesses us in the long term may not make us happy in the short term. Let it therefore be said up front: disciplining ourselves to the way of love may have a beneficial impact on our relationships, but it is not itself a relationship "fix." It is not the means by which we reach our personal goals for self-improvement. That would be closer to the Corinthians' approach to the spiritual life than Paul's.

Nor is the discipline always easy or even rewarding. Jesus' love for the Father and for the human race meant having to endure the suffering of the cross. Paul's love for the Corinthians meant having to endure their backbiting and betrayal. But both persisted in love precisely because they knew it to be God's way. They weren't aiming at happiness. They were aiming at holiness, at embodying all that is right and godly in everything they did.

Don't get me wrong. I'm not saying that love will make you miserable and grumpy. Quite the contrary. The journey should lead us to something even better than happiness: a deep and abiding joy that comes from being aligned to God's way. But the bumps on the road will be many, and our motivation for the journey needs to be right. If God is love, then we must pursue love as we pursue God: not as a solution to a problem, not as a means to some other end. We must pursue love as an end in itself.

In the remainder of this book, therefore, we turn our attention to Paul's high road, the way of love. To my mind, Paul's positive and negative statements—what true love does and doesn't do—group together fairly naturally, so the chapters will take these two or more at a time. We begin with Paul's transition from the supremacy of love to a description of what love is truly like. And if we follow the apostle's logic, there's no better place to start than with a consideration of how God loves us: with extraordinary patience and kindness.

talk or think about it

1. As I've suggested, most people encounter Paul's teaching about love in romantic contexts like weddings. Does anything surprise you about the idea that these verses are about Paul trying to create a pastoral vision for a troubled congregation? What difference does it make to the way you read and apply what he says?

2. You may already be familiar with Paul's image of the church as the body of Christ. But as the earlier quote from N. T. Wright suggests, this isn't just a colorful metaphor for the idea of unity in diversity. It's a way of describing our calling to embody—to demonstrate in our daily, bodily existence—the character of God as revealed in the life of Jesus. Think of two specific people in your life whom you supposedly love, but with whom you've had some difficulties. For each of those relationships, name one concrete thing you might do to embody the love of Christ, and what difference you think this might make.

3. It's hard to embody God's love without an appreciation of its depth and breadth. What can we do, individually and corporately, to grow in our appreciation and understanding of the love of God?

remember god's patience and kindness

Love is patient, love is kind... (1 Cor 13:4a)

When he first became a cab driver on the night shift, Kent Nerburn had no idea that the cab would become a "rolling confessional" as passengers would spill out their stories from the back seat.[1]

One night, he found himself waiting outside a darkened fourplex at two-thirty in the morning. Only one light appeared to be on in the building. Many drivers would have honked once or twice, then driven away. But Nerburn thought differently:

> I had seen too many people trapped in a life of poverty who depended on the cab as their only means of transportation. Unless the situation had a real whiff of danger, I always went to the door to try to find the passenger. It might, I reasoned, be someone who needed my assistance. Would I not want a driver to do the same if my mother or father had called for a cab?[2]

Thus, he went to the door and knocked.

A voice answered weakly: "Just a minute." When the door finally opened, he saw a frail elderly woman dragging a small suitcase. Nerburn could see that she was vacating her home. The walls were bare; the furniture was draped with sheets. She asked him to take her suitcase, give her a few moments alone, then come back to help her to the cab.

Once inside the cab, she gave him the address she was going to and asked him to drive through downtown. That wasn't the most direct route, and he told her so. But she replied that there was no hurry—she was going into hospice. She didn't have long to live, and had no family to care for her. She just wanted to see the sights one more time, to reminisce, before going to her final destination.

Quietly, Nerburn reached over to the meter and shut it off. He decided to take her wherever she wanted to go, for as long as it took.

They meandered the streets for two hours. She showed him the places that had been important to her, sharing memories of earlier, happier times. At length, she grew weary and asked to be taken to the facility, where orderlies put her in a wheelchair. She tried to pay him, but he refused, spontaneously bending down to give her a hug instead. She held him tightly and said thank you for the few moments of joy he had made possible.

Then they wheeled her away, and the door closed behind her. Nerburn writes:

> For the remainder of that day, I could hardly talk. What if that woman had gotten a driver who had been angry or abusive or impatient to end his shift? What if I had refused to take the run, or had honked once, then driven away? What if I had been in a foul mood and refused to engage the woman in conversation? How many other moments like that had I missed or failed to grasp?[3]

Personally, I've never been a cab driver. But I have been a passenger, and I've seen drivers treated like menial servants. A little impatience at the end of a long shift would be understandable.

Yet Nerburn chose patience and kindness instead. It started with giving his passenger the benefit of the doubt and taking the few seconds needed to walk up to the door and knock. In so doing, he treated an unseen stranger as a fellow human being—indeed, he treated her as he would have wanted his mother to be treated. At that moment, he didn't know what his simple act of courtesy might bring. When the evening was over, however, and the door closed behind the woman in the wheelchair, he realized what a moment of impatience would have cost them both.

Reading his story, I'm left wondering two things.

First, why is it that even in our closest relationships, let alone with strangers, we so often leave the meter running?

And second, what would happen if God were the same way with us?

■ ■ ■

I've been asked on occasion to consult with congregations and Christian organizations in conflict. Sometimes, the problem begins with some kind of miscommunication or misunderstanding. They want to do better, and have prayed diligently about the situation. But people don't feel heard, and they've become more entrenched in their positions. Nerves are frayed and relationships strained, and they need a little outside help to find their way forward.

This is the sometimes awkward reality of the church. By God's design, the gospel is embodied by human beings who bring both gifts and vulnerabilities to that vocation. We may wish things to be different, but the presence of the Holy Spirit does not automatically banish selfishness, defensiveness, or arrogance. Just ask the apostle Paul. It was his ongoing pastoral task to encourage believers to live according to the Spirit as he struggled to correct their errant ways.

Imagine, then, that you've been asked to write a letter to a troubled and contentious congregation. Specifically, your task is to help them envision what a true and godly love is like. How would you describe it? Where would you begin?

Paul, writing to the believers in Corinth, begins with the qualities of patience and kindness. Here are his words again:

Love is patient, love is kind, it isn't jealous, it doesn't brag, it isn't arrogant, it isn't rude, it doesn't seek its own advantage, it isn't irritable, it doesn't keep a record of complaints, it isn't happy with injustice, but it is happy with the truth. Love puts up with all things, trusts in all things, hopes for all things, endures all things. Love never fails. (1 Cor 13:4-8a)

As translated above from the Greek, "patient" and "kind" are two of eight adjectives used to tell us what love "is" or "isn't." There are also eight verbs telling us what love does or doesn't do. But as mentioned in the introduction, *all* of Paul's descriptors are actually verbs. Some Christians are therefore fond of saying that love is not a feeling, but an action.[4] Their point is to insist, and rightly so, that one can choose to behave in a loving fashion even if one doesn't feel loving.

It would be a mistake, however, to separate action from feeling, or to define love too narrowly as action alone. First, as we saw in chapter 2, emotions influence our behavior in ways we may not even be aware of. If we leave our emotions out of the equation, we may blind ourselves to deeper motivations that need a closer look.

Second, a little reflection will show that love can't be about right action alone. Consider the love of Jesus himself. By his own words, the cross was the utmost demonstration of his love for the Father and for humanity (e.g., John 15:13). But what if Jesus had only gone to the cross grudgingly? If love is only the action itself, the motivation shouldn't matter. As long as Jesus got the job done, we would have to call it love, even if he griped all the way to Golgotha. That's hardly an ideal picture of love.

Nor is it Paul's. As we've seen, the apostle insists that our acts of piety—even to the extreme of giving away all our possessions or martyrdom—mean nothing without love (1 Cor 13:1-3). True love is known by its fruit and expresses itself in loving action, but the action itself is not love. As Dallas Willard has said:

Love, as Paul and the New Testament presents it, is not action—not even action with a special intention—but a *source* of action. It is a condition out of which actions of a certain type emerge. ... [L]ove is an overall condition of the embodied, social self poised to promote the goods of human life that are within its range of influence.[5]

Love, in other words, is not just a matter of behavior alone but of character. Paul doesn't want the Corinthians merely to clean up their act. Nor is he trying to get them to muster up the willpower to behave in heroically loving ways despite what they feel. He wants them to be transformed. They must learn to see their sisters and brothers through God's eyes, to cultivate the emotions and perceptions that would spur them to love.

That's why, as we saw in chapter 6, Paul tries to give them a vision of being one body in Christ, despite their differences. Their gifts all come from the same Spirit, by the will of the same God, for the good of the one body. They are called to love because they are called to be the living embodiment of the character of Christ.

I believe Paul is still casting that vision as he transitions into talking about the positive qualities of love. As we'll see in the sections below, he begins with patience and kindness because those represent the inexplicably merciful way that God loves us.

▦ ▦ ▦

In the Old Testament, patience, compassion, mercy, and love are all bound up together in the character of God. We hear it in the way God describes himself to Moses (Exod 34:6), words that are echoed in the Psalms: "But you, my Lord, are a God of compassion and mercy; you are very patient and full of faithful love" (Ps 86:15; cf. also Ps 103:8). Or consider the words of the prophet Joel, as he warns God's people of coming disaster and invites them to repent:

> Yet even now, says the LORD, return to me with all your hearts, with fasting, with weeping, and with sorrow; tear your hearts and not your clothing. Return to the LORD your God, for he is merciful and compassionate, very patient, full of faithful love, and ready to forgive. (Joel 2:13).

Come back to God, the prophet pleads. Come back with hearts full of repentance, and find a God who is patient and loving, eager to forgive.

The same portrait of God, of course, is also found in the New Testament. Notably, Jesus himself teaches his disciples about the Father by telling them a parable about a king and his servant.

When you envision a king, what qualities come to mind? Perhaps you imagine someone tall and distinguished, someone of impressive and regal bearing. Even the prophet Samuel thought that way—and had to be corrected by God (e.g., 1 Sam 16:6-7). You might picture someone with a reputation for wisdom, like Solomon, or military prowess, like his father David. Or perhaps the idea of a king is a fearsome one, reminding you of someone who wields power like a hammer, like Herod the Great.

Whatever personal qualities make our lists, patience probably isn't one of them. And yet Jesus' story about the kingdom of heaven describes an astonishingly patient God who is full of compassion and mercy (Matt 18:23-35).

The king in the parable had many servants, one of whom owed the king "ten thousand bags of gold" (vs. 24).[6] It was an impossibly large and unpayable amount. To gain back a small part of the debt, the king ordered that the servant, his family, and all his possessions be sold.

There was nothing unjust or inappropriate about the king's plan. He was entirely within his rights. Knowing this, the servant did the only thing he could: he fell to his knees and begged for mercy. "Please, be patient with me," he cried, "and I'll pay you back" (vs. 26). It was a desperate plea and an empty promise. There was no way to pay back such a debt. But he was out of time and out of options.

The verb translated as "be patient" stems from two words, which when coupled together suggest something like "delayed anger," or in the King James Version (hereinafter, KJV), being "long-suffering" or "slow to anger."[7] Today, we might speak of someone who has a "long fuse." By begging the king to be patient, the servant was asking him to put off the day of reckoning.

Miraculously, the king was deeply moved by the man's plea.[8] In an unexpected act of mercy and compassion, the king forgave the entire debt. No installment plan, no compound interest, no repayment whatsoever. The debt was simply wiped off the books, and the servant was set free.

We are meant to be astonished at the merciful patience of the king. And in next turn of the story, we should be equally astonished at the unmerciful impatience of the servant.

Having been released, the man went out from the king's presence and happened upon a fellow servant who owed him money. The amount owed was next to nothing compared to what he had just been forgiven.[9] But in what seems like a desperate act, the first servant grabbed the second by the throat and demanded to be paid back immediately.

Earlier, the first servant had said to the king, "Be patient with me, and I'll pay you back." In return, he had received mercy. The second servant used the same words to beg for patience as well, promising to pay the money back.[10] It was a reasonable promise. But the first servant was unwilling to wait, and had the second man thrown into prison.

News of these events eventually reached the king, and the former debtor was summoned into the royal presence. This time, however, there was no mercy, only condemnation. The king declared him wicked. The servant had pled for patience and received much more. But he had refused to listen when his fellow servant made the same plea; he had refused to extend the forgiveness he himself had received. The story ends sadly with the king throwing the unforgiving servant into prison until the entire debt could be paid.

The servant's behavior is puzzling. He had received a great gift of unexpected grace. How could he then have been so selfish, so foolhardy? So morally clueless? As I've suggested elsewhere, it may be that the man didn't take the king at his word.[11] He heard the decree of mercy, but couldn't accept the fact that undeserved forgiveness was the only solution for his unpayable debt. He was still a man with a plan, hoping to work his way back into the king's graces. And no sooner did he leave the palace than he began trying to balance the books on his own by squeezing a debt out of someone else.

Whatever the case may be, we need to take the story to heart, because sometimes our own behavior can be equally puzzling. Even when we praise God for his grace toward us in forgiving sin, we may turn right around and act in distinctly ungracious ways toward those who sin against us.

Indeed, Jesus told the parable in response to a question from Peter, who wanted to know just how far he had to go in forgiving someone who had offended him. "Should I forgive as many as seven times?" he offered, probably hoping that Jesus would commend him for being so generous of heart. Jesus' actual response, then, must have been discouraging: "Not just seven times, but as many as seventy-seven times" (Matt 18:21-22).[12]

It's not that Peter needs to work harder and mouth the words of forgiveness more often. Jesus isn't saying, "Nice try, Peter. But seven is for wimps. When you can get it up to seventy-seven, then we'll talk about that promotion to head disciple." Imagine the acts of false forgiveness an answer like that would engender. We would feel obligated to forgive even when we don't feel like it—like doing homework in a subject we hate so we don't fail the test. So we take a deep breath and suppress our emotions. We turn away from the other person; we avoid eye contact. Perhaps we mutter, "Forget about it," or something else equally half-hearted. And when we're alone, we continue to nurse our grievances and pat ourselves on the back for being on a higher spiritual plane.

There. We've done our religious duty. Only seventy-six times to go.

That's not what Jesus means.

Rather, when we wonder whether to forgive someone, Jesus wants us first to remember how much we ourselves have already been forgiven. The mercy of God is meant to transform our attitude and behavior. Indeed, Jesus makes that expectation quite explicit. After the servant is thrown into debtor's prison, Jesus adds this postscript: "My heavenly Father will also do the same to you if you don't forgive your brother or sister from your heart" (vs. 35).

That sounds harsh. But let's be careful not to separate the statement from the parable. At the beginning of the story, the servant was already destined for trouble. He deserved the king's wrath, and he knew it. Thus, he could only beg for patience. What he received was the immeasurable gift of compassion.

We can only speculate as to why, afterward, he would dare to strangle money out of someone else. But one thing seems sure: his heart had not been transformed. He had not received the gift rightly, for if he had, he would at least have made a stab at forgiveness when the other man begged his patience. Mercy, it seems, had found no foothold, and the servant's fate ended up being the same as if he had been offered no mercy at all.[13]

When Paul declares that love is "patient," he uses the same word as in Jesus' parable, in which the patience of the king was expressed in compassion and mercy. If we are to love others with that kind of patience, we must begin by wholeheartedly embracing the patience of God toward us. God has every right to demand a reckoning for our sin, but holds his anger at arm's length out of compassion for our plight.

But wait. For some of you reading this, Peter's question—"How many times must I forgive?"—may be extremely personal, and Jesus' answer disturbing. You've been severely mistreated, perhaps abused. And you've been told that you're obligated as a Christian to forgive. Your version of Peter's question is "Do I have to keep forgiving as if the abuse never happened, and open myself to being a victim of further violence?" And depending on your experience, you may also be asking, "Does the abuser have a right to demand forgiveness from me just because I'm a Christian?"

The answer is no. To both questions.

Forgiveness does not mean turning a blind eye to sin and injustice. God doesn't give grace merely to let us off the hook, but to motivate and empower us toward holiness, toward being more and more like Christ. In other words, God both forgives and demands repentance and change. Forgiveness does not mean, "Let's just forget about it and go back to the way we were." And let it be said clearly: the abuser who demands to be forgiven lacks the humility of true repentance and is guilty of yet one more unloving act of intimidation.

Love is patient and longsuffering. And all who follow Christ are called to give love and compassion, even those who have suffered abuse at the hands of others. At the same time, victims of abuse are also deserving of compassion. The problem in some of our real-life Christian communities is that conflict makes us nervous, and we want to resolve the tension as quickly as possible. We conclude, too quickly, that there must be one right "Christian thing to do." And often, that means either condemning the abuser as inhuman, or demanding that the victim shut up and stop rocking the boat.

To preach patience is not to suggest a one-size-fits-all behavioral prescription for every situation of conflict. Neither Jesus nor Paul was laying out a rule to be simply and slavishly obeyed—that would be more like the neat, simplistic answer Peter wanted rather than the one Jesus actually gave. A gospel of love is about something deeper: creating a people whose hearts and imaginations have been transformed. We need wise and discerning communities that will help us all to remember what the mercifully patient God has done and continues to do, and to revel in that grace.

That's where love begins.

▓ ▓ ▓

Love is also "kind." The word Paul uses is rich with meaning.[14] In general, it suggests someone of a decent, upright, or kind nature. We might think of someone who is "nice," and this may be part of what Paul is describing.

But the word can also suggest moral goodness. To a devout Jew, the word would have brought to mind the goodness of God and of his faithful people, as extolled in the Psalms. God is good, does good (Ps 119:68), and abundantly gives what is good: "How great is the goodness that you've reserved for those who honor you, that you commit to those who take refuge in you—in the sight of everyone!" (Ps 31:19).[15] In response, the faithful are to "Trust in the LORD and do good" (Ps 37:3a), in a corrupt world in which the psalmist declares "no one does good" (Ps 14:3b). God is incomparably good to us, and likewise, what we call "kindness" entails valuing others and working for their good.

In Paul's writings, moreover, the qualities of patience and kindness often go hand in hand. Both describe how God treats us, and thus how we are expected to treat others in turn. For example, as Paul wrote to the church in Rome:

> So every single one of you who judge others is without any excuse. You condemn yourself when you judge another person because the one who is judging is doing the same things. We know that God's judgment agrees with the truth, and his judgment is against those who do these kinds of things. If you judge those who do these kinds of things while you do the same things yourself, think about this: Do you believe that you will escape God's judgment? Or do you have contempt for the riches of God's generosity, tolerance, and patience? Don't you realize that God's kindness is supposed to lead you to change your heart and life?[16] (Rom 2:1-4)

What could have been happening in the church for Paul to write such words? Some Christians, it seems, were being judgmental toward other Christians (imagine that!). We are, of course, expected to exercise good moral judgment. But these folks appear to have been condemning others for things that they were guilty of themselves. Paul warned that God would judge them for their arrogance and hypocrisy.

More specifically, some Bible scholars argue that Paul was addressing Jewish believers who were looking down with disdain on their Gentile brothers and sisters.[17] The problem of hypocrisy seems clear from what Paul says just a few verses later in the chapter:

> But, if you call yourself a Jew; if you rely on the Law; if you brag about your relationship to God; if you know the will of God; if you are taught by the Law so that you can figure out the things that really matter; if you have persuaded yourself that you are: a guide for the blind; a light to those who are in darkness; an educator of the foolish; a teacher of infants (since you have the full content of knowledge and truth in the Law); then why don't you who are teaching others teach yourself? If you preach, "No stealing," do you steal? If you say, "No

adultery," do you commit adultery? If you hate idols, do you rob temples? If you brag about the Law, do you shame God by breaking the Law? (Rom 2:17-23)

These Jewish believers took great pride in their religious and cultural tradition, boasting in their special status as God's chosen people and heirs to the Law of Moses. Paul, of course, could easily have made the same claim and more. He had been an exemplary Jew in every way, including being faultless by the standards of the Law (Phil 3:4-6).

His encounter with the risen Jesus, however, shook him to the core. It wasn't that he suddenly scorned his Jewish heritage. He did not believe, as some in Rome apparently did, that God had now rejected the Jews in favor of the Gentiles (Rom 11:1-32). But he was utterly captivated by the grace that made an apostle out of a violent enemy of the church. '

As a result, Paul had to radically reevaluate his entire religious résumé. Legalistic righteousness had once been a source of personal pride, but no more. In its place was a righteousness he couldn't earn by his own moral effort, a righteousness in and from Christ that left no room for boasting (Phil 3:7-9).

It would have hurt him to know that some of his Jewish brothers and sisters in Rome had not had a similar change of heart. They had received the gospel, and their tradition would already have taught them that God was patient and kind. But such kindness was not to be taken for granted. Rather, in Paul's words, it was meant to change their "heart and life." Jewish and Gentile believers alike, as part of one body in Christ, were to work for the common good by doing good to one another. To have an ungenerous and unkind attitude was to stand in contempt of the generosity and kindness of God.

Patience and kindness go together in Paul's understanding of the grace of God, and in his portrait of those who have been transformed by that grace. The two qualities are mentioned side by side in his list of overlapping and Spirit-empowered character traits headed by love: "But the fruit of the Spirit is love, joy, peace, patience, kindness, goodness, faithfulness, gentleness, and self-control" (Gal 5:22-23a; cf. Col 3:12). Furthermore, patience, kindness, and love are even bound together in Paul's description of himself, as he testifies to how the Holy Spirit has helped him endure the many hardships he's suffered for the gospel (2 Cor 6:4-6).

In short, when Paul teaches the positive side of love in 1 Corinthians 13, he begins with a vision of the longsuffering lovingkindness of God. The God of the Bible has always been patient and kind. And firmly grasping that truth, we as God's people should seek to embody patience and kindness in our relationships to one another.

Do we?

▦ ▦ ▦

Everyone knows the value of patience. It's embedded in folk wisdom, as in the sayings, "A little patience goes a long way" or "Patience is a virtue." It's also embedded in biblical wisdom. The following quote from the book of Proverbs, for example, is worthy of its own motivational poster: "Patience leads to abundant understanding, but impatience leads to stupid mistakes" (Prov 14:29). I can easily think of utterly stupid things I have said or done in my impatience. I've even considered writing a don't-do-it-yourself book entitled, *101 Stupid Tricks with Household Electricity*. I've nearly electrocuted myself more than once while working on home improvement projects, all because I couldn't be bothered with going outside to flip the proper circuit breaker.

Proverbs also links patience with self-control: "Better to be patient than a warrior, and better to have self-control than to capture a city" (Prov 16:32). Here, too, personal examples quickly come to mind. I remember my anger when our children were young and I could hear them squabbling in the other room. *I just told them to stop doing that,* I'd say to myself in frustration. *Why can't they just do as they're told?* I'd stomp down the hallway, ready to lay down the law. Often, thoughts of self-control would flit through my mind: *Hey, calm down. They're just kids. You don't have to be mad. You're the adult here; you know how to manage your temper.* Most of the time (I think?), Patient Dad would win: I'd take a deep breath and calm myself before entering the room.

Other times, though, Warrior Dad would just storm the city.

But love means more than just holding troublesome inclinations at bay. God's love is both patient and kind, and in our love for one another, patience and kindness must also be kept together. As St. John Chrysostom reminds us,

> a patient person is not necessarily also kind. And if that person is not kind, the love itself becomes a vice, and that person is in danger of falling into malice. Therefore, love supplies a medicine, which Paul calls *kindness*, and it is this that preserves the virtue of love.[18]

It's possible, in other words, to put off anger without dealing with it, giving us more time to rehearse unkind thoughts. There's nothing virtuous about having a long fuse if it means smoldering in our resentment. That kind of "patience" is not love.

Imagine praying with our eyes raised to heaven, arms spread in exasperation as if to say, *Why me?* "Lord, give me patience!" we cry, thinking of the people who continually test our resolve. There's nothing wrong with the words themselves. But what about the attitude with which the words are spoken, the heart behind the prayer?

When we're upset, it's easy to exaggerate what we perceive as a person's most annoying traits. We grumble over someone's thoughtless act, as if that person were simply incapable of considering anyone's feelings. We complain about someone being a control freak, as if that person were endlessly accusing us of incompetence. Then they hurt us again, and we grit our teeth and pray for patience.

Our pain and frustration may be understandable. But to the extent that we see others as the very embodiment of thoughtlessness itself, or as nit-picking personified, our prayer for patience will be unkind. It devalues and dehumanizes others by treating them as problems to be solved instead of people to be loved and understood.

Moreover, a prayer for patience can be arrogant. Such a prayer should be offered humbly. Too often, however, it's corrupted by a self-satisfied tone. We pray as if God were automatically on our side: *Lord, you know how annoying that person is. How can anybody put up with it? But look at me—I could have jumped down his throat, and I didn't! I know I'm not perfect, but I think I'm already above average in patience, don't you? If you insist that that person is my cross to bear, well, somehow I'll muddle through. But a little help would be nice. Give me patience!*

We might never be so cheeky as to utter any of this out loud. But as the psalmist says, "God knows every secret of the heart" (Ps 44:21b). We might deceive ourselves, but we can't fool God, and as we've seen, Paul warns that "every single one of you who judge others is without any excuse" (Rom 2:1a). We would be wise, therefore, to search our hearts: are our prayers for patience marred by a proud and superior attitude? If so, then perhaps we should be praying for humility and kindness as well.

If there is any place where I regularly lack patience and kindness, it's behind the wheel of my car. I know I'm not alone in this, for as one popular Internet meme puts it, "Patience is something you admire in the driver behind you, but not in one ahead."[19] I want the person behind me to be patient and kind. But the person in front of me is just plain in my way. I have somewhere I need to be: why doesn't everyone just understand that?

Because they have somewhere *they* need to be. And to them, I may be the person in the way.

As with the freeway, so with life. Moment to moment, my usual concern is not about others and their goals. It's about where I want to go, where I want to be, and others are a help or a hindrance. There's nothing strange about that way of thinking—but it's intrinsically self-centered, and can lead to frustration and even rage. The alternative is to remember that I'm not the only person out here. For the moment, we're in this together. The people around me have their own destinations, and deserve the same courtesy and consideration I want for myself.

▪ ▪ ▪

Thus, patience means more than merely putting up with people whose behavior we find hurtful or annoying, and kindness is more than niceness. Love requires a humble and self-sacrificial attitude in which we step down from the lofty perch from which we judge. It requires us to reimagine others—even the ones with whom we struggle—as creatures of intrinsic worth and value. This is how a gracious God relates to us, and is therefore how we should relate to others.

But loving acts of self-sacrifice needn't be heroic. There are endless opportunities in everyday life to embody love in ways that may seem quite ordinary when compared to the cross. What are these everyday miracles? Where do we see the loving tandem of patience and kindness?

We see it in the cab driver who has empathy for his passengers. Instead of worrying about when he'll get home, he gives a gift of time and attention to a woman on her way to hospice.

We see it in the father who pauses in the midst of his frustration to remember that his kids are just kids. Instead of acting impulsively out of anger, he asks himself how to handle the situation in a way that is best for them.

We see it in spouses who, despite deep feelings of hurt, listen to each other as best they can. Instead of lashing out, they try to understand what their partner is thinking and feeling.

We see it in church members who are learning what it means to be one body in Christ, to value each other as partners in the gospel, even when they find some members of the body insufferable.

We see it in pastors who continue to serve even when their ministry is being taken for granted. Instead of giving up, they endure patiently and work for the good of the congregation. Paul was such a pastor. He wrote to the Corinthians about the glories of love, and was the very embodiment of longsuffering patience and kindness. He endured in his God-given vocation despite the many ways the congregation mistreated him.

But again, Christian love isn't about moral or spiritual heroism. It's about being transformed from the inside out by God's love and the Spirit of Christ. And that transformation begins by reminding ourselves again and again that we are debtors—forgiven debtors—set free by the miraculous mercy of the king. We must never take that mercy for granted, for God's kindness is meant to change our heart and life.

talk or think about it

1. The chapter began and ended with ordinary stories of patience and kindness (e.g., the cab driver taking a woman to hospice). Tell a similar real-life story. If the story is about your own determination to be patient and kind in the face of frustration, say what motivated you and how you felt afterward.

2. Have you ever tried to forgive someone because you believed you were obligated to do so, but found that you had no real forgiveness in your heart? Alternatively, have you ever tried to be patient with people while struggling with unkind thoughts and feelings toward them? What were the circumstances and what was the result?

3. Prayerfully consider this question: is there someone in your life right now to whom you need to show patience and kindness? How can you do so with the humility appropriate to understanding God's patience and kindness toward you?

4. Discuss Jesus' parable of the unforgiving servant (Matt 18:21-35). Do we experience ourselves as those would owe an impossible and unpayable debt, if not for the patience and kindness of God? If not, why not? And what might change if we did?

8

repent of your rivalry

Love...isn't jealous, it doesn't brag, it isn't arrogant... (1 Cor 13:4b)

In 1918, the Friedman family of Sioux City, Iowa welcomed identical twins into the world. They named the girls Esther Pauline and Pauline Esther. You may never have heard of them, but theirs is a well-known story of modern-day sibling rivalry.

As you might guess from their names alone, the twins shared much in common. As children, they often slept in the same bed. Their parents even dressed them the same way—a trend which the sisters continued into early adulthood. As Esther's daughter later recalled, "They would sometimes go to a party or a dance with one escort—these two girls in the same outfits with one guy between them."[1] The sisters married at the same time in an elaborate double wedding, wearing identical bridal gowns and hairstyles.

Pauline—or "Popo"—enjoyed their shared identity. But Esther— or "Eppie"—came to want a more independent identity of her own. In 1955, after moving to Chicago, she won a contest to take over a syndicated newspaper advice column. And with the column, Eppie inherited the pseudonym under which she continued to write for decades: Ann Landers.

Letters from the distraught and lovelorn poured in for Eppie. For the first few months, Pauline helped her sister handle the volume by writing some of the advice herself. But Eppie's editor put a stop to that, prompting Pauline to apply to another newspaper to write a column of her own. She took the pen name of "Abigail Van Buren," and her column, "Dear Abby," became an instant success.

Thus began an on-again, off-again professional rivalry between the two sisters. Pauline's daughter, Jeanne Phillips, took over the Dear Abby column when her mother began to suffer from Alzheimer's. Phillips claims that after Pauline got her own column, Eppie refused to speak to her twin sister for ten years. Eppie's daughter, Margo Howard, also became an advice columnist. The feud that began in one generation continued into the next.[2] And all of this from writers who have helped thousands with their relationship advice.

We shouldn't be surprised. As many who have grown up with siblings can attest, rivalry can be the flip side of closeness. Children don't have just one feeling toward their siblings, but a whole range of conflicting emotions. They don't simply hate each other, even if that's what they're shouting at the moment.

How parents handle these volatile emotions can make all the difference.[3] Unfortunately, parents sometimes make the situation worse—even in the Bible.

There's family drama galore in the line of Abraham, some of which gets scrubbed out in the tidier versions of the stories we feed our children. The twins Jacob and Esau, for example, were rivals from the start, competing at birth and even in the womb. Jacob, ever the schemer, manipulated his brother out of his birthright by capitalizing on his weaknesses.

And if that weren't enough, each parent fanned the flames of rivalry by loving one child more than the other. When Rebekah overheard Isaac promise to give Esau a blessing, she hatched an elaborate plot to steal the blessing for Jacob. To accomplish her ends, she had to betray her loyalty to her husband and take advantage of his failing eyesight. At the end of the day, Jacob walked away with the blessing, and Esau held a murderous grudge against his brother (Gen 25:21-34; 27:1-41).

So much for the biblical example of a loving family.[4]

The problems continued in the next generation. Just as Isaac and Rebekah had played favorites with their children, so did Jacob. Jacob had twelve sons, by two wives and their respective maidservants. But he loved one son more than all the others: Joseph, the firstborn of his favored wife, Rachel.   The other brothers knew Joseph was the favorite, because he wore a robe that Jacob had made just for him.[5]   To make matters worse, Joseph snitched on his brothers, and prattled on about having a dream that they would all one day bow down to him.

So they plotted to get rid of him.   They grabbed Joseph, stripped him of his precious robe, threw him into an empty cistern, and sold him into slavery.   Then they dipped the robe in goat's blood and pretended he had been slaughtered by a wild beast, much to their father's unending grief (Gen 37:1-35).   Centuries later, in the book of Acts, Luke would describe Jacob's older sons as being "jealous of Joseph" (Acts 7:9).   That's putting it mildly.

But neither Jacob nor Joseph were innocent in the matter.   The brothers were stung by Jacob's favoritism and by what they saw as Joseph's braggadocio.   Jealousy and arrogance thus go hand in hand—and this is true even of the sibling rivalry between those who are supposed to be brothers and sisters in Christ.   Jealous rivalry is not love.

As we've seen, Paul wants the Corinthians to rise above their competitive concerns by aspiring to a higher way, the way of love.   In 1 Corinthians 13, therefore, he puts before them a broad and inspiring vision of love.   In verse 4, he begins to describe what love does, choosing patience and kindness as his starting point.   These two qualities are not just a description of how we should love—they're a reminder of how God loves and has always loved.

By the end of verse 4, however, Paul turns to the negative side of his teaching.   He describes what love doesn't do, or to put it more directly, how loving Christians should not behave: love isn't "jealous," doesn't "brag," and isn't "arrogant" (1 Cor 13:4b).   Sadly, these unloving qualities describe the Corinthians themselves.   More sadly still, they sometimes describe us.

In this chapter, therefore, we'll look at these first few aspects of what love doesn't do, how they apply to problems in the Corinthian church, and what they might mean for us.   Following the way of love means that some things need to change, and Paul begins with the jealousy and arrogance that too often fracture our relationships.

▦ ▦ ▦

Before we do that, however, let's pause to consider how Paul makes the transition from what love does to what it doesn't do, from a positive vision of godly love to a negative list of problematic emotions and behaviors. From the ideals of patience and kindness, Paul moves quickly to the bad attitudes that are dividing the church: jealousy, arrogance, self-centeredness, irritability and the like.

If we were to visit a congregation like that today, we might be quick to judge and walk away. But these are the real feelings of real people who are trying—often unsuccessfully—to follow Christ. Despite all of their problems, Paul loves these people and is confident that the Holy Spirit is in their midst.

We need a similar realism. I have argued that even if we shouldn't reduce love to the biology of emotion, neither should emotion be ignored in favor of a more "spiritual" ideal. The calling to embody the love of Christ in our daily lives comes to us in the midst of a messy mix of worldly expectations and real relationships. It does no good to deny the fact that we have hopes and dreams for our love lives that have little to do with the gospel.

Nor can we deny that on any given day, we are quite capable of being envious, selfish, and resentful—all the things for which we might look down our spiritual noses at the Corinthians. If we aspire to walk the high road, our ideals must be accompanied by sober judgment. If Paul's vision of love helps us to say, "This is who I want to be," that budding desire cannot be allowed to ignore "This is who I am."

How does Paul, as a pastor, encourage this way of thinking? He could have written, "God is patient and kind. You Corinthians, however, are anything but. Some of you are arrogant braggarts. The rest of you are green with envy." We've heard sermons like that: *God is holy, and you're an unholy mess. Get your act together!* We leave the building with a firmer grasp on our badness than on God's goodness. And while the accompanying guilt may feel pious enough, it doesn't empower much in the way of change.

Similarly, Paul could have demanded directly, "Stop being so jealous and arrogant!" But notice what he does instead: he comes at the matter indirectly by describing how *love,* personified, behaves. Paul is not, of course, afraid to speak his mind; much of what he writes in other parts of the letter is both direct and critical.

As we've seen, however, his purpose in the love chapter is different. He is trying to give them a vision of the higher road, the more excellent way. He wants them to be captivated by the wondrous superiority of love, so much so that they would rather pursue love than anything else.

The jealousy and arrogance amongst the Corinthians needs to stop, but he wants the people to change for the right reasons. "Knock it off!" would be a more forceful message than "Love isn't jealous." But it would also be a poor pastoral strategy.

Changes in behavior and attitude can't be imposed by fiat. Ideally, they should be the expression of true repentance. Where minds and hearts have been transformed by the love of God, there is both a negative and a positive movement: a turn away from the old and a turn toward what's new and better. Given the loving unity he's trying to foster, therefore, "Love isn't jealous" may be Paul's way of suggesting that when the Corinthians truly desire the way of love, they'll see their jealous behavior for what it is.

▪ ▪ ▪

What, then, is jealousy? And how does it differ from envy?

Again, our language isn't always exact. Although distinctions can be made between the two, many people use the word "jealousy" to mean both. One helpful way to think of the difference is in terms of *losing* something versus *lacking* it.[6] I am jealous when because of you I fear losing something important to me; but I am envious when you have something important to me that I lack.

Both emotions can be normal responses to everyday situations. But each also has its pathological extreme. What's known as "morbid" jealousy is seen, for example, in spouses who suffer from the delusion that their partner is unfaithful. These unhappy souls compulsively check on their partners' whereabouts, and may subject them to interrogations, lie detector tests, and even physical abuse.[7] Similarly, while a benign form of envy can spur us to admiration and self-improvement, maliciously envious people wish failure or harm on their rivals.[8]

In recent years, a less extreme but potentially troubling form of envy has emerged: "Facebook envy." To some extent, it's human nature to compare ourselves to others. That's how we gauge our social standing. But this has become increasingly complicated in today's age of online social networking. The number of people to whom we compare ourselves has grown. We're no longer just trying to keep up with the Joneses next door, but the hundreds of people on our list of Facebook friends, many of whom we don't actually know.

Worldwide, five new Facebook profiles go up every second (and an estimated 83 million of these profiles are fake). There are plenty of people looking: the service boasts over a billion users who visit the site daily for an average of twenty minutes per visit. And what do they see? Among other things, several of the over 300 million pictures that are uploaded every day.[9]

When consumer-friendly film cameras were invented for the masses, we used pictures to chronicle our lives. But often, the images were more about life as we wanted it to be rather than life as it actually was.[10] Vacation photos showed happy families in beautiful places, not kids whining and squabbling in the back seat of the car. Digital photography and social media have only upped the ante on image management. Pictures aren't crammed into photo albums for the occasional walk down memory lane anymore. We put them out there for everyone to see, and curate the content according to the image we want to convey.

Social networking can connect us with others in positive ways. As we scroll through other people's Facebook timelines, we chuckle at the recycled bits of Internet humor, find new inspirational quotes, and share words of support and celebration with our friends. The downside of Facebook usage, however, comes with the more subtle, cumulative effects of comparing ourselves to others. A study of over 400 undergraduates, for example, found that the more time college students spent on Facebook each week, the more they believed that other people had happier and better lives.[11] The more we see our own lives as less desirable and the more we envy what we see in other people's profiles, the greater the chance that Facebook use will leave us depressed.[12]

Psychologists have been studying the invidious effects of social comparison since the 1950s.[13] We have an intrinsic need, it seems, to evaluate our opinions and abilities, and we do so by comparing them to the opinions and abilities of others.[14] The more frequently we engage in such comparison, however, the more likely we are to experience envy, defensiveness, and regret; we're even more likely to lie in self-protective ways.[15] Comparing ourselves to someone who seems more successful is a potent occasion for envy, particularly if the other person's good fortune seems undeserved and we see little opportunity to improve our own lot.[16]

Think for a moment about your own situation. Perhaps you've experienced Facebook envy. Your Facebook friends are posting selfies from exotic locations that you'd love to visit but can't afford. Or you're struggling with family issues and all those pictures of joyous reunions and cute little babies are getting on your nerves. Or perhaps someone else at your job landed the promotion you believe should have been yours. If that person seems less qualified, you might even be hoping in secret that they'll fail.

Social groups have yardsticks by which we measure our relative standing. As a professor, I inhabit the hallowed halls of academia, in which the marks of social status are like the common air we breathe. Your official title gives your "rank": one aspires eventually to be promoted to "full" professor, as if for all the previous years you weren't quite the real thing. And there are numerous other marks. Who's awarded tenure and who isn't? Who reels in the most or the largest research grants? Who publishes the most articles, or gets the book contract with the most prestigious publisher? Who's honored with the endowed chair or public lectureship? That's not to say that any of these things are illegitimate in themselves. But concerns about status automatically invite comparison, and with it, the whole package of competitive emotions.

The church is far from immune to such concerns. For example, as much as we might want to say that the "success" of a congregation is measured by the spiritual maturity of its members, that's too abstract a criterion. In our productivity- and stats-obsessed culture, attendance and growth lend themselves much better to numbers and charts. Even pastors can get caught up in the numbers game, judging their own worth by the size of the membership. At denominational meetings and conferences, you might overhear pastors telling others about how their congregations have grown numerically. On the surface, it's a way of giving thanks for God's goodness and grace. But underneath, it can be a subtle (or not so subtle!) reminder of who has bragging rights.

Social comparison. Self-doubt, envy, and resentment. Arrogance and bragging. All of these things, apparently, were fueling discord in the church at Corinth. That's why Paul needed to write to them about love.

■ ■ ■

"Love isn't jealous." That's the translation found in some Bibles, while others translate Paul as referring to envy.[17] As explained earlier, there's a distinction between the two concepts, even if we tend to use the word "jealousy" for both. So which translation is right? Is Paul speaking of jealousy or envy?

Both. And neither.

Paul's word (in its noun form) is actually the root from which we get our English word "zeal."[18] It suggests the eager pursuit of some goal, and the meaning of the word takes its cue from the nature of that goal. If the end goal is praiseworthy, the word takes on a positive tone. At the end of 1 Corinthians 12, for example, as Paul leads into the love chapter, he advises them to zealously pursue the greater spiritual gifts (1 Cor 12:31a).[19] He knows the Corinthians to be an ambitious people, and wants to encourage that zeal in the right direction: toward prophecy as the gift that's best for the church, and toward love as superior even to prophecy.

If the goal is a selfish one, however, the same word takes on a negative tone, and suggests jealousy or envy. Consider, for example, this passage from James:

> What is the source of conflict among you? What is the source
> of your disputes? Don't they come from your cravings that are
> at war in your own lives? You long for something you don't
> have, so you commit murder. You are *jealous* for something
> you can't get, so you struggle and fight. (James 4:1-2a,
> emphasis added)

Here, the people's zeal is for something they want but don't have.
Unexamined, frustrated desire is leading to conflicts that are damaging
the community and distracting them from the gospel. Something
similar was probably the case in Corinth.

Thus, when Paul states that love isn't "jealous," he uses a word
that doesn't mean either jealousy or envy exclusively, but a zeal that
can be applied toward good or bad ends. The meaning has to be
determined in context by the rest of what Paul writes in the letter.
And the picture of the congregation that we get from his earlier
chapters is one in which Christians are competing with each other for
social status, evoking a toxic mix of pride, jealousy, envy, and
resentment.

▦ ▦ ▦

Paul begins 1 Corinthians with his usual words of greeting and
encouragement. Then he gets down to business, addressing a
troublesome situation that was reported to him secondhand. The
Corinthians, apparently, had been quarreling with each other in a
curiously divisive way:

> What I mean is this: that each one of you says, "I belong to
> Paul," "I belong to Apollos," "I belong to Cephas," "I belong to
> Christ." Has Christ been divided? Was Paul crucified for you,
> or were you baptized in Paul's name? (1 Cor 1:12-13)

It's not clear whether there were actual rival factions in the church,
like competing political parties or even fan clubs. But the people

seemed to take pride in boasting of their allegiance to a specific figurehead (1 Cor 3:21). Each leader had something to commend him. Paul was their founding pastor and spiritual father (1 Cor 4:14-16), and those who boasted of belonging to him may have prided themselves on their loyalty. Apollos was the more eloquent speaker (Acts 18:24-28; 1 Cor 2:1), an important qualification in a culture in which people paid to hear good rhetoric. Cephas, or Peter, had been Jesus' right-hand man and was one of the leaders of the mother church in Jerusalem. There's no record in the Bible that he ever visited Corinth, but if he had, some of the believers there were apt to be impressed.

And not to be outdone, some of the Corinthians were proclaiming their allegiance to Jesus himself. The words "I belong to Christ," of course, are theologically correct; Paul himself would have agreed. But there was something wrong with the way it was being said, a way that promoted division in the body of Christ instead of unity.

That's not hard to imagine. Haven't we all heard someone declare the truth with a self-satisfied air that seems to say, "I'm smart and you're stupid," or, "I'm spiritually enlightened and you're not"? Have we done that ourselves without realizing it? Because when that happens, even a truth that is spoken quietly can be drowned out by an attitude that screams of arrogance.

The problem was significant enough that Paul was still addressing it all the way into chapter 4 of the letter. In chapter 3, for example, he writes:

> Brothers and sisters, I couldn't talk to you like spiritual people but like unspiritual people, like babies in Christ. I gave you milk to drink instead of solid food, because you weren't up to it yet. Now you are still not up to it because you are still unspiritual. When *jealousy* and fighting exist between you, aren't you unspiritual and living by human standards? When someone says, "I belong to Paul," and someone else says, "I belong to Apollos," aren't you acting like people without the Spirit? (1 Cor 3:1-4, emphasis added)

In calling them "unspiritual," Paul isn't saying that they don't have the Holy Spirit, but that they're not living by the Spirit. They're still living according to their old cultural values and habits of thought, jockeying for social status in ways that provoke jealousy and conflict.

Similarly, in chapter 4, he points to pride as a root issue:

> Brothers and sisters, I have applied these things to myself and Apollos for your benefit. I've done this so that you can learn what it means not to go beyond what has been written and so none of you will become *arrogant* by supporting one of us against the other. Who says that you are better than anyone else? What do you have that you didn't receive? And if you received it, then why are you bragging as if you didn't receive it? (1 Cor 4:6-7, emphasis added)

The word translated as "arrogant" suggests the image of a person whose chest is swelled with pride, puffed up like a balloon.[20] This attitude was affecting the congregation in numerous ways, not just in their conflict over leaders. They were puffed up and arrogant in their opposition to Paul (1 Cor 4:18-19), in their inappropriate response to flagrant sin in their midst (1 Cor 5:2), and in their self-serving use of knowledge (1 Cor 8:1).

Thus, the Corinthians were plagued by jealousy or envy on the one hand, and arrogance or boastful pride on the other. Consequently, the first problem that Paul tackles in his letter—the argument over leaders—also provides the lead-in for his description of love's opposite. Love doesn't act in jealous, boastful, or arrogant ways—though the Corinthians, unfortunately, did all these things.[21]

In addition, one might reasonably speculate about how such troublesome tendencies could complicate the matter of spiritual gifts in the congregation. As mentioned in an earlier chapter, Corinth was a prosperous city. There were obvious divisions of social class and a culture of upward mobility, not unlike city life today. Even in the church, people were used to thinking in terms of personal status, of how to climb another rung on the social ladder.

In such a climate, the Corinthians would not have been inclined to think, "You have one spiritual gift, and I have another. That's so we can complement each other and work together to accomplish God's purposes." It was easier to think of gifts as signs of divine favor. To the Corinthians, those with showier gifts like speaking in tongues seemed to have been singled out by God as special, even if nobody could say why.

Add to that a further complication: for whatever reason, some of the Corinthians had stopped believing in a future resurrection of the dead (1 Cor 15:12). The upshot is a congregation in which success means winning the game of religious status, against the background belief that this life—the one that begins with physical birth and ends at death—is the only one there is.

When I was a kid, Christmas was all about presents. I'd drop hints about what I wanted, usually some toy I'd seen in a television commercial. Then the long-awaited morning would come. My sister and I would tear into the packages and hope for the best. Sometimes, our wishes came true, or we'd get something even better than expected.

And sometimes we'd get...underwear. Functional, yes. But not something you'd take much pride in or show off to your friends.

Thus we might reimagine the concerns over spiritual gifts that Paul describes in 1 Corinthians 12. Christmas was over, all the gifts had been given, and Santa wasn't coming back next year. Worse, he had played favorites instead of treating all the good little boys and girls the same. Some seemed to have hit the jackpot, while others had received far less glamorous presents. The end result was that some of the children were tempted to crow over their good fortune, though they had done nothing to earn their gifts. Others felt neglected and envious: *Why him? Why her? Why not me?* Feeling left out, they were tempted to believe that they weren't really part of the family.

That would have been a situation ripe for sibling rivalry.

As one New Testament scholar has written, "If any assembly in the first century was torn by envy it was Corinth."[22] The people had received the gospel, and the Holy Spirit was clearly active in their midst. But whatever its cause, the presence of envy meant they were still living according to those unspiritual human standards Paul had warned them about (1 Cor 3:3)—or in modern terms, the rules of social comparison they took for granted. Who's important, and who's not? Who's a success, and who's a failure? Evaluating themselves against such standards and against each other, some went the way of boasting and others the way of envy. And neither was the way of love.

This points to the core of how love functions in Paul's letter. Love is known by its attitudes and actions, but is neither an attitude nor an action in itself. Love is not simply a feeling, whether of warmth, intimacy, or compassion. Moreover, Paul's words can't be used to "define" love as the presence of patience nor the absence of arrogance, and so on. He's writing more as a pastor than a philosopher, and if he were to address a different congregation with a different set of problems, he might describe love somewhat differently.

Rather, when Paul speaks of love, he means the embodiment of the life of Jesus in the lives of his followers, in such a way that the truth of the gospel is demonstrated in their relationship to one another. In and through the life, death, and resurrection of Christ, we have been redeemed by a loving God. But that's not the end of the story. We have been redeemed for a purpose: to show, here and now, the transformative power of that love.

And that truth changes—*must* change!—the standards by which we assign worth and value to ourselves and others.

■ ■ ■

What are the implications of all this for our usual ways of thinking and speaking about love? Again, my goal is not to define love in some narrow way that excludes romance and all its cultural trappings. Like it or not, erotic attraction and romantic affection will always be part of how we use the word "love" in its more general sense.

But if what I've said above about the embodiment of the life of Jesus is correct, then we have both the right and the responsibility to ask how our attitudes and behaviors are shaped by our culture's ideals regarding love. Specifically, we can ask whether and when they give rise to standards of comparison that lead us away from our calling.

It's a bit like the conversation that prompted the so-called Parable of the Good Samaritan (Luke 10:25-37). An expert in Jewish law put Jesus to the test by asking what he had to do to gain the eternal life for which Jews hoped. He was caught by surprise when Jesus turned the rhetorical tables on him by asking him to answer his own question.

The lawyer promptly quoted the two great commandments to love God and love your neighbor. Jesus' response was authoritative and straight to the point: "You have answered correctly. Do this and you will live." That may sound rather matter-of-fact. But the words implied, *You already know the answer to the question. You can talk the talk. Now, walk the walk.*

The lawyer was on the spot. In a crafty attempt to save face, he came back with another and more controversial question: "And who is my neighbor?" (Luke 10:29). There was, of course, no question about the first commandment, to love God. But the second? *Interpret it for me, Jesus. Give me a definition. Who is my neighbor, and who isn't?*

In response, Jesus told the story of a man beaten and robbed by thieves, and left for dead by the side of the road. Soon after, a priest happened by, and then a Levite. Both would have known God's commandment—and both hurried past the injured man, ignoring his plight. Then a third traveler happened by: a Samaritan, someone whom the lawyer would have treated with contempt. In Jesus' story, it was neither the priest nor the Levite, but the despised Samaritan who was moved by compassion. He bandaged the victim's wounds, took him to an inn to recuperate, and gave the innkeeper a blank check for the expenses.

When he had finished the parable, Jesus turned the tables again. He hadn't answered the lawyer's question. He hadn't drawn a line between neighbors and enemies—though surely the lawyer himself would have put any Samaritan in the latter category. Instead, Jesus had told a story of compassionate love in which a Samaritan was the surprise hero. Then he asked the legal expert, "What do you think? Which of these three was a neighbor to the man who encountered thieves?" (Luke 10:36).

The lawyer had asked, "Who is my neighbor?" The question had probably been intended to prompt the kind of debate he thought he could win. But Jesus took the conversation to a different level. He raised the question of character: "Who was neighborly?"

We might adopt a similar strategy for our questions about love and romance. One can ask whether it's right to include secular ideals in the ways Christians think and speak of love. But given the flexibility of the word itself, we're apt to disagree over matters of definition and conceptual boundaries.

I propose a slightly different line of questioning. Instead of asking, "What is love?" we can ask, "What is loving?" Instead of trying to draw a clear line between secular and Christian ideals, we can ask how our embodiment of either is actually loving in the way that Paul describes.

For example, consider again the notion of love as something you fall into by a twist of romantic fate or destiny. The pious version of the myth is that God in his providence and grace will eventually reveal to the faithful their one true soul mate. I know Christian couples who would say that they fell madly in love at first sight, and are now happily married to their God-given match. And I have no desire to spoil their romantic story.

The problem comes when the story invites social comparison— when it becomes a standard by which others are encouraged to measure their own lives. A happily married couple, for example, trying to be supportive, tells a distraught unmarried friend, "Don't worry. Look at us. God has someone for you, too." Then, as if to reinforce the point, the spouses turn and look lovingly into each other's eyes.

Here, the question "What is love?" might mean interrogating the soul mate myth: is there any real biblical or theological justification for it? But the question, "What is loving?" points us in a different direction. What are the subtle ways in which the couple communicates their superiority? *We were faithful, and see how God rewarded us!* How might their mooning over each other provoke their friend to envy?

That version of the problem is at the weaker end of the continuum. It gets worse when the story represents the shared mythology of a group. In some congregations, for example, unmarried visitors quickly get the impression that they're deficient in some way—as when they're quickly directed to a "singles group" whose unspoken purpose is to pair people off. We can and should question the social and theological assumptions that stand behind the practice. But we should also ask in what way the practice is hurtful and unloving.

Or think back to chapter 4 and the romantic woes of many Christian college students. Where, exactly, does a campus' culture of purity go off the theological rails? That's an important and legitimate question. But Paul, I think, would be just as concerned about how the fairy-tale mythology plays out in a painful game of social comparison that results in winners and losers. As we've seen, those who win the game are tempted to smugness and arrogance, while those viewed as losers are bathed in shame and envy. We can argue about whether the ideals of the Christian purity culture are properly biblical. But one thing seems clear: the rivalry that often results from those ideals is not loving.

Moreover, the typical vision of love given to us in romantic fiction and fairy tale isn't terribly helpful when it comes to dealing with the ups and downs (particularly the downs!) of real-life relationships. Let's face it: sooner or later, even in the most ideally romantic of relationships, we will stumble over disappointment. *Cinderella leaves her glass slippers all over the floor! Prince Charming doesn't want to go to the ball anymore!*

Most people, I think, realize at some level that the happily-ever-after ending isn't as neat or automatic as the stories would have us believe. Still, it's hard to know to what extent the mythology shapes our disappointment, the vague feeling that our relationships *should* be different or easier. And if people in general are discouraged from being honest about the challenges they face in their relationships, where will we find a realistic standard of comparison?

Not in the myth itself.

Romantic mythology, in other words, lacks the realism of Paul, who calls people to love even in the midst of their quarrels. His description of what love doesn't do is like the flip side of Elizabeth Barrett Browning's famous sonnet: *How are you hurting each other? Let me count the ways.* People don't become Christians and then live happily ever after, at least not this side of the final resurrection.

The reality is that congregations are human social organizations. Certainly, they are more than that, but they are also at least that. And that means that they wrestle with some of the same issues of social comparison—in both life and love—that other people do. They have similar concerns over power and status, over success, self-worth, and significance.

The rivalry fostered by social comparison is not unique to Corinth. God's people have always struggled with envy and arrogance, right up to the present. But again, we are called to love, to embody the life of Christ even in the midst of these struggles. Only one kind of boasting is appropriate in the church: "The one who brags should brag in the Lord" (1 Cor 1:31; cf. Jer 9:24; 2 Cor 10:17). It is God who establishes us, who declares our worth by the love he has demonstrated through his Son. And when we finally begin to grasp the depth and breadth of that love, we can also begin to let go of our anxious need to compare ourselves to others. Embraced by the longsuffering patience and kindness of God, we can relax and repent of our rivalries.

talk or think about it

1. Name one or two social contexts, past or present, that are or have been important to your sense of worth or success (e.g., family, work, school, friends, church, neighborhood). What kinds of social comparisons do people make in these groups? How do people know who's higher or lower in status?

2. If you've ever felt like you were on the losing end of some social comparison, how did you feel and what did you do about it?

3. In what ways, if at all, have you seen rivalry and competition play out between members of the same congregation? What can Christians do to help one another be more loving in the face of all the ways we engage in social comparison?

4. More specifically, consider the ways we compete with one another in terms of who's more "successful" in the realm of romance, marriage, and family life. *I got my ring by spring, and you didn't. Most of us here are married, so why aren't you? My kid gets all As in school and loves Jesus, and yours...doesn't.* What's the more loving alternative, and what would it take to get there?

9

look out for number two

Love isn't rude, it doesn't seek its own advantage... (1 Cor 13:5a)

As Christians, we talk a lot about "witnessing" and of our "witness." The first generally refers to sharing the gospel with others, verbally. But the second is broader: it refers not just to the words we speak, but the life we live in the sight of others. The distinction is important, because people may not believe what we say about the faith unless it is matched by the faithfulness of what we do.

So what do people see when they look at the way we live, especially the way we relate to others?

Karen Ehman was standing in line to order lunch at a coffeehouse. An elderly woman ahead of her had paid for her order and was awkwardly trying to gather her things. But it was too much for her to handle. She faltered and fumbled as she tried to open the door and balance her purse, food, and drink all at the same time.

Even though Ehman had just reached the front of the line, she sacrificed her place to lend a hand. She quickly walked over and held the door open for the woman, then offered to help carry her food. Ehman describes the woman's reaction:

> She stopped in her tracks, her bright blue eyes looking up at me with gratefulness. "Oh, dear...you must have a grandmother living that you're so kind to an old woman."
>
> "No, ma'am, I don't," I answered. "I just love Jesus, and he wants me to help you."

Her face softened. She shook her head and decidedly declared, "Of course! You people have always been so helpful to me. I don't know what I'd do without you."

You people. I'm pretty sure she meant, "You Christians."...[S]he referred to me—and others who loved Jesus—as "you people." It made me wonder, how had other Christians helped her? ... It reminded me of an age-old truth: more is caught than taught. It also demonstrated that people are watching. ...What do they see?[1]

I find Ehman's story encouraging. For the woman she helped, at least, the label of "Christian" was a positive one. It gathered together under the name of Christ all the people who had reached out to her in love and kindness.

Sadly, however, what people see in Christians is not always loving.

In recent years David Kinnaman, president of the polling organization the Barna Group, has forcibly argued that millions of people in today's younger generation view the church in a negative light. Many know the basics of the gospel message and have even spent time around Christians. But what they've seen hasn't been inviting. Christians are often perceived as hypocritical and oppositional, defining themselves more by what they stand against than by what they stand for.[2]

Even those who grew up in the church often drift away in their twenties, citing a host of negative reasons. For example, they see the church as overprotective, suspicious of secular culture in a way that's more isolationist than redemptive. The church relies too much on shallow platitudes that don't help young people make sense of a rapidly changing world. The church is not a safe place for them to express doubt and ask hard questions about the faith. These young people may thus spend years exploring alternatives to the church. And if they find people of other faiths whose lives seem to be more congruent, they may abandon Christianity altogether.[3]

In the previous chapter, I suggested that we need a healthy dose of realism with regard to the church. Jesus taught, "This is how everyone will know that you are my disciples, when you love each other" (John 13:35). From the time of the New Testament to the present, however, Christians have too often done a poor job of living out that kind of loving witness to the world. Even in the church, we can be downright rude to one another, in ways that make people want to leave and never come back.

Paul had no illusions about the state of the church in Corinth.

But that didn't stop him from calling them to love.

"Love isn't rude," Paul taught, nor does it "seek its own advantage" (1 Cor 13:5a). At root, the issue is a kind of self-centeredness in which we're always looking out for number one, always seeking what's best for ourselves. There's nothing intrinsically wrong, of course, with pursuing our own goals and desires. The question is what happens when our needs conflict with someone else's.

Americans live in a highly individualistic culture in which it's common for people to reason, *Hey, I'm not breaking the law—if they don't like it, that's their problem.* But a people called to embody the love of Christ can't afford to think that way. That doesn't mean we have to do whatever others tell us to do. It does mean, however, that we need to realize that our choices aren't made in a vacuum. Like pebbles in a pond, our behavior creates ripples that affect other people. And what love does is to desire the best for the others around us, even if it means some sacrifice on our part.

In other words, we need to look out for number two.

■ ■ ■

When we use the word "rude," we usually mean some behavior that's offensive because it's impolite. Some social nicety has been neglected. A restaurant server is curt and inattentive; the patron is demanding and belligerent. Each goes home thinking the other rude, perhaps even blaming the other as the reason for their own ungraciousness.

But that's not the kind of behavior Paul means. When I read that love isn't rude, I don't think of people who need a lesson in manners. I think of Peter Pan.

Well, actually, I think of Captain Hook.

J. M. Barrie's 1904 stage play, *Peter Pan; or, the Boy Who Wouldn't Grow Up*, gave the world one of the most enduring characters of children's literature. Barrie later turned the play into a novel, and the story has been adapted and retold again and again.[4] One ambitious attempt at a sequel, in fact, tries to answer the question, "What if Peter *had* grown up?"

In the 1991 film *Hook*, Peter Banning (Robin Williams) is a ruthless corporate lawyer who is becoming more and more estranged from his children.[5] He's forgotten his earlier life as Peter Pan, with no memory of Neverland, the Lost Boys, or even his old nemesis Captain Hook. Hook (Dustin Hoffman), however, remembers, and wants his revenge. To lure Peter to Neverland, Hook kidnaps his son, Jack (Charlie Korsmo). And to sweeten his revenge, he tries to win Jack over by being the fun and attentive father that Peter is not. In order to win his son back and defeat Hook, Peter will have to reconnect with his magical, youthful self—with Tinkerbell's (Julia Roberts) help, naturally. I'm sure you can guess how the story ends.

When I hear Paul's words, a scene from the movie plays out before my mind's eye. Hook knows Jack's fondness for baseball, so he arranges a game between his men (and yes, they call themselves the Pirates). When a runner tries to steal second base, the catcher rears up and shoots him dead, to the crowd's delight. But Hook immediately objects. "No, no, no!" he cries. "No, no! Stop it! We're playing this game according to Master Jack's rules. Bad form!"

Implication: according to pirate rules, shooting the base runner is a legal play. But we wouldn't want to upset Master Jack.

To show "bad form" gets us in the neighborhood of what Paul says. Taken literally, Paul's word suggests a problem in the outward form or appearance of something. Earlier in the letter, he uses the same word to refer to inappropriate behavior (1 Cor 7:36). In another place, he uses the corresponding adjective to describe parts of the body that "aren't presentable" and therefore shouldn't be seen in public (1 Cor 12:23).[6] In other words, the Corinthians were suffering from more than just a case of bad manners. Some of their behavior was downright shameful—and they weren't ashamed.[7] The most flagrant example was a case of open incest:

> Everyone has heard that there is sexual immorality among you. This is a type of immorality that isn't even heard of among the Gentiles—a man is having sex with his father's wife! And you're proud of yourselves instead of being so upset that the one who did this thing is expelled from your community. (1 Cor 5:1-2)

You can hear Paul's incredulity: *You've got to be kidding me! Everyone's talking about this; it's all over social media. And you're proud???* He probably doesn't mean that the Corinthians are proud of the incestuous behavior itself. Rather, they're patting themselves on the back for their spiritually sophisticated, open-minded attitude. It was as if to say, "People worry too much about what they do with their bodies. There are too many pesky religious rules about things like food and sex. But look at us! We're beyond all that."[8]

As both a Jew and a Christian, Paul was horrified:

> Your bragging isn't good! Don't you know that a tiny grain of yeast makes a whole batch of dough rise? Clean out the old yeast so you can be a new batch of dough, given that you're supposed to be unleavened bread. (1 Cor 5:6-7a)

Paul used a metaphor that everyone would have understood. Even a tiny bit of yeast, even the smallest bit of leaven, will eventually have an effect on the entire lump of dough.[9] Sin spreads like a contagion.

Note Paul's concern. He's not trying to make a case for how morally reprehensible the behavior is. He takes that for granted, as if it should be obvious: *Not even pagan Gentiles would do something like this!* What he's worried about is the effect of the behavior—and their attitude toward it—on the congregation. He wants them to kick the man out before his behavior brings down the whole church (1 Cor 5:9-13).

We need to be careful here, for Paul's words can be abused. I've written elsewhere about a troublesome pattern that can crop up in anxious congregations: scapegoating.[10] Something's happened to stir up controversy and set the congregation on edge (a case of incest would certainly qualify). The people are divided and unable to discuss the matter calmly. So what do they do? One way to restore emotional balance is to lay all the blame for the congregation's ills on one person. *He's the problem. He's the enemy. If we just get rid of him, everything will be fine.*

Thus, instead of addressing their inability to work out their difficulties and differences, the people simply vilify and oust the troublemaker. And when the dust settles, everything seems fine— problem solved, crisis averted. Until the next problem or crisis. Then a new scapegoat has to be found.

Yes, Paul is bold enough to tell the Corinthians to expel someone who persists in flagrant sin. But he also pushes for loving restoration when a person repents (2 Cor 2:6-8).[11] That's the kind of people he wants the Corinthians to be: driven by love, not anxiety.

When someone in the church acts like a pirate, it's not just between that individual and God. The church is the body of Christ, a family. What one does affects the whole. The choices made by individual Christians can have negative consequences for the witness of the church outside its walls and for the relationships inside.

That's what makes bad form the enemy of love.

■ ■ ■

From soap operas to reality television, sensationalist headlines to fake news and tabloid journalism: we seem to have a taste for scandal. Google the phrase "church scandal" and you'll be treated to a depressing catalog of the hypocritical sexual sins of Christian evangelists, pastors, and church leaders.

Scandalous behavior happens in the church. That's nothing new. But the technology now exists for both rumors and reports to go viral in the blink of an eye. That makes it even more important for Christians to consider the social consequences of their behavior. The reputation of the church is always on the line, and with it, the gospel message that people so desperately need.

But what fuels the shouts of hypocrisy? Why are some people almost gleeful to catch Christians in scandalous behavior? Often, it's the pleasure of taking an arrogant person down a notch. When Christians project an air of moral superiority—"I'm better than you!"—it invites retaliation.

Such a lack of humility is actually a betrayal of the gospel. The good news of a gracious God is exchanged for just another religion of good works and moral rules. But the world doesn't need another religion. It needs to see the evidence of God's love embodied in a humble people, in a community of believers who sacrifice for each other in the name of love.

And that means that sometimes those who follow Christ must willingly give up something to which they're entitled.

Imagine, for example, that two members of the same church have a business agreement with each other, and one fails to live up to their part of it. Perhaps some service hasn't been rendered as agreed, or a customer refuses to pay. What then? Do they go to court over their disagreement?

Although we don't have the details, some such situation happened in Corinth. One believer was taking another to court, meaning that there would have to be a public trial. Paul vehemently opposes this, and tells them they should be ashamed:

> When someone in your assembly has a legal case against another member, do they dare to take it to court to be judged by people who aren't just, instead of by God's people? Or don't you know that God's people will judge the world? If the world is to be judged by you, are you incompetent to judge trivial cases? Don't you know that we will judge angels? Why not ordinary things? So then if you have ordinary lawsuits, do you appoint people as judges who aren't respected by the church? I'm saying this because you should be ashamed of yourselves! Isn't there one person among you who is wise enough to pass judgment between believers? But instead, does a brother or sister have a lawsuit against another brother or sister, and do they do this in front of unbelievers? (1 Cor 6:1-6)

Here, Paul seems to look forward to a day in which Jesus has returned and God's people have been given authority to judge.[12] Against the backdrop of that envisioned future, lawsuits in the present seem utterly trivial.

Moreover, he hates the idea that believers would make fools of themselves in public. He resorts to sarcasm to make his point: *Some of you like to boast about how spiritually wise you are. All right, then: do you mean to tell me that there isn't a single person in the congregation who's wise enough to decide the matter without having to air your dirty laundry in front of unbelievers? Shame on you!*

Thus, the situation posed two problems. The first was the fraudulent or unethical behavior that gave rise to the lawsuit to begin with. Paul doesn't ignore the fact that someone had been mistreated. Indeed, he chastises the congregation for cheating their brothers and sisters in Christ (vs. 8).

But the second and more far-reaching problem had to do with the consequences of how they handled the situation. As we've seen, the Corinthians already tended to lean toward arrogance. What must the scandal-mongers have thought as they watched them batter each other in court? "The fact that you have lawsuits against each other means that you've already lost your case," Paul writes. "Why not be wronged instead? Why not be cheated?" (vs. 7).

In other words, Paul grieves that they would cheat each other in the first place. But he also grieves that the situation would deteriorate to the point that they would sue one another in public, which is an embarrassment to the church and to her Lord. Pointedly, he asks the plaintiff a rhetorical question: *Wouldn't it be better to drop the lawsuit instead?* He doesn't say that based on his evaluation of the legal merits of the case. He says it out of concern for the church's witness to an unbelieving public. It's one thing to win the legal battle. It's another to lose the war for people's destinies by turning them away from the gospel.

Again, we must go carefully here. What happened in Corinth still happens today: sometimes, Christians cheat and defraud one another. And they sue each other for offenses both real and imagined. Is Paul saying that we have no right to seek redress when we've been wronged? Is he making a rule that Christians can never take one another to court?

I've had that conversation from time to time with Christians who have found themselves embroiled in legal battles. They know that Paul says, "Why not be cheated?"—and are worried that he's telling them to roll over and play dead. Other Christians, in fact, have explicitly told them they would be violating Scripture to bring a lawsuit against another believer, even if the suit clearly had merit.

Is that what Paul means?

I don't believe the apostle was making a blanket rule of conduct, to be imposed without regard to the particulars of a situation. Paul would certainly never tell Christians to turn a blind eye to sin or injustice. Again, he assumes that some wrong has been done, and scolds them for it. But how they handle the situation matters. For the sake of the gospel and the church's witness, whatever they do should be done in-house, not in the spotlight of a public forum.

Ultimately, it's not a question of whether one believer has the legal or moral right to sue another. It's a matter of when, and for what reason, one might choose to forgo that right for the sake of a higher cause, such as preserving the church's witness in a litigious society. Paul himself enumerates all the rights he should enjoy as an apostle—only to say that he would rather give up those rights than "put any obstacle in the way of the gospel of Christ" (1 Cor 9:12).

In other words, Paul embodied a love that doesn't seek its own advantage.

■ ■ ■

"I don't care what anyone else thinks."

"It's a free country."

"I know my rights."

How often have you heard such things said? By whom, and in what context? Or how often have you said them yourself?

In America, argues law professor Mary Ann Glendon, political discourse has become thoroughly saturated with "rights talk."[13] There's no question that as a nation and as a world, we need some shared understanding of basic civil rights. Oppression and injustice are real. The problem is that we also need a shared understanding of civic responsibility. Rights and responsibilities should be like the two sides of one coin, the matching expressions of a society's vision of a well-lived human life.

A shared vision of the good, however, is hard to come by in a pluralistic and increasingly self-oriented society. We are more and more becoming a nation of people who want to be left alone to do our own thing, and the language of "rights" points us less and less to higher goods than to personal preferences. In that way, rights talk is no longer just for politicians and pundits. Whatever I think I should be free to do, I frame in the language of rights. You do the same. And unless we agree on a grander vision of what's right—such as a vision of love—all we're left with is a contest of rights, mine versus yours.[14]

When Paul says that love "doesn't seek its own advantage," he's writing to a congregation in which some believers have hurt others with their behavior.[15] We've seen two examples of this already. The man who was carrying on an incestuous relationship was hurting the congregation. The believers engaged in a public lawsuit were hurting non-believers by damaging the church's witness. Each shows bad form in a different way. Incest clearly crosses the line of what's permissible, whereas lawsuits may be permissible but unwise.

A third and more complicated situation that Paul addresses in his letter seems to be the one most closely related to his teaching on love. As a colony of the Roman Empire, Corinth was dotted with pagan temples in which people made sacrifices to idols. Many of the Corinthian converts had once been idol worshippers themselves. Some continued to attend the feasts held there, using the logic that it couldn't possibly matter if they ate meat sacrificed to idols, since idols weren't real gods anyway (1 Cor 8:4).

Paul doesn't challenge that part of their reasoning. *Yes, yes,* he seems to say, *we all know idols aren't real, blah, blah, blah. Good for you. Go to the head of the class.* But he corrects them for the unloving way in which they put their knowledge into practice:

Now concerning meat that has been sacrificed to a false god: We know that we all have knowledge. Knowledge makes people arrogant, but love builds people up. If anyone thinks they know something, they don't yet know as much as they should know. But if someone loves God, then they are known by God. (1 Cor 8:1-3)

There's that arrogance again; they're puffed up and proud of their theological sophistication. If they really knew what they needed to know, Paul suggests, they would make love their first priority: a love of God that seeks to be known by him, and a love of others that seeks to build them up.

The problem was that not everybody in the church thought the same way as these supposedly more sophisticated believers. For some, eating meat sacrificed to idols was still a matter of conscience. They were torn between what they were being told was permissible, their desire to do what they saw others doing, and the feeling that it was somehow wrong.

Paul doesn't mince words as he writes to the believers who were creating this crisis of conscience:

Suppose someone sees you (the person who has knowledge) eating in an idol's temple. Won't the person with a weak conscience be encouraged to eat the meat sacrificed to false gods? The weak brother or sister for whom Christ died is destroyed by your knowledge. You sin against Christ if you sin against your brothers and sisters and hurt their weak consciences this way. (1 Cor 8:10-12)

And again, using himself as an example, Paul insists that he would sooner give up his right to eat meat ever again than cause a fellow Christian to stumble and fall (vs. 13).

The problem went further. Whatever was sacrificed to idols but not eaten at the temple found its way into the local meat market. Could Christians buy such meat, eat it, serve it to others? What if you were a guest in someone else's home? Did you need to ask where your hosts did their shopping?

The "knowledgeable" Corinthians had a ready answer for their more skittish brothers and sisters: everything is permitted. *It's all okay, so stop worrying and eat your meat loaf.*

Paul's response is worth quoting at length:

> Everything is permitted, but everything isn't beneficial. Everything is permitted, but everything doesn't build others up. *No one should look out for their own advantage*, but they should look out for each other. Eat everything that is sold in the marketplace, without asking questions about it because of your conscience. ... But if someone says to you, "This meat was sacrificed in a temple," then don't eat it for the sake of the one who told you and for the sake of conscience. Now when I say "conscience" I don't mean yours but the other person's. Why should my freedom be judged by someone else's conscience? If I participate with gratitude, why should I be blamed for food I thank God for? So, whether you eat or drink or whatever you do, you should do it all for God's glory. Don't offend either Jews or Greeks, or God's church. This is the same thing that I do. I please everyone in everything I do. *I don't look out for my own advantage*, but I look out for many people so that they can be saved. (1 Cor 10:23-25, 28-33, emphasis added)

Again, Paul doesn't argue with them about whether it's okay to eat the sacrificial meat. It is. They can eat it with a clear conscience.

But then Paul offers a "what if" scenario. You're a dinner guest in someone's home. The person next to you leans over and says, "This meat was sacrificed in an idol temple." You have the right to eat it. The question is, should you?

Paul is vague about the speaker's motives, and interpreters disagree. Some envision the speaker as a fellow believer, with the comment implying an anxious question: "Isn't it wrong to eat this?" Others see the speaker as a non-believer who's trying to be helpful: "Listen, I know you have some scruples about this, so I thought I'd let you know."[16] Either way, the recommendation is the same: don't eat it, lest you offend the other person's conscience. If the speaker is a believer, your eating may cause a spiritual crisis for them. If the speaker is a non-believer, they're watching to see what you do, and eating the meat could hurt your witness.

Note that when Paul says, "I please everyone in everything I do," he doesn't mean, "I try to be a 'people-pleaser,' and so should you." We use that term to refer to those whose sense of self-worth is dependent on the good opinion and approval of others. That's a poor description of Paul, who is willing to suffer any hardship for the sake of the gospel. Indeed, that's the point: in love, he is willing to forgo his rights if it means bringing someone closer to the God who saves.

Whether in Paul's time or ours, there's nothing unusual about people acting in their own best interest. At a fundamental level, we are built to learn from experience and survive. But in a broken world, my interests will sometimes clash with the interests of others. Then what?

We prize our freedom to do as we please. And as Christians under the grace of God, we have a great deal of freedom, provided we don't compromise the essentials of the faith. But in an imperfect church, my interpretation of what's essential may clash with someone else's. Again, then what?

What Paul wants us to know, I think, is that love is one of those essentials.

■ ■ ■

I once went to rent a pickup truck from my local home improvement store. I didn't know at the time that I would have to show proof of insurance. The document was in the glove compartment of my car, and I started to leave the rental counter to go get it. But the clerk stopped me. "Never mind," she said, with a wave of her hand. "I know who you are. I trust you."

Curious, I asked how she knew me. We were members of the same church. The congregation was too large for me to have recognized her, but she had seen me in the pulpit many times. That was proof enough that I would be responsible for the truck. And immediately, it became that much more important to me personally to bring the pickup back without a scratch. I would not betray the trust I had so graciously been given.

Experiences like this have reminded me how public my life can be, despite the fact that I'm actually quite private by nature. Time and again, I've been greeted by perfect strangers—at conferences, in stores and parking lots, even out on the street. One gentleman, a regular reader of my blog, actually approached me one morning when I was out for a walk and passing his house. Through his living room window, he saw me coming and popped outside to say hello. In his words, it was like having a "movie star" walk by.

People know me, even if I don't know them.

And they're watching.

Pastors know the feeling, especially solo pastors in small communities. They live under the watchful eye of their congregations. How they behave in public matters, and sometimes, even what they do in private becomes known. They are, in effect, local celebrities.

But this isn't just about people with some kind of celebrity status. It's about anyone who is known by others as a follower of Christ.

Over the years, I've read hundreds of letters of reference for students applying to graduate school. Many are so filled with flowery words of praise that it's almost embarrassing. And I've written scores of reference letters for my own students, with the understanding that my job is to help them put their best foot forward. If I can't say something nice—really nice—it would be better to say nothing at all.

It's stunning to me, therefore, that the apostle Paul considered the Corinthians to be the letter of reference by which people would evaluate his ministry.

Yes, the Corinthians—the congregation with all the problems we've discussed.

The issue had been raised by Paul's opponents: *Other people who make a living from their rhetoric carry letters of introduction. Why doesn't he? Doesn't that seem suspicious?* Paul's answer, essentially, is that he doesn't need such letters, because the Corinthians *are* his letter:

> We don't need letters of introduction to you or from you like
> other people, do we? You are our letter, written on our
> hearts, known and read by everyone. You show that you are
> Christ's letter, delivered by us. You weren't written with ink
> but with the Spirit of the living God. You weren't written on
> tablets of stone but on tablets of human hearts. (2 Cor 3:1b-3)

Paul almost seems to get carried away. At first, the Corinthians are
Paul's letter of introduction to others. Then they're Christ's letter to
the world, delivered by Paul. Then, as Christ's letter, they are written
by the Spirit. The commandments were once engraved on tablets of
stone by the finger of God. But now, by God's grace and through the
Spirit, a new day has dawned; the law of God has been written
directly on the hearts of his people (Jer 31:31-33).

Let Paul's words sink in for a moment. The Corinthians were
struggling with envy and arrogance. They were acting out sexually.
They were suing each other in court. They were continuing to
frequent idol temples, and standing on their rights in a way that hurt
the conscience of others.

And yet Paul can say that they are Christ's letter of reference,
written by the Spirit of God, out there for all the world to read.

Seriously? That's exactly the kind of behavior that makes people
today shout "Hypocrite!" and run as fast and far from the church as
possible.

Again, Paul isn't blind to the Corinthians' faults. Yet he sees what
others on the outside might miss: that despite all their problems, the
Corinthians are a work of the Spirit. A work in progress, to be sure,
but of the Spirit nonetheless.

That is the truth of every congregation, then and now. Moreover,
even healthy congregations need to be reminded of the importance of
a humble concern for the interests of others. If Paul had asked me to
pick a congregation to be his letter of reference, for example, I would
have chosen the one in Philippi. But even to them, Paul felt
compelled to write, "Instead of each person watching out for their

own good, watch out for what is better for others" (Phil 2:4).

Because if we're going to Christ's letter of introduction to the world, it never hurts to be reminded of the essentials.

■ ■ ■

What do people see when they look at the way we as Christians live? What do they see in the way we relate to others, in our homes and in our churches?

What do people see, for example, in our marriages? Much of the romantic ideology of love is essentially selfish: I love you for what you can do for me, to complete me, to help me feel whole. But romance can falter when confronted with the reality of two people trying to make a life together despite their different wants and needs. A marriage in which the spouses both insist on having things their way won't survive. Each must care for the other's interests, and do so in love.

My wife needs the house to be more orderly than I do. Being surrounded by clutter stresses her out. Knowing this, I try to tidy up after myself—not because I need to for my own sake, but because it would make her life easier. Even when I don't feel like doing a particular chore, I tell myself, "It would make her happy," and that becomes reason enough. In exchange, she ignores the chaos in other areas of the house, knowing that I will never be neat by nature. That's one way I know she loves me.

What do people see in our churches? It saddens me to think of all the unloving encounters people have endured when visiting congregations, from suspicious stares and judgmental comments to basic, garden-variety rudeness. Young people looking for a place to belong feel excluded by cliquish youth groups. And this isn't simply a matter of how believers treat non-believers, but how believers treat each other.

The church as a social organization provides a place for people to find meaning and significance. That can be a good thing. But that sense of significance must be thoroughly grounded in a gospel vision: as God has loved us in Christ, so too must we love one another.

Without such a vision, we will be more concerned about what the church can do for us than what we can do for others.

Some congregations, like the one in Philippi, are on the more loving end of the continuum; others, like the one in Corinth, are less loving. But by the sheer grace of God, they are all letters of Christ to the world. And in sheer gratitude for that grace, we should all want to be the best and most loving letters we can be.

talk or think about it

1. In what ways, if at all, are you conscious of how others see you as a Christian? What difference does it make to how you behave or make decisions?

2. Think of the congregations of which you have been a part. What behaviors have you seen personally that might be considered rude or scandalous, that could fuel negative perceptions of the church? Tell the story of what happened. Then consider the multitude of problems that faced the church in Corinth, and the fact that Paul still saw this troublesome congregation as his "letter of reference," a group among whom the Holy Spirit was active. What do you find either encouraging or challenging about Paul's willingness to see them that way?

3. Americans live in a culture that tends to put more emphasis on our individual rights and freedoms than our responsibility to others. We are taught to "look out for number one." But being called to love one another within the body of Christ will sometimes mean looking out for number two: we go the extra mile, give up something we want, or relinquish a right—for someone else's benefit. What examples of this can you think of in your own life?

get off the merry-go-round

Love...isn't irritable,
it doesn't keep a record of complaints... (1 Cor 13:5b)

In some ways, my grandmother was a remarkable woman. She came from China to the United States to do a college degree in business. That might not seem particularly revolutionary in today's world. But for an immigrant woman in the early years of the twentieth century, that was quite an accomplishment.

To my knowledge, she never put her education to formal use. But for as long as I can remember, she was interested in investment. She used what money my grandfather made as a university professor to dabble in stocks and mutual funds, working with financial advisors to tinker with her portfolio. I personally am one of the beneficiaries of her dabbling. She paid for my college education and helped my wife and I make it through graduate school. For that I am forever grateful.

She had an accountant's mindset. And the stock market wasn't the only place she used it.

I remember listening in on some of the conversations (arguments, really) she had with my mother. If Grandma had been invited to a wedding, she would decide whether or not to go—and how expensive of a present to buy—on the basis of a kind of social accounting. How much respect or honor did she "owe" that family? What favors had she done them? Had that family been stingy or generous in their gifts to her own relatives? And so on. She had a long memory for what she considered to be social slights, and would repay accordingly.

It was an education for me as a boy. I had naively thought that if you had been invited to a friend's wedding, you simply went if you could, and you'd bring a "nice" present. I had no idea that there was such a complicated calculus of who owed what to whom. I know better now.

It reminds me again of Jesus' parable of the unforgiving servant, which we discussed in the chapter on patience. Peter had asked Jesus if it would be sufficient to forgive someone up to seven times. I imagine Peter must have thought he was being magnanimous by suggesting seven. But that bubble was quickly burst. Jesus' answer can be translated as "not seven times but seventy-seven," or even "seventy times seven" (Matt 18:22).

Was Jesus telling Peter that his number wasn't high enough and that he needed to try harder? No. He was trying to get Peter to stop counting altogether.

Think back to the parable. The servant's debt was ridiculously high, and the king's mercy in forgiving it was therefore ridiculously generous. In such an economy of sheer grace, it makes no sense to go out of the palace thinking stingy thoughts. Thus Jesus' answer of seventy-seven—or 490!—is not meant to be the "correct" number, but a ludicrously exaggerated one meant to shock Peter out of keeping a mental record of offenses.

As we'll see below, there are perfectly good reasons why we remember the offenses we've suffered. Even in our closest relationships, it sometimes feels like the same hurtful thing happens again and again. Our resentment builds as we mutter and grumble to ourselves about how selfish or thoughtless the other person is. It's not long before we develop a hair-trigger sensitivity to every perceived slight, ready to retaliate should they offend us again.

And then we read Paul, who warns us away from the resentful and unforgiving way we keep track of how others have wronged us.

In this chapter, therefore, we'll begin by taking a closer look at

Paul's teaching before exploring how the resentment he warns us against can damage relationships. Paul isn't saying that we shouldn't have any memory of past hurts. As much as we might like to, we can't simply say "Forgive and forget!" and have it be true.

The question is not whether we remember past hurts, but how we handle them when we do remember. "Don't keep a running account," Paul says. Stop rehearsing your grievances. Stop ruminating over how you've been wronged. You'll put yourself on a merry-go-round of negative thoughts and feelings that will draw you further and further away from God and from a life of love.

It's perfectly normal to find ourselves on the merry-go-round from time to time. But what love does is to get off as soon as possible.

▥ ▥ ▥

As we've seen, Paul's previous teaching about love can be linked to particular problems in the church which are addressed elsewhere in the letter. The Corinthians were acting in envious, arrogant, and self-centered ways, as demonstrated in their confusion and conflict over leadership, sexuality, and other matters of conscience.

Paul now insists that love "isn't irritable" and "doesn't keep a record of complaints" (1 Cor 13:5b). In contrast to envy and the other negative attitudes and behaviors Paul describes, these two seem less directly tied to specific problems addressed in the letter.

Yet given the way the Corinthians were behaving toward each other, it's easy to imagine the cloud of mutual bad feeling that must have hung over the congregation. The people had numerous complaints against each other. They felt demeaned by each other's pride and arrogance. They remembered all too well how others had offended them, and were primed to be offended again. It was not a climate conducive to love. Thus Paul continues with his description of what love doesn't do, to motivate the Corinthians to stop what they are in fact doing and to aim higher.

The word Paul uses to say that love isn't "irritable," is a rare one.[1] The verb appears only twice in the New Testament, once here, and once in Acts 17:16, where it describes Paul's deep distress at finding the city of Athens filled with idols. Literally, the word means "to sharpen." Metaphorically, therefore, it can describe the "sharpness" of being provoked to anger.[2] In fact, it's the root from which we derive the English "paroxysm"—a sudden and violent outburst of anger or rage.

Again, we can't be certain what Paul may be pointing to in the Corinthians' attitude or conduct. But whatever it is, strong negative emotions like anger are involved. Their irritability is more than mere grumpiness.

Paul also says that love "doesn't keep a record of complaints." The verb he uses and its relatives have a wide range of meaning.[3] In its most general sense, the word can refer to "thinking" or "reasoning" (e.g., 1 Cor 13:11). More specifically, however, it can take on the nuance of calculation and the keeping of accounts. Paul uses the same word, for example, to teach that God "credits" righteousness to believers—not the way wages are credited to a worker who has earned them, but by grace (Rom 4:4-6).

Love, therefore, doesn't keep accounts. What is it, though, that love doesn't keep an account of? Translated literally, Paul says that love doesn't keep a record of "the bad/evil thing."[4] That sounds vague, and it is. But put the phrase together with the previous idea of irritability, of being easily provoked to anger. What Paul seems to be describing is a resentful attitude in which people keep ongoing accounts of the perceived wrongs done to them by others.

That habit of thought promotes an eye-for-an-eye, tit-for-tat approach to relationships. It's also a self-perpetuating vicious cycle. If I dwell on your past offenses, I'll be sensitive to new ones. And with every new offense, I'll become even more easily provoked. It may take very little to make me explode in anger or descend into stony silence.

It's sobering to think that a congregation as young as the one in Corinth would already have built up such a history of resentment. But anyone who has been around the church long enough has probably seen something similar. Sisters and brothers in Christ sometimes act more like a dysfunctional family than a functional one. People feel hurt. Some leave to find another congregation. Some leave the church altogether. And all are wary of letting themselves be hurt again.

I've often had the opportunity to give workshops and seminars on church dynamics to pastors and ministry students. It's interesting to see how the different groups react. When I describe some of the challenges of ministry and the ways congregations can mistreat their pastors, the pastors in the room will often nod, or look at each other knowingly, or share their own stories. Occasionally, there's a spontaneous "Amen," as if to say, "Finally! Someone's acknowledging what I've been through!"

The less experienced among the ministry students, however, are sometimes shocked and disillusioned. One young woman sat through much of a presentation with her mouth hanging open and her eyes wide with disbelief. A similar expression was on the face of a young man sitting nearby. Shakily, he raised his hand to ask a question. I don't remember what he asked. I do remember, however, what he said first: "Okay, so you're like freaking me out!"

Again, that's what I appreciate about the deep realism of Paul's letters to the Corinthians. Love is not to be taken for granted among the followers of Christ. Just as the gospels show Jesus teaching love to fickle and thick-headed disciples, so too are Paul's words about love given to a congregation that has a lot to learn.

When it comes to how irritability and resentment play out in our life together, we are no different than the Corinthians. Such negative emotions are an inevitable part of life. But they need to be understood and handled well if we are to learn to love.

■ ■ ■

All the way back in chapter 1, I asked you to do a simple sentence completion task. Here's another experiment to try. Sit down at a table with pen and paper. Set a timer for five minutes. Then quickly think of as many emotion words as you can and write them down.

Done? Now look over your list. How many of the words describe "positive" emotions, like joy? How many describe "negative" emotions, like anger? I've put the words "positive" and "negative" in scare quotes because the distinction isn't absolute; anger, for example, is usually considered negative, but can serve a positive purpose. But typically, people can easily distinguish the emotions they consider desirable or pleasant from the undesirable or unpleasant ones. If you're not sure about a particular word you wrote, just call it "neutral" and move on.

Here's the question: did you have more positive or negative words?

In general, people have an easier time coming up with negative words. The same task was given to over 400 students in six countries. The researchers made a list of the twelve emotions mentioned most frequently in each country, then compared. Only four emotions made all six lists: joy, sadness, anger, and fear.[5] Add disgust to the list, and you have the five basic emotions portrayed in one of my favorite films, Pixar's *Inside Out*.[6] Moreover, these five emotions—four of them negative!—are the ones eminent emotion researchers generally agree have been most firmly established by science.[7]

That's a simple illustration of what appears to be a universal fact of our psychological makeup. As Roy Baumeister and his colleagues have argued, when it comes to the effect of emotions on our lives and relationships, "bad is stronger than good."[8] Study after study illustrates the fact that compared to "good" or pleasant events, "bad" or unpleasant events have a greater impact on our emotions and mood.

When good things happen, we feel happy and optimistic—at least temporarily. The good is soon forgotten, and we go back to feeling as we did before.[9] Conversely, when bad things happen, we feel unhappy and pessimistic—and these feelings, unfortunately, last longer than their positive counterparts. As Baumeister illustrates, "you are more upset about losing $50 than you are happy about gaining $50."[10] The loss will generate the stronger emotion and will bother you for a longer time.

Why should this be so? As suggested in chapter 2, emotions have survival value. Negative emotions in particular, working in the background of consciousness, can help keep us safe. Imagine, for example, eating two different foods; both are delicious, but the second makes us violently nauseous. What do we need to remember from the experience? Forgetting that we ate something delicious won't kill us. But forgetting what made us sick might. That's why we're apt to have an automatic sensation of nausea or disgust at the very sight or smell of the offending food. The impact of bad experiences lingers to teach us to be careful.

A single traumatic event, in fact, can impact us for a lifetime. Psychiatrist Norman Rosenthal, for example, tells of the horrific experience that led to his professional interest in the power of emotions. At the time, he was a medical intern. It was a warm evening, and he and his girlfriend were driving back from a dinner out with friends. They parked a few blocks from her home to sit and chat.

Suddenly, a rock shattered the windshield. Someone smashed Rosenthal's window and began stabbing him repeatedly with what was later discovered to be a sharpened screwdriver. Terrified, Rosenthal acted on instinct. He grabbed his attacker's hand, forced it against the broken glass, and blew the horn. His girlfriend screamed. The commotion got the attention of the neighbors. Doors and windows were opened; lights came on. The attackers fled.

Numb and in shock, Rosenthal drove his girlfriend home, only to collapse in her living room from the loss of blood. At the hospital, he was found to have multiple stab wounds and punctured organs. Being young and strong, he recovered quickly from the physical trauma—but the emotional trauma lingered. For months afterward, a whiff of the perfume his girlfriend had worn that night would automatically trigger feelings of fear. Even decades later, he found himself unable to stomach the dish he had eaten for dinner that evening, though it had been one of his favorites. Nor could he sit parked in a dark place without feeling anxious.[11]

Few of us, hopefully, have experienced that level of terror.

Rosenthal's point, however, is that it was precisely his terror—his body's automatic response to a life-or-death situation—that helped him fight back and hold on until he could get to safety. Negative emotion, in other words, saved his life.

Trauma is an extreme example of the way emotional memory is designed to shield us by warning us that danger may be near. In Rosenthal's case, that danger was actually life-threatening. Most of the time, the alarm will be unnecessary. But better safe than sorry. As long as the anxiety doesn't interfere with normal life, a hundred false alarms are better than no alarms at all if just one moment of wariness actually saves us from harm.

Our lives don't have to be on the line, of course, for the alarm to go off. Any remembered threat will do, even an unconsciously remembered one. Think back to the story in chapter 2 of the patient who had her hand pricked by a hidden pin. Our brains register the experience of pain and the circumstances associated with it, and reacts automatically when faced with what seems like a similar threat. That includes social and emotional pain, like the pain of being jilted by a lover, rejected by a parent, belittled by a bully, or betrayed by a friend or spouse.

Note, however, that not all of the remembered associations are helpful. Being wary of dark parking lots makes sense; being wary of perfume does not. Imagine Rosenthal on a first date with a woman wearing the same scent his girlfriend had worn that fateful night, unaware of the reason for the feeling of panic rising in his chest. There probably wouldn't be a second date.

At some point, others will push buttons that activate the negative emotions associated with past injuries. When we feel hurt and threatened by someone, part of our reaction is due to the other person's behavior, and part of it is due to old memories (like parking lots and perfume). In the heat of the moment, however, our emotions will unfairly assign all the blame to the person in front of us.

The reaction is understandable. But it can send a relationship spinning off in the wrong direction.

■ ■ ■

Meet Ron and Sonja.[12] When they first married, they were very much in love. Part of the attraction was that each admired the other for qualities they found lacking in their respective families. In Ron's childhood home, emotions were kept tightly zipped. Children were expected to do as they were told. Ron's parents doled out precious little praise or encouragement. Growing up, he was uncertain of his parents' love and felt like nothing he did was ever good enough. But he never dared to say it aloud. He simply coped as best he could.

When Ron met Sonja, he marveled at her warmth and expressiveness. Here was a woman who was unafraid to speak her mind or voice her feelings. He found her family a little intimidating at first. There, emotions flowed freely—both positive and negative ones. On the one hand, they were openly affectionate. On the other, they fought with an intensity he had never seen before. When that happened, he usually found himself escaping to another room until the argument was over.

Ironically, Ron's reluctance to join the fray was part of what drew Sonja to him. To her, Ron was a quiet and stable man who could anchor her in the midst of her family's storms. She knew from conversations with her friends that she had a "big personality" that tended to take over a room. But Ron adored her nevertheless. When she was with him, she felt calm and safe.

Like many couples in their first year together, they stumbled over mundane matters like household chores. Who was expected to do what, when, and how? Both of them worked full-time, and their hours were sometimes erratic. Ron wanted more order and predictability in the way they kept their home, while Sonja naturally preferred a more spontaneous approach.

At first, Ron said nothing and quietly accommodated to his wife. *I'm the one who wants things more organized*, he reasoned, *so I guess I should just take care of it myself. Besides, when she realizes how much nicer it is to have everything in its place, and sees all the extra work I'm doing to keep it that way, she'll change her mind and start pitching in.*

It didn't work. Not that Sonja was completely unappreciative. When she noticed that Ron had done something for which she was grateful, she was affectionate in her thanks. But much of what Ron did simply went unnoticed, and he resented it. Wasn't he doing all of this for her, for them? He felt slighted, as if Sonja was taking all of his effort and sacrifice for granted. The more slighted he felt, the more he noticed her sins of omission, and the more he seethed inside.

For her part, Sonja was mystified. What was wrong with Ron? Why was he being so moody and sullen? She energetically tried to pry the problem out of him. But the more she pressured him to talk, the more tight-lipped he became. When they were dating, she had found his quietness endearing. Now, it felt threatening. She would have preferred an all-out shouting match to his brooding; anything was better than feeling coldly judged from a distance. Why couldn't he talk to her? Why wouldn't he tell her what he was feeling? Sonja could feel the questions swirling in her mind, and she began to wonder if their marriage had been a mistake.

Sometimes in our relationships, we feel like we're stuck on a merry-go-round of hurt and resentment. When someone offends us, we understandably feel pain. But dwelling on the offense typically makes matters worse. As Barbara Fredrickson has written:

> Studies show that when people experience negative emotions, they selectively call to mind negative thoughts. That's simply the way our brains work: we create a chain of thoughts that are linked by their negative tone. So when you ruminate, you dredge up thoughts that only add fuel to the fire of your negativity. And because negative emotions and narrowed, negative thinking feed on each other, they drag you down.[13]

At first, we simply smart over an offense. But ruminating about it sets us on a downward spiral. We begin attributing hostile motives to the other person. Sonja, for example, was certain that Ron was intentionally freezing her out just to spite her, and she couldn't understand why.

Then we begin questioning or attacking their character; Ron began thinking of Sonja as flighty and selfish. Negativity begets more negativity as we become increasingly watchful for anything that confirms our suspicions, ignoring evidence to the contrary, and overreacting to further insults.[14] We may even begin to resemble the following description of someone suffering from chronic anger:

> When someone says something nice to them, they hear it as neutral. If someone says something neutral, they hear it as negative. And if someone says something that's actually negative, they hear it as a total attack.[15]

The merry-go-round, however, isn't just about our private thoughts and feelings as individuals. There are two people in a relationship. Each of us has some responsibility for how the interaction plays out. And how I respond to you in the present may depend in part on the emotional memory of things that happened before we even met.

It's easy for me to see your faults and to resent the way you seem to be mistreating me. But it's harder for me to notice how I myself may be overreacting. True, your behavior toward me may be unpleasant in some way, but there's no real danger. You mean me no harm—but it feels like you do, because you've tripped an alarm. Suddenly, I need to protect myself. I may get angry as a way of repelling or overpowering the threat. Or I may try to escape the threat by running away or shutting down emotionally.

In close relationships, moreover, the chances are that what I do to protect myself when I feel threatened will set off one or more of *your* alarms as well.[16] This triggers what my colleague Terry Hargrave aptly calls *the pain cycle*.[17] Something in your behavior stirs negative emotions in me; I feel unloved or unsafe. My attempts to cope stir negative emotions in you, and your attempts to cope in response circle back and exacerbate my pain. Around and around we go, each feeling victimized by the other.

Until Ron and Sonja began living in the same household, for example, they had not experienced firsthand the impact of their different habits and attitudes regarding housework. Such differences, of course, are perfectly normal. It matters greatly, though, how couples handle them.

Ron thought he was being noble for taking on extra chores to keep their home neat. But if the truth be told, he didn't do it out of love. He was annoyed with Sonja, and couldn't tell her so. Growing up, he had never felt safe dealing with negativity. Now, in his marriage, it was easier to put up with the chores than it was to take responsibility for what he was feeling.

Though he didn't recognize it as such, bearing the extra load was his way of simultaneously being the good guy and making her feel guilty enough to change—all without having to say anything negative. When he didn't get what he wanted, Ron became more and more annoyed, grumbling to himself about how he had to do all the work. Feeling unseen and unappreciated, he withdrew.

His stoniness set off Sonja's alarms. It was true that the conflict in her family had sometimes been frighteningly loud. But to her it still expressed a kind of loyalty: *I love you enough to fight with you. We need to clear the air and hash it out, even if we have to scream at each other to do it.* Ron's moody silence left her feeling rejected and abandoned. She coped by nagging him to communicate, and got louder and more verbally abusive when he didn't. He responded by pulling even further into his protective shell—and so on, and so on.

They needed to get off the merry-go-round. But they didn't know how.

■ ■ ■

"Bad is stronger than good." That's a psychological principle, not a theological one. Indeed, Paul tells the Corinthians that there's a proper order to things that begins with the resurrection of Christ and ends with the final defeat of all God's enemies, including death itself (1 Cor 15:23-26).

But when Paul says that love isn't irritable and doesn't keep a record of complaints, he's pointing to a fact of emotional life that we've all experienced and which had probably affected the life of the church in Corinth. People had offended one another. As a result, they carried self-protective grudges: *How do I resent thee? Let me count the ways.* And that brooding resentment only widened the divide. People became even more sensitive to insult, and more likely to get angry and hurt each other again.

Paul insists that this is not how love behaves. But please note what Paul does *not* say. He doesn't say, "Love doesn't get angry in the first place." There are legitimate reasons for anger, as when Jesus drove the sellers and money-changers from the Jerusalem temple (e.g., John 2:14-17). Paul himself taught that it was possible to be angry without sinning (Eph 4:26).

The problem, therefore, is not anger, but what we do with it—and everything else Paul has said about love is relevant. Anger is fed by our envy, arrogance, and self-centeredness. Nursing anger by dwelling self-righteously on the sins of others turns it toward resentment and bitterness. If we forget the patience and kindness of God toward us, what might otherwise be a momentary emotional response can begin to harden into an unloving disposition.

This side of heaven, we will never live a completely conflict-free existence. We will hurt and annoy one another, both in our families and in our churches. Bad things happen, and bad is stronger than good. How much stronger? Evidence suggests that we need at least three times as many positive experiences as negative ones in order to flourish.[18] Knowing this, we can be more purposely proactive in breaking negative cycles and cultivating more positive and loving ways of thinking and behaving.

So how do we get off the merry-go-round?

Begin by noticing when you're indulging resentment. Perhaps you find yourself obsessing over what someone did to hurt you. You're locked in a spiral of negative thoughts: *How dare they treat me like that? Who do they think they are?* In your mind, you attack their character or even fantasize petty ways to get revenge.

That kind of thinking is a slippery slope and needs to be interrupted as soon as possible. Barbara Fredrickson's simple suggestion is to distract yourself. Find something else to occupy your attention, something diverting enough to take your mind off the problem. It's an added bonus if the activity lifts your spirits, but that's not necessary. Be careful to avoid doing anything that will make you angrier or steep you in negative emotions, as some music, movies, and video games can. And prepare your plan in advance, before you actually need it, rather than trying to decide what to do when you're in a hostile frame of mind.[19]

Distracting yourself will help keep you from spiraling downward. Is there a way to spiral upward? Yes. The good news is that if negativity breeds further negativity, then positivity also breeds positivity.[20] As John Gottman insists, it's not a matter of trying to eliminate negativity altogether, but of being intentional about cultivating the positive. His suggestions for couples aren't relational rocket science. For example:

- Show that you're paying attention to and interested in what your spouse is saying.
- Find a variety of ways to express affection.
- Do small, thoughtful things to show that you care.
- Be supportive when your spouse is upset.
- Respect what your spouse is saying, even if you don't agree with it.
- Have fun together (but beware of hurtful uses of humor).
- When you're experiencing positive feelings like joy or excitement, share them with your spouse.[21]

Moreover, how we think about our relationships matters. For example, research suggests that when a relationship is characterized by trust, the people in it actually remember things differently than people in less trusting relationships. To be sure, they are at first stung by their partners' transgressions, just as anyone else is. Over time, however, they tend to remember those transgressions in a more positive light. Even when they've been instructed to keep a diary of offenses, they eventually remember those offenses as being fewer and less severe than before.[22] That's because in a relationship built on trust, partners "cherish" one another: "they think fondly of their partner even when they are apart, and have a habit of mind that dwells on being *grateful* for the partner's positive qualities."[23]

Resentment is the enemy of relationships—but gratitude is the enemy of resentment. As Paul himself writes:

> Make sure no one repays a wrong with a wrong, but always pursue the good for each other and everyone else. Rejoice always. Pray continually. Give thanks in every situation because this is God's will for you in Christ Jesus. (1 Thess 6:15-18)

Leon Morris' comment on Paul's text is apt: "The refusal to nurse grudges and to retaliate when provoked is not something that is to be attempted in a spirit of suffering resignation."[24] It all goes together: what God wills for us is a life of joy, prayer, and gratitude, in a loving community of those who shun retaliation and always look out for number two.

We have a choice: we can dwell on what's wrong with a relationship, or on what's right. We can ruminate on the negative, or learn to cherish the positive. Indeed, telling others what we cherish about them is one of the most positive things we can do for a relationship. Numerous scientific studies demonstrate that practice of gratitude is good for our mental and physical health. That's why gratitude researcher Robert Emmons declares, "Indulging resentful habits of thought makes about as much sense as watering weeds."[25]

How do we cultivate a more thankful disposition? Again, it's not rocket science. Emmons, for example, recommends beginning with the intentional commitment to practice gratitude: "I vow to not take so many things in my life for granted. I vow to pause and count my blessings at least once a day."[26] One effective way to do this is to keep a written journal of the things for which we are thankful. People may do this in different ways, whether in the morning or evening, whether handwritten or typed. What seems to matter is that we reflect carefully on what we're actually grateful for, write those thoughts down, and do it every day.[27]

Perhaps it sounds trite to say that we should "count our blessings" in the face of all that we've suffered, all that others have done to hurt and offend us. I suspect that the reason for our cynicism is that people have sometimes used that phrase to ask us to engage in denial or to stop making them uncomfortable with our complaining. It's as if to say, *Don't you know that in Christ we are victorious in everything? So you shouldn't be feeling bad. Quit your faithless whining and smile!*

Nothing of value, however, is won by denial. To be grateful for the good requires honestly facing up to the bad as well.[28] Here, we might turn to the Psalms for inspiration. They demonstrate over and over how deep gratitude for God's grace can be expressed even in the midst of deep lament.

Our troubles are real, and tend to grab our attention. People will hurt us and let us down—just as we will hurt them and let them down. Relationships are like that. And it's perfectly natural that our thoughts and emotions would drift toward the negative.

But counting complaints leads to resentment and a downward spiral of negativity. It may sound simplistic, but counting blessings instead can lead to gratitude and trust. As Christians in particular, we need to cling to the truth that we have a heavenly Father who loves and embraces us. That one astonishing fact helps put the rest of life into perspective. When we understand how our loving Father has nailed our debt to the cross (Col 2:14), it helps us let go of the resentful accounts we keep.

That's the way of love. And as I'll suggest in the next chapter, that's the importance of learning to celebrate the gospel. Our love for others is one sure sign that the gospel is transforming us from the inside out. But as Jesus himself taught, anyone can love one's friends. The real miracle is loving one's enemies (Matt 5:43-48).

■ ■ ■

In 1940, the Nazis invaded the Netherlands. Two years later, Corrie ten Boom and her family began hiding Jewish refugees from the Gestapo. When their work was discovered, the entire family was arrested. Corrie and her sister Betsie eventually ended up at the women's concentration camp at Ravensbrück, where the sisters quietly ministered to the other prisoners.

Betsie died soon after, but not before giving Corrie what would end up being her commission to preach the message of God's gracious presence in the midst of great suffering. "We must tell them that there is no pit so deep that He is not deeper still," Betsie whispered, as she lay dying. "They will listen to us, Corrie, because we have been here."[29]

After the war was over, Corrie began a worldwide ministry of telling her and Betsie's story. Once, after speaking at a church in Munich, she was approached by a man in an overcoat. With a shock of recognition, she realized he had been one of the guards from Ravensbrück. In an instant, she was flooded with traumatic memories and filled with angry, vengeful thoughts.

The man didn't recognize her. Since the war, he had become a Christian. He came to her with his hand outstretched to thank her for her message, and to ask forgiveness for his past crimes.

She knew as a Christian that she was commanded to love and forgive him, to take his hand. But her heart was empty and her arm was frozen at her side. All she could do was silently confess her inability. Praying that Jesus would forgive the man through her, she obediently took his hand. And then, she writes, "From my shoulder along my arm and through my hand, a current seemed to pass from me to him, while into my heart sprang a love for this stranger that almost overwhelmed me."[30]

I've heard that story many times, and it never fails to move and inspire me. By the power of the Holy Spirit and the grace of God, it is possible to love even the worst of one's enemies.

And yet...how many of us have been tortured and traumatized in prison camps? How many of us have been faced with such a stark choice to forgive? Who would fault her for feeling hatred toward the man, for not being able to wipe the slate clean, just like that? Her story may seem impossibly heroic in a way that rises far above our everyday, petty annoyances. Corrie forgave someone who was for her the very embodiment of evil, of all the months of suffering and humiliation she and her sister had to endure.

Me? I'm just trying to get over that little thing my wife said that hurt my feelings. And she didn't even know she had said it.

We might imagine that once Corrie had experienced that triumph, once she had been flooded miraculously with the love of God, she never again struggled with resentment or bitterness. If she could forgive that man, she should be able to quickly and easily forgive anyone for anything.

Not so, she insists: "I wish I could say that merciful and charitable thoughts just naturally flowed from me from then on. But they didn't."[31]

She recalls a time in which some trusted Christian friends hurt her. She ruminated over the offense for weeks, until she finally turned to God and asked for another miracle of love. It was granted. She made a deliberate decision to forgive, and was promptly flooded with the joy and peace that comes from letting go.

End of story? Not quite.

Even after that prayer of surrender, she found herself still lying in bed awake, brooding in the darkness over what her friends had done. She prayed for help again that night.

And the next.

After two sleep-deprived weeks of struggling to forgive, Corrie sought help from a Lutheran pastor. Here's how she recalls his wise counsel, which she would come to call "the ding-dong principle":

"Up in that church tower," he said, nodding out the window, "is a bell which is rung by pulling on a rope. But you know what? After the sexton lets go of the rope, the bell keeps on swinging. First *ding* then *dong*. Slower and slower until there's a final *dong* and it stops. I believe the same thing is true of forgiveness. When we forgive someone, we take our hand off the rope. But if we've been tugging at our grievances for a long time, we mustn't be surprised if the old angry thoughts keep coming for a while. They're just the ding-dongs of the old bell slowing down."[32]

Corrie ten Boom's story is instructive. We are called to love those who have hurt us, whether the injury is small or impossibly large. It may take a miracle to do so. But even then, we should expect that the bell may keep ringing for a while. That's not faithlessness on our part; it's the way our emotions work.

Our job is to keep our hands off the rope.

Why should we do so? What motivation do we have? One might argue that we should take Paul's advice for psychological reasons. Even if we have a right to our anger, resentment is bad for us. It eats away at our soul, making us unhappy. Gratitude and forgiveness, by contrast, are good because they free us from resentment's burden. We should get off the merry-go-round—and stay off!—because we'll be happier if we do.

That's legitimate as far as it goes. But Paul's reasons are different and higher, in accordance with the teaching and example of his Lord. *Don't count other people's sins against them*, he insists, *because you belong to a loving and patient God who doesn't count yours against you.*

In other words, if we're going to keep our hands off the bell rope of resentment, it should be for more than just our personal happiness. The more biblical reason, as we'll see in the next chapter, is that we want to embody true love, and love celebrates whatever embodies the truth of the gospel.

think/talk about it

1. "Bad is stronger than good": negative experiences seem to have a deeper and longer-lasting effect on us and our emotions than do positive experiences. What examples can you think of in your own life?

2. Go back and review the story of Ron and Sonja as an example of the cycle of hurt and resentment that people sometimes fall into. We bring certain sensitivities with us into a relationship, areas in which we are already more likely to take offense because of past relationships. Then someone does something to slight or offend us. We resent them quietly, and may dwell on the offense; we behave in ways that offend them; they resent it and respond negatively in turn. Around and around it may go, *ad nauseam*. Do you recognize this pattern in your own relationships? How does it play out? What would it take to get off the merry-go-round, and what would motivate you to do so?

3. I've included Corrie Ten Boom's story of the so-called "ding-dong principle" because I find it encouraging that someone of her spiritual reputation can still struggle with resentment and forgiveness as I do. To what extent can you identify with her story? What can you do to "keep your hands off the rope"? How can we help each other to do so?

4. Earlier, I listed several suggestions from marriage expert John Gottman for building more positivity into your marriage (or other relationship): show that you're interested and paying attention; express affection in a variety of ways; do small, thoughtful things; be supportive; always show respect for what your partner says; have fun together; talk about your positive feelings and experiences. What are one or two ways can you begin building more positivity into your relationships, and how will you actually put this into practice?

11

celebrate the gospel

Love...isn't happy with injustice,
but it is happy with the truth. (1 Cor 13:6)

Dreams are strange, mysterious things. Sometimes, I'm not sure if I'm asleep or awake. I seem to have one foot in the dream world and one in reality, as if I were someone else watching me dream from the outside. Part of me is aware that the things happening in my dream are impossible. But the feelings and reactions are real, and I can awake with a start, pulse racing.

Similarly, in waking life, we have dreams and aspirations. We live in a tangible world, where we have to deal with all the complexity of our relationships, of who did what and said what to whom. But we also live in the world of imagination, of how we interpret what people say and do against the background of our hopes and fears. Our emotional responses draw from both worlds.

We have hopes and dreams for our dating relationships and for marriage. Everyone wants to be loved and accepted. But we may have different ideas of what it would look like to be cherished the way we want. As I've suggested before, some of us—whether we realize it or not—are looking for Mr. or Ms. Right, Prince Charming or Sleeping Beauty, or our one true and God-given soul mate. Some are much more pragmatic: *I'd really like to settle down with someone.*

I admit that I'm not head over heels in love with this person, but we get along fine. I think we can make a go of it.

And we may have hopes for our church relationships. What does it mean to us to be part of the body of Christ, the so-called family of God? Is church just a place we go once a week to pay religious respect to God, or to have our own individual experience of worship? Do we expect anything of other believers, like care or friendship—or maybe even just civility? And if so, what happens when someone violates those expectations? How do we respond?

As I've suggested before, Corinth was the kind of congregation we might visit once and leave, never to return. Yet Paul, despite the mistreatment he had received, saw these people as a miracle of God, a people among whom the Holy Spirit was active. Given the level of commotion in the congregation, however, the Corinthians themselves probably had a much dimmer view of each other. Paul needed to reshape their imagination, and he did so by teaching them about love.

Do our imaginations need to be similarly reshaped? There's nothing intrinsically wrong with having hopes and dreams for our romantic relationships. Nor is it necessarily wrong to hope that one day we'll find that special church we're looking for, where people say and believe all the "right" things and always treat each other with love and respect.

Meanwhile, however, we must learn to love in the context of the flawed relationships we have. To do that, we'll need something greater than our typical romantic dreams and worldly ambitions can provide. As we'll see shortly, what we need is a vision of love that takes joy in seeing the truth of the gospel triumph in our life together.

■ ■ ■

As suggested in chapter 6, Paul sets a broad vision of love in front of the Corinthians, as part of his response to their concerns about spiritual gifts. Within that vision, he describes in positive terms what love does. And in the midst of that, he also describes in negative terms what love doesn't do. The negatives point to problematic, unloving behaviors and attitudes that were already troubling the congregation, while the positives point the way to the higher road of love.

Now, in 1 Corinthians 13:6, Paul transitions from the negative back to the positive. He teaches that love "isn't happy with injustice, but it is happy with the truth." But that sentence might sound a little odd. First, why would anyone actually be happy with injustice? Second, even if that made sense, why don't the two parts of the sentence match? In other words, why is the contrast between injustice and *truth*? Wouldn't it make more sense to talk about injustice versus *justice*, or *falsehood* versus truth?

To get at these questions we need to take a closer look at Paul's wording. The word translated as "happy" in the first phrase is a commonly used verb meaning "to rejoice."[1] In general, it can suggest something like merrymaking. But more specifically, what we see over and over in the New Testament is that rejoicing is associated with the success of the gospel.

The book of Acts provides numerous examples. When the apostles dared to preach the gospel openly in Jerusalem despite the warnings of the ruling council, they were arrested and severely beaten. Upon their release, the apostles didn't skulk off into the shadows. Instead, they "left the council rejoicing because they had been regarded as worthy to suffer disgrace for the sake of the name" (5:41). Philip was sent by an angel to explain the gospel to an Ethiopian eunuch, who became a believer, was baptized, and "went on his way rejoicing" (Acts 8:39). Barnabas rejoiced to see how, by God's grace, the gospel had spread in the city of Antioch (11:23), the place where believers were first called "Christians" (11:26). Later, in another city also named Antioch, Paul and Barnabas preached the gospel in the synagogue, with great success.[2] But some of the Jews there, out of jealousy, tried to sabotage their ministry. Paul therefore declared that by God's command he would henceforth devote himself to bringing the gospel to the Gentiles—at which the Gentiles "rejoiced and honored the Lord's word" (13:48).

One of Paul's greatest joys as an apostle—perhaps *the* greatest joy—was to see the gospel spread and take root in the lives of believers (e.g., Phil 1:18). Anything that served that purpose, even his own weakness and suffering, was cause for joy (e.g., 2 Cor 13:9; Col 1:24). And he wanted the Corinthians to find their happiness in the same way.

For Paul, both love and joy are marks of the spiritual life (Gal 5:22). The gospel brings joy and is embodied in the life of love; love, joy, and the gospel are inseparable. It should thus be no surprise that Paul would insist in 1 Corinthians 13 that a godly love can't be "happy with injustice." The word "injustice"—which can also be translated as "unrighteousness"—points to everything from individual sins to the whole sad gamut of ways in which world is out of alignment with God.[3] Love doesn't rejoice over such things.

This statement stands at the climax of his negative description of what love doesn't do, which as we've seen is something of a pastoral reprimand. To say that love isn't happy with injustice may thus be meant as a pointed reminder of a specific situation, as in their arrogant bragging over the case of incest we discussed earlier.[4] Or it may be meant as a punchline for the whole. Paul isn't talking about injustice in the abstract, but all the ways in which the Corinthians are failing to embody the gospel. Envy. Boastfulness and arrogance. Selfish unconcern for the well-being of others. Irritability and resentment. Who knows what else Paul could have included in the list?

But I think Paul is pointing still further, beyond criticism of the Corinthians' misdeeds to a vision of love that will inspire them to aim higher. That's why Paul doesn't just say what love doesn't do. He says what it does: it rejoices in the truth.

■ ■ ■

To be perfectly honest, part of me bristles at the idea that Paul might accuse me of rejoicing over injustice or unrighteousness. That sounds like the description of a sociopathic or criminal mind. Surely, nobody's perfect. We all have room—okay, *lots* of room!—for improvement. But were the Corinthians really "rejoicing" over their bad behavior and attitude? Were they "happy," for example, about their arrogance or selfishness?

Is Paul implying that I'm happy about mine?

The statement that love "isn't happy with injustice" has to be held together with its counterpart, that love "is happy with the truth." Paul isn't accusing anyone of being sadists or sociopaths, of deriving pleasure from hurting others. He's making a fundamental contrast between two orientations in life, and forcing us to examine where our loves and loyalties lie. Do we define ourselves by worldly values and standards? Or is our identity grounded in the truth of the gospel?

Similar contrasts can be found throughout the New Testament. Think, for example, of the words of Jesus: "No one can serve two masters. Either you will hate the one and love the other, or you will be loyal to the one and have contempt for the other" (Matt 6:24). The wholehearted pursuit of God and God's kingdom is incompatible with the pursuit of worldly wealth.

The apostle James makes the same point regarding worldliness in general: "Don't you know that friendship with the world means hostility toward God? So whoever wants to be the world's friend becomes God's enemy" (James 4:4). He says this to explain why Christians fight. Not only does worldliness make us enemies of God, it also makes us enemies of each other. And perhaps most pointedly, John writes, "Don't love the world or the things in the world. If anyone loves the world, the love of the Father is not in them" (1 John 2:15).

As discussed in chapter 6, the Corinthians were recent converts who were accustomed to the values and commitments of a highly pagan society that knew little to nothing about Jesus. As one New Testament scholar describes it, Corinth was shot through with a culture of self-promotion and social climbing, "a highly competitive environment, with people vying in business, politics, and claims to status."[5] Naturally, they brought their worldly habits of thought and behavior with them into the life of the congregation, giving rise to boasting and envy, and concerns about status even in spiritual matters. As their pastor, Paul had to teach them the subversive implications of their newfound faith. It could no longer be business as usual.

Thus, Paul chooses "truth" as the counterpoint to "injustice"—and he does the same elsewhere. In his letter to the Romans, for example, he declares that God's wrath is against those who "silence the truth with injustice" (1:18), and who "obey wickedness instead of the truth" (2:8).[6] In one of his letters to the Thessalonians, he teaches that when Jesus returns, "everyone will be judged who is not convinced by the truth but is happy with injustice" (2 Thess 2:12).[7] To stand against or reject the truth of the gospel, in other words, is tantamount to a worldly love of unrighteousness. Similarly, he tells the Corinthians:

> Examine yourselves to see if you are in the faith. Test yourselves. Don't you understand that Jesus Christ is in you? Unless, of course, you fail the test. But I hope that you will realize that we don't fail the test. We pray to God that you don't do anything wrong, not because we want to appear to pass the test but so that you might do the right thing, even if we appear to fail. We can't do anything against the truth but only to help the truth. (2 Cor 13:5-8)

Here, being in the faith means recognizing that the Spirit of Jesus dwells in them, and that they are called to live accordingly. Paul wants their lives to "pass the test" of Christlikeness, and offers himself as an example of one utterly compelled to live the truth of the gospel.

Let the implications of what Paul is saying sink in for a moment. *Christ is in you*, Paul tells the Corinthians. And yet there's a lack of Christlikeness in the church. There's a question of whether they understand and live by the truth they have supposedly believed.

Does that sound at all familiar? It's as Jesus, James, and John all warned: the worldly values that we so easily take for granted can draw us away from God and cause us to act in unrighteous, unloving ways toward each other. Love, as Paul teaches it, means more than merely replacing wrong behavior with the right. It means displacing worldly values and habits of thought with the gospel.

Thus, as Paul transitions back from what love doesn't do to what love does, his words are appropriately visionary. *Look at what you're doing,* he seems to say. *You're being envious and resentful, self-centered and arrogant toward one another. You need more than just a refresher course in good manners—you need to examine what's important to you and why. Love is the way of God. You owe your life to that love, and you're meant to be living demonstrations of it. That's your highest calling, whatever other ambitions you may have. That's where your true joy lies—in the embodiment of the truth, in the day-to-day practice of love and grace.*

When conducting marriage workshops in church settings, I often begin by asking the participants, "Why are you here?" Some of them stare back at me blankly, as if to say, *Isn't it obvious?*

So I press on: "I know that some of you are here because you were dragged here, and you'd really rather be somewhere else. Most of you are probably here because you want to improve your marriage, to make your home a happier place. And I hope that all of you will learn a few things today that you'll find helpful.

"But let me ask you another question. What if you learn something here, try it at home once or twice, and it doesn't seem to work? What if your spouse doesn't respond the way you want? Let's say you try really hard to be a better listener, but your spouse is still mad, or won't listen to you. What then? Will you consider it just another failed experiment and give up?

"Most meaningful change in a marriage doesn't happen overnight. It takes a while to reestablish the trust on which a good relationship is built. You have to stick with it.

"So whatever you learn today, don't do it to change your spouse. Do it to change yourself. If you're convinced that what I'm teaching you is a step in the right direction for you and for your marriage, then commit to it *because* you know it's right. Remember how God loves you, and commit to being the person that God in his grace is already making you to be."

Our highest calling is to embody the truth of the gospel, the truth that a loving God has cleared a path for us to find our joy in him. If we are to truly learn the way of love, that truth must transform us from the inside out.

■ ■ ■

That brings us to one more observation about Paul's contrast between truth and injustice. In the English, it looks like Paul uses the same verb twice, first to say what love doesn't rejoice over, then to say what it does. In the Greek, however, there's a small but important difference. While the first verb means simply "to rejoice," the second means to "rejoice *together*," or if you like, to "co-rejoice."[8]

Think, for example, of Jesus' parables of lostness. As we saw in chapter 5, Jesus tells the story of a loving father who embraces his prodigal son. The story is actually the third of three parables about joy in finding the lost, told in response to the scribes and Pharisees who grumbled that Jesus seemed to enjoy spending time with social outcasts.

In the first parable, a shepherd rejoices when he finds his lost sheep (Luke 15:4-6). He returns home with the sheep draped across his shoulders, and then calls his friends and neighbors together. "Rejoice with me!" he says. Literally, it's an invitation to "co-rejoice," to join him in celebration. In the second parable, a woman loses a precious coin, and diligently searches her house until she finds it (vss. 8-9). When she does, she too calls her friends and neighbors together and says, "Rejoice with me!" And in the third and longest parable, about the Prodigal Son and his father, there is an even greater emphasis on bringing people together to celebrate (vss. 11-24).[9]

Three parables, three parties.

In these stories, in other words, we see both individual joy and its cousin, the gathering of a community for the purpose of celebration. Paul himself uses both words—rejoice and co-rejoice—side by side, and not just in 1 Corinthians 13. To the church in Philippi he writes:

But even if I am poured out like a drink offering upon the altar of service for your faith, I am glad. I'm glad with all of

you. You should be glad about this in the same way. Be glad
with me! (Phil 2:17-18)

I'm glad; be glad with me! There are those words again: *I rejoice; let's
rejoice together!*

Paul's words remind me of memorial services that I have attended
or officiated. Some believers, knowing that death is near, look
forward as the apostle did to leaving this life behind to go be with
Jesus (Phil 1:23). But they also know that their friends and family will
grieve. So they leave instructions with their loved ones: *Please don't
let my funeral turn into some dreary, somber affair. My suffering is
done and I'm going home. Be happy for me! Rejoice together, rejoice
with me!*

Paul takes personal joy in his ministry and the progress of the
gospel. He wishes the same joy for the Corinthians—but not, I think,
as a matter of individual happiness. The whole point of teaching them
about love is to change how they relate to one another in community.
And for that to happen, they must be united in purpose. A
community of godly love celebrates when the lost are found. It
doesn't settle for the status quo of individual ambition and self-
preoccupation. Instead, it rejoices when the truth of the gospel
triumphs in their life together over things like envy and resentment.

This kind of communal celebration was missing in Corinth. Why,
for example, was there the kind of division in which some members of
the body took pride in proclaiming their loyalty to one teacher over
another? To a large extent, it's because of the worldly values which
the Corinthians had imported into their life together. As Paul writes:

When jealousy and fighting exist between you, aren't you
unspiritual and living by human standards? When someone
says, "I belong to Paul," and someone else says, "I belong to
Apollos," aren't you acting like people without the Spirit?
After all, what is Apollos? What is Paul? They are servants
who helped you to believe. Each one had a role given to them
by the Lord: I planted, Apollos watered, but God made it

grow. Because of this, neither the one who plants nor the one who waters is anything, but the only one who is anything is God who makes it grow. (1 Cor 3:3-7)

Here, we have to imagine a culture in which some people made their living by rhetoric, by being clever and entertaining public speakers. Many came to Corinth seeking the patronage of the wealthier citizens. It was a social bargain: *If you support me financially, then whatever glory I get becomes yours, too!* These so-called "sophists"—think "public philosopher"—competed with each other and had rival followings.

Paul considered himself and Apollos to be on the same team, working together under God. But the Corinthians were primed by their cultural training to think differently. Their own sense of personal prestige depended in part on following the "right" leader. Social competition was the common wisdom. Thus, Paul was forced to respond bluntly: "This world's wisdom is foolishness to God. ...So then, no one should brag about human beings" (1 Cor 3:19a, 21a). To boast in that way was a grand exercise in missing the point. They were deriving satisfaction from following one man as versus another, instead of celebrating the fact that God was the one giving the Spirit and making things grow.

Perhaps the most ironic example of the Corinthians' worldliness, however, had to do with the way they were observing the Lord's Supper. What better time in the church's life to celebrate and embody the truth of the gospel than in their remembrance of the body and blood of the Lord? Sadly, the ritual had become another place for ingrained cultural habits to sabotage any sense of loving unity. Deeply dismayed, Paul tackles their misbehavior head-on:

Now I don't praise you as I give the following instruction because when you meet together, it does more harm than good. ...[W]hen you get together in one place, it isn't to eat the Lord's meal. Each of you goes ahead and eats a private meal. One person goes hungry while another is drunk. Don't

you have houses to eat and drink in? Or do you look down on
God's churches and humiliate those who have nothing? What
can I say to you? Will I praise you? No, I don't praise you in
this. (1 Cor 11:17, 20-22)

The congregation in Corinth was small by today's standards. They
met in groups in people's homes. Here, Paul seems to be describing a
time in which the groups would come together all at once, probably
in the evening, for what was supposed to be a common meal and then
a celebration of the Lord's Supper.

To accommodate this larger gathering, it would have to have been
held in the home of one of the richer members of the church. The
host's dining room would not have been able to hold everyone, so the
majority of people would have eaten in an adjoining courtyard or
entrance hall.[10]

In Roman custom, feasting was often a noisy, wine-soaked affair.
The quality and elaborateness of one's meal, moreover, was itself a
mark of social status. The majority of the members of the church
would likely have been slaves, many of whom could afford nothing
fancy in the way of food.[11] What then would happen when these
members of the lower class arrived at a wealthy person's home?

What Paul describes can be interpreted in different ways. The
host would have been accustomed to inviting other members of the
upper class to enjoy an extravagant meal. This may have been done in
conjunction with or before the arrival of the poorer guests. Either
way, class distinctions prevailed. The rich feasted on fine food and
got drunk while the poor went hungry. The wealthy may not have
intended to rub their brothers' and sisters' noses in their low status.
But that was the effect. As we might well imagine, it was a
humiliating experience.

How, after that, were they supposed to celebrate the Lord's
Supper together?

Paul is directing his comments at the rich: "Don't you have houses
to eat and drink in?" But he doesn't tell them to dial back their
gluttony. Nor does he chastise them for getting drunk. Instead he

insists that if they must gorge themselves on food and drink, they should do it in private, at home. Why?

Every society has its designated signs of social status, the ways of marking who "counts" and who doesn't. In the context of the Roman Empire, bringing together people of such different social classes to worship together and share a common meal signaled a new reality. In the new creation called the church, the old status distinctions had no place. People came together to celebrate the Lord's Supper, with the one loaf of bread signifying their oneness in the crucified Christ (1 Cor 10:16-17).

In theory, at least. In the case of Corinth, old cultural habits got in the way of loving behavior and the embodiment of the truth.

The challenge is not just for early Christians living under the imperial shadow. It's for us. We have our own taken-for-granted marks of status. Listen in on the conversations that happen around a church on Sunday morning. For that matter, as suggested in the chapter on envy and rivalry, look at what people post on their Facebook pages. How much of it—if the truth be told—has to do with trying to climb a little higher on some social ladder?

The avenues of comparison are endless. They can begin as invitations to celebrate someone's good fortune, as in, *Hey, come on out to the parking lot and see my new car!* or *Look at the beautiful vacation photos I posted on my timeline!* But social comparison is never far behind. There's only one short step from showing people pictures of your grandkids to thinking, *And mine are cuter and better behaved than yours.*

More darkly: we may sort people into categories and treat "us" differently than "them." We see the color of someone's skin or the way they dress; we hear them speak with a national or regional accent that's different than our own. And we respond accordingly, deciding who is equal to us and who is not. In all of this, we implicitly or explicitly seek to win the game of social comparison.

But who gets pushed lower if you climb higher?

It's perfectly natural to compare ourselves to others. It's natural to take pleasure in fortunate circumstances.

But the gospel isn't "natural." Grace doesn't follow the logic of social comparison, as if salvation or membership in the body of Christ was a prize awarded to the best and brightest of society. Paul tries to establish that fact early in his letter to the Corinthians, in a way that some of them must have found insulting:

> Look at your situation when you were called, brothers and sisters! By ordinary human standards not many were wise, not many were powerful, not many were from the upper class. But God chose what the world considers foolish to shame the wise. God chose what the world considers weak to shame the strong. And God chose what the world considers low-class and low-life—what is considered to be nothing—to reduce what is considered to be something to nothing. So no human being can brag in God's presence. (1 Cor 1:26-29)

And if the gospel isn't natural, neither is the church to which it gives rise. Being one body in Christ is part of God's miraculous, post-resurrection new creation (2 Cor 5:17). And in that body, "There is neither Jew nor Greek; there is neither slave nor free; nor is there male and female, for you are all one in Christ Jesus" (Gal 3:28). By stringing together a short list of some of the most important social distinctions of his world, Paul implies that other distinctions between those who are in Christ are null and void as well. In the church, there is no us and them.

That's the reality we should celebrating in our life together.

For if we do what comes naturally, we may end up celebrating the wrong thing.

▪ ▪ ▪

As ethicist Oliver O'Donovan has written, "every determination of love implies a corresponding hatred. For a community to focus its love on *this* constellation of goods is to withdraw its love from *that*."[12] A church which celebrates the gospel must recognize and turn its back on its unjust and unrighteous ways. In other words, the love to which Paul calls believers doesn't begin with a seminar on how to improve your relationships (and I've taught plenty of those myself). It begins with a love for the gospel itself, with a shared desire to be the kind of people who embrace and embody its truth. That's the love that grounds and sustains the community—not the ups and downs of how loving we happen to be toward each other at the moment.[13]

One of the unsettling implications of this is that we need communities in which it's possible to admit difficulty or failure. A true appreciation and celebration of grace goes hand in hand with a correspondingly humble and honest recognition of sin. Typically, our habits of social comparison tempt us to sort our congregations into sheep and goats based on outward criteria that comfortably show us to be sheep. But the gospel is not served by people trying to be on their best behavior outwardly while inwardly maintaining judgmental thoughts.

Consider how this might play out with respect to our attitude toward marriage and relationships. What happens when active members of a congregation go through times of marital strain? Many of us would find it nearly unthinkable to even admit that we had a fight in the car on the way to church—forget letting anyone know that we were contemplating separation or divorce.

Too many couples have found their communities unwilling to walk with them in their pain. When they admit to struggling in their marriages, they're met with a variety of unloving and unhelpful responses. Some people respond in withering judgment, saying some version of "Obviously you're not trying hard enough." Some offer sunny platitudes designed to sweep away their own anxiety: "Just trust God and it'll all be okay, you'll see." And some simply react with shocked silence, leaving sufferers wondering where they stand.

Over the years, there's been much hand-wringing in the church over the divorce rate among Christians. Some studies seem to indicate that so-called "born-again" Christians are just as likely to divorce as people in the American population overall.[14]   Others, however, dispute these findings on the basis of different data, claiming that

Christians and other religiously affiliated people divorce at lower rates than those without a religious affiliation. They also argue that other variables need to be taken into account. Christians who go to church more often, for example, seem to divorce less often than less frequent attendees.[15]

I agree that there's cause for concern. In the arena of love and marriage, we take too much for granted, which is one of the reasons for this book. I suspect, however, that some of the anxiety over the Christian divorce rate is driven as much by social comparison as a love for the gospel. Statistics that show Christians failing in some way make good fodder for social media and the popular press. It's understandably tempting to respond in kind: *No, that's a lie. We really are as good as we say!*

Please don't get me wrong. I want the stats to show Christians succeeding at marriage. I want marriage vows to be meaningful and to stick. I want us to take the call to love seriously in ways that make a concrete positive impact on our relationships. What people outside the church see inside the church matters.

But a knee-jerk kind of defensiveness over the church's public image won't serve us well. It won't create communities in which it is safe to admit our weaknesses to one another or to seek compassionate guidance and support. Whether we are struggling in our marriages or some other area of life, what we need are communities who are able to ask the hard questions and seek the answers together. We need communities committed to understanding, celebrating, and embodying the truth: we are broken people whom God in his love and grace wants to make whole.

And as we'll see in the next and final chapter, though people may fail, God's love never will.

talk or think about it

1. Surely none of us would want to be accused of being "happy with injustice." But to the extent that we fail to celebrate the gospel—including the truth of who we are and what God has done—we may be failing to take our own sin and God's grace seriously. Think about a conflict you have had with someone close to you, and how you would tell someone else the story of what happened. Does "your side of the story" have an element of self-righteousness to it? If so, what would it mean in that situation to "celebrate the gospel" instead?

2. Much of the way we speak about "happiness" has to do with how we feel as individuals. That's not the same thing, however, as the idea of a community "rejoicing together" because of their shared love for the gospel. For example, churches rightly celebrate when they hear that someone has committed his or her life to Jesus. What might it look like to celebrate the gospel together as a community when it comes to marriage and relationships?

3. What "us versus them" distinctions have you noticed within your congregation, or between Christians generally? How do these play out in people's attitudes and behaviors? And how is the gospel being impeded by the division that results?

12

love story

Love puts up with all things, trusts in all things,
hopes for all things, endures all things.
Love never fails. (1 Cor 13:7-8a)

For much of the first part of our life together, my wife and I lived on a shoestring budget, particularly in graduate school. Every month, more money went out than came in. We had to rely upon on financial help to make ends meet. Of necessity, we had to find ways to economize. We ate food that was simple and cheap, scouring grocery store ads, clipping coupons, and driving all over town to get the best deals. We rarely ate out, but when we did, we ignored anything on the menu that cost more than ten bucks.

When we became homeowners, I had to learn to make things we needed and fix what was broken. I built cabinets, replaced faucets and toilets, installed flooring, hung drywall, tiled the shower—and sanded, scraped, varnished, or painted just about every surface in the house.

Things are a little different now that we're older. Admittedly, I still have a knee-jerk aversion to spending a lot of money in restaurants. But more often than not, we hire others to do the repair work around the house, to save both time and energy.

Our philosophy about how and what we buy has changed too.

We used to buy everything on discount, regardless of its quality, because it was all we could afford. "How much does it cost?" was always the most important question. Even now, by reflex, we still look for the best deal possible. But more and more, the primary question has become, "How long will it last?"

A case in point: for years, we relied on vinyl flooring in our kitchen. It would get nicked, scratched, and stained. But it was inexpensive, and I could replace it myself. Our mentality was, "It'll do for a few years, then we'll get a new one."

The vinyl is gone now, never to return. In its place is porcelain tile, professionally laid. It cost more, and we have to work to take care of it. But this floor will not only outlast vinyl, it will probably outlast *us*. That's the new mentality. We don't settle for today's bargain if it means having to replace it tomorrow. We're willing to sacrifice more for things we know will endure.

"It'll do for a few years, and then we'll get a new one." We live in an era of disposable everything. It's not just a matter of cheap construction. It's an obsession with newness and convenience. I think of the collection of ballpoint pens we have scattered in various drawers around the house. Some are cheap stick pens; they're meant to be thrown away. I have a few expensive pens that were given to me as gifts, but I never use them. And in between I have several pens that are, in principle at least, refillable. What happens when one of them runs out of ink? I scribble furiously on a scrap of paper to make sure, then toss it in the trash. It's easier to throw it away than to bother with refilling it. Why not? I have lots of other pens just waiting to be used.

Are we the same way with our relationships?

There's a memorable movie line to that effect: "Husbands should be like Kleenex—soft, strong, and disposable."[1] It's meant to be funny, coming in the middle of a dialogue peppered with risqué one-liners. But the line plays on the fact that we already live in a culture of replaceable relationships. I remember being at a therapy conference and hearing the story of a real-life wedding reception at which the mothers of the bride and groom were chatting amiably. "She'll make him a good first wife," one was overheard to say, while the other just smiled and nodded.

That's not to say that people don't care if their relationships last. But it's getting harder to imagine good reasons for investing time and emotional energy into relationships that are bothersome or difficult. It's easier to walk away from people we're having problems with, to unfriend them or ignore their text messages. It's easier to walk away from a church and find a new one than it is to learn to love one another.

Unless, of course, you happen to live in ancient Corinth. Then you're stuck with each other.

We can't live on the fairy tale view of life, on the hope that someday we'll stumble into relationships that hum along happily by themselves. Even the most successful of marriages, for example, have their hiccups—issues the spouses argue about again and again without ever coming to a resolution.[2] What matters for the health and longevity of the relationship is not ridding it of conflict. It's being willing to turn toward one another instead of away. It's the commitment to persist, to endure, to hang in there.[3] It's the day-by-day decision to keep reaching out across the chasms that inevitably threaten to divide.

What vision of love can help us do that? We are flawed people with flawed homes and congregations. Neither the romantic ideal of finding one's already perfect partner nor a culture of disposable relationships will do.

What we need is Paul's vision of a love that never fails.

■ ■ ■

As Paul brings his teaching to a climax, he rapidly fires off four more things that true love does: it "puts up with all things, trusts in all things, hopes for all things, endures all things." Paul's Greek is much simpler than most English translations. He uses a mere eight words. The single word meaning "all things" is repeated four times in succession, and each time it is followed by a single verb.[4] In my mind I can hear Paul preaching, hammering home his message about love, pounding the pulpit with each of the four verbs.

The meaning of the first verb, however, is difficult to pin down, as a quick survey of different Bible translations will show. Some translations read that love "puts up with" all things. Others, similarly, say that love "bears" all things. One has Paul saying that love "always protects."[5] And at least one commentator prefers the translation that love "supports" all things.[6] We don't have to insist that one is right and the others wrong, because Paul may have more than one meaning in mind. But what might he be trying to say?

The basic sense of the verb is "to cover." There's a related noun, for example, which means "roof," as found in the story of the paralytic who is lowered down to Jesus through a hole dug in the roof (Mark 2:4).[7] To cover something in this way thus has more to do with protection than concealment. This in turn leads to a host of metaphoric possibilities from which translators can choose.

For example, the word could be used in the ancient world for things that were waterproof, keeping fluids out like a roof. Conversely, it could describe things that were leakproof, keeping fluids in. Paul may therefore mean that love "doesn't leak," in the sense that a loving person always protects others by keeping confidences.[8] If you've ever had a friend blab something embarrassing you told them in secret, you've experienced this lack of love. One can easily imagine, moreover, that gossip was a problem in a contentious congregation like Corinth. A word from Paul may very well have been needed on that score.

Personally, however, I prefer the more traditional translation: love "bears" all things, in the sense that a true and godly love doesn't quit; it's able to endure or put up with anything without giving up.[9] Paul is the only New Testament author to use the word, and does so only four times. One use, of course, is here in Paul's love chapter. Two more appear in the same paragraph in 1 Thessalonians, where the word clearly suggests bearing up under difficult circumstances (e.g., 1 Thess 3:1, "when we couldn't stand it any longer").

Even more pertinent, perhaps, is the fact that the other remaining use occurs earlier in his letter to the Corinthians:

If others have these rights over you, don't we deserve them all
the more? However, we haven't made use of this right, but
we *put up with* everything so we don't put any obstacle in the
way of the gospel of Christ. (1 Cor 9:12, emphasis added)

Here, Paul is dealing with the question of why he doesn't make his
living from preaching the gospel as others apostles do. He seems to
believe that receiving money from the Corinthians will somehow
contaminate his relationship with them, so he works with his hands as
a tentmaker instead. That decision makes his life considerably more
difficult. But he endures the added hardship for their sakes—because
he loves them.[10]

Obviously, for Paul to "put up with everything" doesn't mean that
the Corinthians can do as they please. If that were so, there would be
no need for him to teach them about love, or to describe the things
that love doesn't do. The point is not that love tolerates all behavior,
but that it is willing and able to "hang in there" no matter what
happens.

How does love do this? In part, love is able to put up with
hardship in the present because it also has an eye toward the future.
When a dear friend we haven't seen for a while makes a date to spend
time with us, we say, "I'm looking forward to it!" And somehow,
living in the sure anticipation of the good that will happen tomorrow
makes today's burden a little lighter.

The attitude of the Christian life should be one of "looking
forward." The last three verbs in Paul's sequence of four can be
translated as "to have faith (or 'believe' or 'trust')," "to hope," and "to
endure."[11] Faith, hope, and love have traditionally been known in the
church as the three "theological virtues," and we already see Paul
holding them tightly together at the end of the love chapter itself:
"Now faith, hope, and love remain—these three things—and the
greatest of these is love" (1 Cor 13:13). In Paul's vision of God's
future, love is the virtue that abides.

There's clearly a close relationship between faith, hope, and love
in Paul's letters. But given his forward-looking vision, endurance
must also be part of the mix.

He writes, for example, of the faith and endurance of the Thessalonians in the face of persecution (2 Thess 1:4). Furthermore, he counsels Timothy to pursue faith, love, and endurance (1 Tim 6:11), and tells Titus to teach the same three things to the older men in the church (Tit 2:2). And in his letter to the Romans, Paul writes of how Christian hope grounds our ability to patiently endure suffering (Rom 8:25). Indeed, in chapter 5 of that letter, he brings everything together in one stirring description of the Christian life:

> We have access by *faith* into this grace in which we stand through him, and we boast in the *hope* of God's glory. But not only that! We even take pride in our problems, because we know that trouble produces *endurance*, *endurance* produces character, and character produces *hope*. This *hope* doesn't put us to shame, because the *love* of God has been poured out in our hearts through the Holy Spirit, who has been given to us. (Rom 5:2-5, emphasis added)

Everything begins with the grace of God, into which we are allowed to enter by faith. Through faith, we also have hope (Heb 11:1). We look forward in confident trust to a future in which God's glory will be fully revealed, knowing that it is our destiny as God's children to share in that glory (Rom 8:17).

That confidence, in turn, empowers us to "take pride in our problems." For Paul, this is not some airy abstraction; it's an autobiographical statement. As we've seen earlier, "endurance" is a word he uses to describe himself as he lists for the Corinthians' benefit all the woes he suffers as an apostle (2 Cor 6:4). He knows firsthand that following Jesus wholeheartedly in a world such as ours will bring difficulties. But he wants us to trust that through our trials and tribulations, God is making us more like the One we follow. When suffering is seen through the eyes of faith, it leads to courageous endurance, which over time proves us to be people of character.

Character, in turn, feeds back into hope, for those who have endured have even more confidence in the love of God. And we won't be disappointed. As John Stott has written, "The reason our hope will never let us down is that God will never let us down. His love will never give us up."[12]   How can we know this?   By the Holy Spirit, given to us a gift.   It is through the Spirit, Paul says, that God's love is so lavishly poured out into our hearts.[13]

In some ways, this description of the Christian life resembles what we already know about how children grow to develop character.   As parents, we can't shield our kids from every scraped knee and broken heart.   Nor should we.   To become confident and courageous adults, children need to learn how to walk through their problems and not around them.

But not alone. Never alone.

The world can be a scary place for children.   They don't have the resources in themselves to survive.   Moreover, raising kids means more than just providing for their physical needs.   They need consistently available, loving adults in whom they can put their trust. They need the sense of safety, security, and deep belonging that only a committed love can provide.   As Gordon Neufeld and Gabor Maté have put it, "We liberate children not by making them work for our love but by letting them rest in it."[14]   By internalizing that love, they gain the confidence they need to explore the world and handle adversity.

Paul, of course, isn't talking about the physical or emotional bumps and bruises of childhood, but the challenges of following Christ.   Still, when I read this passage, I think back to all that I said earlier about the embrace of our loving Father.   The Christian life is expressed in the love that we as human beings show toward one another.   But it is not grounded there.   We love, because he first loved us: our life, our love, is grounded in the sure knowledge of the Father's love for us.

Trusting faith. Confident hope. Proven endurance. These come from knowing that we don't have to work for our Father's love, but can rest in it instead.

We are never alone, because God's love never fails.

■ ■ ■

"Love never fails," Paul insists. That's how many modern translations read. The verb, however, literally means to "fall" or "fall down."[15] A person, for example, can fall down by prostrating themselves in worship (1 Cor 14:25) or by stumbling over a stone (Luke 20:18). Walls, like the ones surrounding ancient Jericho, can collapse and fall (Heb 11:30) as can entire cities (Rev 16:19).

Metaphorically, then, falling may suggest failure or coming to an end. Particularly relevant is Paul's warning to the Corinthians that they should stop being so cocky about their spirituality: "So those who think they are standing need to watch out or else they may fall" (1 Cor 10:12). It's similar to the well-known lesson from the book of Proverbs: "Pride comes before disaster, and arrogance before a fall" (Prov 16:18).[16]

Love, of course, can't literally be said to "fall down." But that's the translation Kenneth Bailey prefers: "Love doesn't fall." He doesn't want us to move too quickly past the literal sense of the word and miss the possible significance of the image it conveys. Quoting the ancient Greek geographer and historian Strabo, Bailey notes that the road from Athens to Corinth was steep and mountainous. Travelers had to pass close to rocky cliffs, and the possibility of falling was dangerously real.[17] Paul would have traveled that road. Ditto for the Corinthians. If Paul wanted to encourage them to aspire to the high road of love, it would make sense to assure them that love doesn't fall.

As with the whole of the love chapter, Paul's words are rich with layers of meaning. Falling is a good summary of all the things that love doesn't do. But as such, it can be both a word of admonishment and of encouragement. Paul warns his congregation, "Be careful! Don't fall down!" At the same time, however, he reassures them: "Stick close to God's love and you *won't* fall down."

When it comes to love, we need to be both admonished and encouraged, to be reminded of what love doesn't do and what it does. If we're paying attention, living neither in delusion nor denial, we are painfully aware of the failures of love. Perhaps our parents weren't there for us consistently in the way we needed them to be. People we counted on as friends betrayed us. The person whose eyes we so lovingly gazed into as we took our wedding vows has begun to feel like an enemy. The congregation we visited treated us rudely, or the one we served for years took us for granted.

And if the truth be told, whether we know it or not, whether we choose to admit it or not, to others *we* are the ones who weren't there. We are the betrayer, the enemy, the one who just doesn't get it, the one who has failed at love.

In our quest to walk the road that Jesus walked, we will fall down. We may fail in all the ways Paul has described. Take some time to thoughtfully and prayerfully read through the following list of questions:

- Recently or in the past, have you been impatient with someone for what you perceived as a fault or shortcoming? How did you show it?
- In what way have you treated someone unkindly?
- Have you felt envious of what seemed like someone else's good fortune? What other thoughts or feelings arose because of it?
- Conversely, have you ever bragged about your own good fortune or accomplishments in a way that left you feeling superior? How? Would anyone have reason to consider you arrogant, and if so, why?
- Do you ever behave in ways that you consider acceptable, but that might wound someone else's conscience? More generally, in what ways do you put your own desires ahead of the needs of others?
- In what areas are you the most easily irritated, and how do you respond to others when that happens?
- What resentments do you carry? Against whom do you have an ongoing grudge—even a small one—and how do you treat them?

If that little exercise was less than enjoyable, here's more bad news. Paul isn't giving a definition of love that we can turn into a checklist or scorecard. There are many, many ways to describe what love does and doesn't do. Had Paul been writing to a different church, he might have highlighted different concerns. The list we have, in other words, is potentially just the tip of the iceberg.

But the bad news is meant to point us to the good news. Our loving heavenly Father is unbelievably patient with us and treats us with kindness. He puts up with so much from his wayward children. He has sacrificed so much on our behalf. But he never stops loving us, never stops waiting to receive us with open arms.

People fail, sometimes spectacularly. Our love for one another fails. But God's love doesn't. That's the good news we must continually celebrate. That's the gospel we must grab onto with both hands to pull ourselves up when we fall. God's love is the foundation of our faith, the source of our hope, the engine of our endurance.

If we learn anything from Paul's relationship to the church in Corinth, it's this: Christians are fallible people, relationships are messy, and somehow in the midst of all of that, we can still catch an occasional glorious glimpse of the unfailing love of God. The good news is that we have a loving God who won't give up on us. We must learn to rejoice in that truth if we want to do better at not giving up on each other.

■ ■ ■

One of the most successful romantic films of all time is entitled, appropriately enough, *Love Story.*[18] The movie follows the romance between Oliver, played by Ryan O'Neal, and Jenny (Ali MacGraw), a contemporary Romeo and Juliet who fall in love and marry despite their class differences and the disapproval of their families. The film ends tragically as Jenny dies from leukemia and Oliver utters the film's famous tagline: "Love means never having to say you're sorry."

Those words quickly became a pop-culture catchphrase.[19] Two years later, O'Neal was cast opposite Barbra Streisand in the screwball romantic comedy *What's Up, Doc?*[20] Against type, he played a nerdy and socially inept musicologist named Howard, to Streisand's loopy misfit, Judy. At the end of the film, Howard declares his love to Judy and apologizes for things he said earlier. "Love means never having to say you're sorry," she responds, batting her eyes coquettishly.

Howard pauses to take in the words. Then he states flatly, "That's the dumbest thing I ever heard."

Which film has it right?

I vote for the nerdy musicologist. Mostly.

I suppose it's nice to imagine a relationship in which the people are so understanding and accepting of each other that apologies are never needed. Perhaps we hope one day to find the church to which we can belong with never a cross word nor a regret.

But that's not the love story the Bible tells.

That story tells of a God who is loving in essence, and who creates the universe as an outpouring of that love. In love, God calls a people to be his own, rescues that people from slavery and gives them a home. In love, God sends his Son to show us how to live and how to die. In love, God redeems and restores, promising a future day of resurrection, giving us a taste of that newness through the gift of his Spirit. We have yet to reach the story's final happy ending. But we are invited to be part of the ongoing adventure, by living in a way that demonstrates our confidence that the divine Author will bring the tale to its promised conclusion.

God's love matters more than anything in the universe. But the story also tells us why *our* love matters. Our vocation as followers of Jesus is to be the living embodiment of God's love in our life together, so that people may know that God exists and that God is love. Our calling, in other words, is to live truthfully so that people will know that the story is true.

We may find ourselves living other stories. We may marry for romantic reasons, hoping to live happily ever after. But then we fail each other, again and again. How will we keep our vows? What will keep us going when the romantic story loses its luster?

We may join a congregation for social reasons, hoping to find instant friendship and a supportive community. But churches, too, fail. So do Christian organizations. People still get into arguments and power plays, still treat each other with disdain or disrespect. Why not just walk away? Why hang in there?

We will struggle to answer such questions. As we do so, we need to make sure we're living the right love story.

God extends to us an impossibly gracious love. We cannot, we *must* not take that grace for granted, as if love meant never having to say we're sorry. Indeed, quite the opposite. The grateful love we return to God includes repentance. We see our sin for what it is: envy, arrogance, selfishness, resentment, and all the rest. We humbly apologize for it, even as we bask in forgiveness and renew our joy in the gospel. And with our eyes fixed on Jesus, we ask for help to be made more like him.

Our love matters because we are called to embody God's love, to show the truth of God's story by the way we live. Let us therefore take Paul's prayer for the Ephesians as his prayer for us:

> I ask that he will strengthen you in your inner selves from the riches of his glory through the Spirit. I ask that Christ will live in your hearts through faith. As a result of having strong roots in love, I ask that you'll have the power to grasp love's width and length, height and depth, together with all believers. I ask that you'll know the love of Christ that is beyond knowledge so that you will be filled entirely with the fullness of God. (Eph 3:16-19)

Can we really be the kind of people Paul envisions? Yes, if the Spirit of Jesus lives in our hearts, strengthening us from within.

Can we have marriages and churches in which people can see something of a love that never fails? Yes, if by the Spirit we can begin to understand the richness of God's love for us in Jesus, and if in community we are deeply rooted in that soil.

And at last, when we begin to grasp why and how much our love matters, we will be able to sing Paul's doxology:

> Glory to God, who is able to do far beyond all that we could ask or imagine by his power at work within us; glory to him in the church and in Christ Jesus for all generations, forever and always. Amen. (Eph 3:20-21)

Yes, Paul. Amen, indeed.

talk or think about it

1. Prayerfully contemplate the bulleted list of questions on page 215. Which of these questions resonate the most strongly with you? Why? Thinking back on core themes from this book represented in those questions, what are one or two personal insights that you could begin implementing in your relationships today?

2. "We need to make sure we're living the right love story." There is nothing intrinsically wrong with having hopes and dreams for romance, marriage, or friendship. But in all of our relationships as Christians, we must first imagine ourselves as those who have received the riches of God's love and mercy. How can we help one another do this, and what difference might this make?

about the author

Cameron Lee, PhD, is Professor of Family Studies at Fuller Theological Seminary, where he has taught since 1986. He is both a Certified Family Life Educator and a teaching pastor, and speaks or preaches regularly on topics related to marriage and family life. In his writing ministry, he is an avid blogger ("Squinting Through Fog," www.the-fog-blog.com) and the sole or senior author of seven previous books including, most recently, *Marriage PATH: Peacemaking at Home for Christian Couples* (2015). He and his wife Suha have been married since 1978 and have two grown children. Though he now enjoys receiving senior discounts at a variety of places of business, part of him still wants to be Spider Man.

notes

Read Me First

[1]Robert M. Polhemus, *Erotic Faith: Being in Love from Jane Austen to D. H. Lawrence* (Chicago, IL: University of Chicago Press, 1990), p. xi.

[2]See, for example, the sermons of St. John Chrysostom, a 5th century bishop of Constantinople, collected under the title of *The Love Chapter: The Meaning of First Corinthians 13* (Brewster: Paraclete Press, 2010). Note also that the book we know as "First" Corinthians is not the first letter Paul wrote to the congregation, but the first of two surviving letters we have from a longer correspondence.

[3]Polhemus, *Erotic Faith*, p. 2.

[4]Some of these verbs have no direct English equivalent, forcing translators to use adjectives like "patient" and "kind."

Chapter 1: Words Can Never Be Enough

[1]The story is anonymous. See Sarah Karlan, "14 People Share the Story of Their First 'I Love You'," posted 12 Feb 2015, at https://www.buzzfeed.com/skarlan/people-share-the-story-of-their-first-i-love-you?utm_term=.mfYX5L mkv#.rfG3wY9LW.

[2]See Solomon, *Love: Emotion, Myth and Metaphor* (Garden City: Anchor/Doubleday, 1981), chapter 11. In Solomon's work, the word is not hyphenated.

[3]"Sonnet XLIII," lines 1-4, from *Sonnets from the Portuguese*, published 1850. See Elizabeth Browning, *The Poetical Works of Elizabeth Barrett Browning*, ed. Harriet Waters Preston (Boston: Houghton Mifflin, 1974), p. 223.

[4]As Angela Leighton has written, "Such passion catches up a lifetime into significance, but leaves out its first inspiration"—the beloved inspires the sonnet, but the sonnet goes beyond. See Leighton, *Elizabeth Barrett Browning* (Bloomington: Indiana University Press, 1986), p. 103.

[5]Thérèse of Lisieux, *The Autobiography of Saint Therese of Lisieux: The Story of a Soul*, trans. John Beevers (New York: Image Books, 1989), p. 109.

[6]Thérèse of Lisieux, *Story of a Soul*, p. 101.

[7]As Trevor Hart has said, "It is not that he loves like us, but that we are urged to love like him." Trevor Hart, "How Do We Define the Nature of God's Love?" in *Nothing Greater, Nothing Better: Theological Essays on the Love of God*, ed. Kevin J. Vanhoozer (Grand Rapids: Eerdmans, 2001), Kindle location 1237.

[8]Marianne Meye Thompson, *1-3 John* (Downers Grove: InterVarsity Press, 1992), p. 120.

[9]The first is pronounced "stor-gay," and the last "a-gah-pay." All four are nouns; each represents an entire word group that includes not only nouns but verbs and adjectives. For the sake of simplicity, I will only refer to the noun forms, even though in some of the biblical texts cited the word "love" is actually a verb.

[10]C. S. Lewis, *The Four Loves* (New York: Harcourt Brace & Company, 1960), p. 91.

[11]E.g., Robert Solomon, who describes *agape* as "the love of humanity"; see Solomon, *Love: Emotion, Myth and Metaphor*, p. 136. Similarly, Ronald de Sousa characterizes *agape* as an "indiscriminate" and "universalized" love directed toward "the mass of humanity," while *eros* is the romantic desire for one person who is "irreplaceably special." See de Sousa, *Love: A Very Short Introduction* (Oxford: Oxford University Press, 2015), p. 3.

[12]John Alan Lee, "Love Styles," in Robert J. Sternberg and Michael L. Barnes, eds., *The Psychology of Love* (New Haven: Yale University Press, 1988), p. 48.

[13]Anders Nygren, *Agape and Eros*, trans. Philip S. Watson (Philadelphia: Westminster, 1953).

[14]The terminology is probably best known from C. S. Lewis' *The Four Loves*, but is also taken up in more recent works, e.g., Gary D. Badcock, "The Concept of Love: Divine and Human," in *Nothing Greater, Nothing Better: Theological Essays on the Love of God*, ed. Kevin J. Vanhoozer (Grand Rapids: Eerdmans, 2001), chapter 2, and John C. Peckham, *The Love of God: A Canonical Model* (Downers Grove: IVP Academic, 2015).

[15]Lewis, *The Four Loves*, p. 1-2.

[16]For an extensive critique of Nygren's one-sided use of biblical texts, see Thomas Jay Oord, *The Nature of Love: A Theology* (St. Louis: Chalice Press, 2010), chapter 2. Unfortunately, he sometimes seems to make the same mistake of which he rightly accuses Nygren—reinterpreting texts to fit a preferred definition of love (e.g., see his comments on John 17:24, p. 48).

[17]See Samuel Terrien, *Till the Heart Sings: A Biblical Theology of Manhood and Womanhood*, new ed. (Grand Rapids: Eerdmans, 2004). In chapter 3, Terrien writes of an "*eros-agape* continuum" rather than a hard distinction; the story of Shechem shows an "*agape* which permeates *eros*" (p. 35).

[18]D. A. Carson, *Exegetical Fallacies,* 2nd ed. (Grand Rapids: Baker Academic, 1996), p. 28.

[19]Carson cites French scholarship demonstrating that *agape* was becoming more widely used throughout Greek literature centuries before the New Testament was written. See *Exegetical Fallacies*, pp. 51-52.

[20]Badcock, "The Concept of Love," pp. 37-38.

[21]Ryken, *Loving the Way Jesus Loves*, Kindle location 291-293. Ryken interprets Paul as describing the love of Jesus in 1 Corinthians 13. I would prefer, however, to say that Jesus as God Incarnate demonstrates God's loving character. To the extent that Christians embody the Spirit of Jesus, they too will act in ways that are resemble the love of Jesus. The character of Jesus is thus never far from Paul's mind. But I don't believe that his purpose in the love chapter is to describe that character. The various qualities of love he lists are chosen to directly challenge specific unloving behaviors of the Corinthians toward each other.

[22]Christina Rossetti, "Love Came Down at Christmas," first published in 1885. http://www.hymnary.org/text/love_came_down_at_christmas

[23]The "one substance" language can be found in both the Nicene Creed of 325 CE and the revised Nicene-Constantinopolitan Creed of 381 CE.

Chapter 2: Love and Emotion

[1]*That Touch of Mink*, dir. Delbert Mann, Universal Pictures, 1962. We'll further examine the role of romantic comedy and fiction in chapter 3.

[2]Dorothy Tennov, *Love and Limerence: The Experience of Being in Love* (New York: Stein and Day, 1979). A corrected edition with a new preface was published 20 years later (Lanham: Scarborough House, 1999), and is the one referenced here.

[3]Tennov, *Love and Limerence* (1999), p. 18.

[4]See Helen Fisher, *Anatomy of Love,* rev. ed. (New York: Norton, 2016), chapter 1, for a review of the research on male and female courtship behavior; there are remarkable similarities between cultures.

[5]Tennov, *Love and Limerence* (1999), pp. 21-22.

[6]For a summary of characteristics, see Tennov, *Love and Limerence* (1999), pp. 23-24.

[7]Fisher, *Anatomy of Love*, p. 22.

[8]Sue Johnson, *Love Sense* (New York: Little, Brown and Company, 2013), p. 66. The words "emotion" and "feeling" are often used interchangeably. For the sake of readability, I will do the same. For many scholars, however, the word "emotion" refers to unconscious physiological states and responses that only become "feelings" when we become aware of them, e.g., Joseph E. LeDoux, *The Emotional Brain* (New York: Simon and Schuster, 1996). The distinction is not trivial. What is important, however, is to remember that there are both unconscious and conscious aspects to what we feel.

[9]Mary K. Rothbart, *Becoming Who We Are: Temperament and Personality in Development* (New York: Guilford, 2011), p. 69.

[10]As philosopher Robert C. Solomon argues, emotions are intelligent in the sense that they undergird purposive behavior; see, e.g., Solomon, *The Passions: Emotions and the Meaning of Life* (Indianapolis: Hackett, 1993). This is related to but somewhat different from the various notions of "emotional intelligence," such as that popularized by psychologist Daniel Goleman in *Emotional Intelligence* (New York: Bantam, 1995). Psychological concepts of emotional intelligence emphasize the ability to be accurately aware of one's own emotional state and the states of others in a way that serves self-regulation.

[11]Stephen W. Porges calls this "neuroception," the unconscious neurological process that lies beneath our conscious perception. See Porges, *The Polyvagal Theory: Neurophysiological Foundations of Emotions, Attachment, Communication, and Self-Regulation* (New York: Norton, 2011).

[12]See Elizabeth Johnston and Leah Olson, *The Feeling Brain: The Biology and Psychology of Emotions* (New York: Norton, 2015), especially chapter 4. Many of the early insights on the biology of emotions came from the study of fear and the brain structure known as the *amygdala*. As Johnston and Olson note, however, more recent research gives us a broader picture: the amygdala becomes active "when a stimulus has personal significance that requires action" (p. 86). As suggested in the earlier quote from Sue Johnson, this significance can be positive or negative: our emotions implicitly direct toward what appears helpful, and away from what appears harmful.

[13]The experiment described is known as the Iowa Gambling Task. See, e.g., chapter 9 of Antonio Damasio, *Descartes' Error: Emotion, Reason, and the Human Brain* (New York: Putnam, 1994). The separation of reason and emotion is the "error" of Damasio's title, exemplified by the highly influential work of the 17th century French philosopher René Descartes.

[14]These patients suffered damage to an area of the brain called the ventromedial prefrontal cortex (vmPFC). Part of the function of the vmPFC seems to be the integration of emotion and reasoning.

[15]The story is told repeatedly, e.g., Douwe Draaisma, *Metaphors of Memory: A History of Ideas About the Mind*, trans. Paul Vincent (Cambridge: Cambridge University Press, 2000), p. 197.

[16]See, e.g., Thomas Lewis, Fari Amini, and Richard Lannon, *A General Theory of Love* (New York: Vintage, 2001), see especially chapter 3. They call this "limbic resonance" in reference to the limbic structures of the brain, which are central to the experience of emotion. Similar concepts go by a variety of names, such as *emotional contagion*.

[17]The visual cliff was originally created to test depth perception. Later researchers used it to study how mothers and children communicate through non-verbal emotional expression. See James F. Sorce, Robert N. Emde, Joseph Campos, and Mary

D. Klinnert, "Maternal Emotional Signaling: Its Effect on the Visual Cliff Behavior of 1-Year-Olds," *Developmental Psychology* 21 (1985): 195-200.

[18]Lewis, Amini, and Lannon, *A General Theory of Love,* p. 61.

[19]In some books and the popular press, this would typically be explained through the function of so-called "mirror neurons." There is intriguing evidence in studies done with monkeys that some neurons (nerve cells) have a mirroring function. If Monkey A sees Monkey B pick up and eat a banana, the motor neurons that A would use to do the same thing will fire—even if A sits there and does nothing. Mirror neurons have been widely and plausibly touted as the basis of human empathy, but as of this writing, they are still a matter of controversy.

[20]Norman Doidge, *The Brain that Changes Itself* (New York: Penguin, 2007), p. 98. Similarly, Lewis, Amini, and Lannon write, "People differ in their proficiency at tracing the outlines of another self, and thus their ability to love also varies. A child's early experience teaches this skill in direct proportion to his parents' ability to know *him.* A steady limbic connection with a resonant parent lays down emotional expertise. A child can then look inside someone else, map an emotional vista, and respond to what he senses." *A General Theory of Love,* p. 207.

[21]This is known as her "broaden-and-build" theory of positive emotions. See e.g., Barbara L. Fredrickson, *Positivity* (New York: Three Rivers Press, 2009).

[22]Barbara L. Fredrickson, *Love 2.0: How Our Supreme Emotion Affects Everything We Feel, Think, Do, and Become* (New York: Hudson Street, 2013), pp. 9-10, 35.

[23]Fredrickson tends to emphasize the role of oxytocin, the so-called "love hormone" that has been implicated in studies of mating behavior, even in the animal kingdom (see Fredrickson, *Love 2.0,* chapter 3). Others researchers, like Robin Dunbar, prefer a more complex picture that includes various neurotransmitters and the neurohormone vasopressin. See Dunbar, *The Science of Love* (Hoboken: Wiley, 2012), chapter 2. Either way, the point remains: there is an underlying biology of love of which lovers themselves are unaware.

[24]Fredrickson, *Love 2.0,* p. 6.

[25]Fredrickson, *Love 2.0,* pp. 35-36.

[26]Fredrickson, *Love 2.0,* p. 189.

[27]From his autobiography, as quoted in Walter Isaacson, *Benjamin Franklin: An American Life* (New York: Simon and Schuster, 2003), p. 37. As Isaacson observes, "A recurring theme in his [writings] was his amusement at man's ability to rationalize what was convenient" (p. 37).

[28]See, e.g., Hans Walter Wolff, *Anthropology of the Old Testament* (Philadelphia: Fortress, 1974).

[29]Phillip Cary, *Good News for Anxious Christians* (Grand Rapids: Brazos, 2010), pp. 97-98, emphasis in original. As Cary notes, in the Old Testament, the Hebrew words *leb* and *lebab* refer to the heart, but are often translated into English as "mind,"

because the heart is the organ not only of feeling but understanding. Though New Testament Greek has more than one word that can be translated as "mind," this is never in contradistinction to the heart. See Cary, *Good News for Anxious Christians*, chapter 6.

[30]See, e.g., Mark Noll, *The Scandal of the Evangelical Mind* (Grand Rapids: Eerdmans, 1994).

[31]Elizabeth Achtemeier, *Minor Prophets I* (Peabody: Hendrickson, 1996), p. 95.

[32]This is contrary to the argument made by Rob Bell in *Love Wins* (New York: HarperOne, 2011). A useful corrective to Bell is provided by Mark Galli, *God Wins* (Carol Stream: Tyndale, 2011).

[33]Matthew A. Elliott, *Faithful Feelings: Rethinking Emotion in the New Testament* (Grand Rapids: Kregel, 2006), p.111.

[34]See Matthew Elliott's argument in *Faithful Feelings*, as well as Jonathan Edwards' work on *The Religious Affections* (reprint ed., Edinburgh: Banner of Truth Trust, 1961), originally published in 1746. The orientation of our affections can be a sign of the work of regeneration. Though some of Edwards' conceptualization is based on antiquated notions of physiology, his understanding of emotion fits well with the idea of unconscious inclination as described earlier in this chapter.

[35]Robert Solomon, *True to Our Feelings: What Our Emotions Are Really Telling Us* (New York: Oxford, 2007), p. 3. This is an argument Solomon made throughout his career. The question, of course, is whether the ideas of "judgment" and "decision" must necessarily refer to conscious as opposed to unconscious mental processes; they too have a neurological basis.

[36]Solomon, *True to Our Feelings*, chapter 1.

Chapter 3: Making Sense of Our Sensibilities

[1]*Pride and Prejudice and Zombies*, dir. Burr Steers, Lionsgate, 2016. The film was adapted from the novel of the same name by Seth Grahame-Smith (Philadelphia: Quirk Books, 2009). Considering that the bulk of the book is Austen's original text, she is listed as first author. One wonders, however, if she would have approved.

[2]See, e.g., Lawrence Stone, *The Family, Sex and Marriage in England 1500-1800*, abridged ed. (New York: Harper Torchbooks, 1979), especially chapter 6, on the rise of "affective individualism." This must be balanced against the finding that passionate, romantic love can be found in both individualistic and collectivist societies alike. See Elaine Hatfield and Richard L. Rapson, "Passionate Love, Sexual Desire, and Mate Selection: Cross-Cultural and Historical Perspectives," in *Close Relationships: Functions, Forms, and Processes*, ed. Patricia Noller and Judith A. Feeney (New York: Psychology Press, 2006), pp. 227-243.

[3]"Before we can love rationally, somebody must fall in love." Polhemus, *Erotic Faith*, p. 49.

[4]Karen Stohr sees the novel as an illustration of Aristotle's ethics of virtue and practical wisdom, and views Elinor's moral imagination as more developed. See Stohr, "Practical Wisdom and Moral Imagination in *Sense and Sensibility*," *Philosophy and Literature* 30 (2006): 378-394.

[5]Stohr, "Practical Wisdom and Moral Imagination."

[6]Deborah Kaplan, "Mass Marketing Jane Austen: Men, Women, and Courtship in Two Film Adaptations," in *Sense and Sensibility* by Jane Austen, ed. Claudia L. Johnson, Norton Critical Edition (New York: Norton, 2002), pp. 402-410.

[7]*Silver Linings Playbook*, dir. David O. Russell, The Weinstein Company, 2012. The film was nominated for all the major Academy Awards, with Jennifer Lawrence winning the Oscar for Best Actress.

[8]*The Princess Bride*, dir. Rob Reiner, 20th Century Fox, 1987. William Goldman's screenplay was adapted from his 1973 novel of the same name (25th anniversary ed., New York: Ballantine, 1998), a sendup of romantic fiction. The final line of actor Peter Falk's voice-over narration, as the two lovers reach for each other, is: "Since the invention of the kiss, there have only been five kisses rated the most passionate, the most pure. This one left them all behind." For a farcical romantic comedy that satirizes the entire genre itself, again, including the final kiss, see *Paris When It Sizzles* (dir. Richard Quine, Paramount Pictures, 1964). It's less watchable than *The Princess Bride*, but blatant regarding the stereotyped elements of the romance plot.

[9]For a description of the shape or trajectory of "comedy-romance" and "happily-ever-after" plot lines, see Kenneth J. Gergen, *Realities and Relationships: Soundings in Social Construction* (Cambridge: Harvard, 1994), chapter 8. The happily-ever-after ending is typical, but not all fairy tales end well. See, e.g., Marina Warner, *Once Upon a Time: A Short History of Fairy Tale* (New York: Oxford, 2014); Sheldon Cashdan, *The Witch Must Die: How Fairy Tales Shape Our Lives* (New York: Basic Books, 1999). Ultimately, the fairy tale is a fluid form with a complex history, and may be impossible to define. See Jack Zipes, *The Irresistible Fairy Tale: The Cultural and Social History of a Genre* (Princeton: Princeton University Press, 2012).

[10]*La La Land*, dir. Damien Chazelle, Summit Entertainment, 2016.

[11]One of the oldest of these seems to be yournovel.com, started in 1992 by Kathy M. Newbern and J. S. Fletcher, a married couple who write together under the pseudonym of Fletcher Newbern.

[12]Eva Illouz, *Consuming the Romantic Utopia: Love and the Cultural Contradictions of Capitalism* (Berkeley: University of California Press, 1997), Kindle location 2251.

[13]Tennov, *Love and Limerence* (1999), p. 8.

[14]This is despite the fact that research has typically shown that "most people end up with demographically similar partners." See Brian G. Ogolsky, Sally A. Lloyd, and

Rodney M. Cate, *The Developmental Course of Romantic Relationships* (New York: Routledge, 2013), p. 56.

[15] *That Touch of Mink*, 1962; *The Lady Eve*, dir. Preston Sturges, Paramount Pictures, 1941; *Sabrina*, dir. Billy Wilder, Paramount Pictures, 1954, and its remake, dir. Sydney Pollack, Paramount Pictures, 1995; *Notting Hill*, dir. Roger Michell, Universal Pictures, 1999; *Love Actually*, dir. Richard Curtis, Universal Pictures, 2003.

[16] *Serendipity*, dir. Peter Chelsom, Miramax Films, 2001. Similar storylines can be found regularly on the Hallmark Channel, though usually with less ambitious production values.

[17] Such exaggeration is probably what earned the film a special honor: to be briefly made fun of as the most egregious example of the genre in *The LEGO Batman Movie* (dir. Chris McKay, Warner Bros., 2017), itself a sendup of the whole Batman corpus.

[18] Randall Munroe has tried to do the math. Assuming that you have one soul mate, that he or she is about the same age as you, that you wouldn't know them until you looked them in the eye, and that you made eye contact with roughly two dozen new people each day, his estimate is that "you would find true love only in one lifetime out of 10,000." See Munroe, *What If? Serious Scientific Answers to Absurd Hypothetical Questions* (Boston: Houghton Mifflin Harcourt, 2014), Kindle location 415.

[19] *Sleepless in Seattle*, dir. Nora Ephron, TriStar Pictures, 1993.

[20] *An Affair to Remember*, dir. Leo McCarey, 20th Century Fox, 1957.

[21] *Hello, Dolly!*, dir. Gene Kelly, 20th Century Fox, 1969.

[22] *WALL-E*, dir. Andrew Stanton, Walt Disney Studios, 2008. The name is an acronym for "Waste Allocation Load Lifter, Earth-Class."

[23] "EVE" is an acronym for "Extraterrestrial Vegetation Evaluator." Created by the humans who abandoned the Earth, her job is to periodically evaluate whether the planet is capable of sustaining plant life.

[24] *Titanic*, dir. James Cameron, 20th Century Fox/Paramount, 1997. Nominated for a record-tying 14 Academy Awards, the film won 11, including Best Picture.

[25] To be fair to the complexity of the script of *Love Actually*, only some of the vignettes have the usual happy ending.

[26] Rotten Tomatoes, a website that aggregates movie reviews, posts lists of the best romantic comedies of all time. As of this writing, six of the top ten are from the 1930s and 1940s (http://editorial.rottentomatoes.com/guide/best-romantic-comedies-of-all-time/), the golden age of the genre. One study examined a representative sample of 100 films from the 1930s: 95 of them "had romance as one of their plot lines." See Illouz, *Consuming the Romantic Utopia*, Kindle location 444.

[27] E.g., Craig A. Anderson, Leonard Berkowitz, Edward Donnerstein, L. Rowell Huesmann, James D. Johnson, Daniel Linz, Neil M. Malamuth, and Ellen Wartella,

"The Influence of Media Violence on Youth," *Psychological Science in the Public Interest* 3 (2003): 81-110.

[28]See, for example, Dorothy C. Holland and Margaret A. Eisenhart, *Educated in Romance: Women, Achievement, and College Culture* (Chicago: University of Chicago, 1990). Holland and Eisenhart describe the negative effects of the "culture of romance"—including norms of attractiveness and gender-based expectations of how to behave in dating relationships—on the educational and career paths of college women.

[29]*High Fidelity*, dir. Stephen Frears, Buena Vista Pictures, 2000.

[30]Indeed, there is an entire profession of music therapy, dedicated to using music to address a wide range of "physical, emotional, cognitive, and social needs." See, e.g., the website for the American Music Therapy Association, http://www.musictherapy.org.

[31]See, e.g., Myriam V. Thoma, Stefan Ryf, Changiz Mohiyeddini, Ulrike Ehlert, and Urs M. Nater, "Emotion Regulation through Listening to Music in Everyday Situations," *Cognition and Emotion* 26 (2012): 550-560.

[32]Lisa Bevere, *Kissed the Girls and Made Them Cry: Why Women Lose When They Give In* (Nashville: Thomas Nelson, 2002), p. 33.

[33]Illouz, *Consuming the Romantic Utopia*.

[34]See, for example, J. Courtney Sullivan, "How Diamonds Became Forever," *New York Times* (May 5, 2013), http://www.nytimes.com/2013/05/05/fashion/weddings/how-americans-learned-to-love-diamonds.html. The marketing campaign began as a way to increase demand for diamonds in the years after the Depression.

[35]These questions are similar to those used by therapist Athena Androutsopoulou. Her goal, however, is different: she wants to mine favorite stories for their therapeutic potential. By adopting the perspective of a favorite character in a story, clients may be able to perceive new possibilities for themselves, or give voice to parts of their own stories that otherwise could not be told. See Androutsopoulou, "Fiction as an Aid to Therapy: A Narrative and Family Rationale for Practice," *Journal of Family Therapy* 23 (2001): 278-295.

[36]As Laura Kipnis has said, the question of what happens next "must not be posed, which is precisely why the strategically timed fade-to-black is the love film's signature shot." See Kipnis, *Against Love: A Polemic* (New York: Pantheon, 2004), p. 100.

Chapter 4: Happily Ever After...?

[1]Peggy Orenstein, *Cinderella Ate My Daughter: Dispatches from the Front Lines of the New Girlie-Girl Culture* (New York: HarperCollins, 2011), pp. 13-14.

[2]See the Disney Princess website: http://blogs.disney.com/oh-my-disney/2015 /08/19/9-steps-for-turning-yourself-into-a-disney-princess/.

[3]See the Disney Princess website, e.g., http://blogs.disney.com/oh-my-disney/2016/ 02/01/quiz-whos-your-disney-soul-mate-based-on-your-zodiac-sign/, as well as http:/blogs.disney.com/oh-my-disney/2015/10/05/quiz-how-many-of-this-disney-guys-would-you- date/.

[4]See, for example, Bruno Bettelheim, *The Uses of Enchantment* (New York: Alfred A. Knopf, 1976). Sheldon Cashdan argues that the characters of fairy tales often possess personal flaws that must be mastered before the witch, wicked stepmother, or other evil character can be defeated. For that reason, the stories serve as mirrors to real-life internal struggles. See Cashdan, *The Witch Must Die.*

[5]This is what Jack Zipes, following the lead of other scholars, has called the *naive morality* of fairy tales. Zipes, *The Irresistible Fairy Tale*, p. 14.

[6]Peter J. Jordan, "Emotions in Comics: Why the Silver Age of Comics Made a Difference," in *Our Superheroes, Ourselves,* ed. Robin S. Rosenberg (New York: Oxford, 2013), chapter 4. This was an intentional creative strategy on the part of publisher Stan Lee.

[7] *Wonder Woman*, dir. Patty Jenkins, DC Films/Warner Bros., 2017.

[8]Rebecca-Anne C. Do Rozario, "The Princess and the Magic Kingdom: Beyond Nostalgia, the Function of the Disney Princess," *Women's Studies in Communication* 27 (2004): 38. *Snow White and the Seven Dwarfs* (dir. David Hand, Walt Disney Productions/RKO, 1937) was the first full-length animated feature. *Cinderella* (dir. Clyde Geronimi, Hamilton Luske, and Wilfred Jackson, Walt Disney Productions/RKO, 1950) premiered 13 years later, and *Sleeping Beauty* (dir. Clyde Geronimi, Walt Disney Productions/ Buena Vista, 1959) nine years after that.

[9]See, e.g., Ken Gillam and Shannon R. Wooden, "Post-Princess Models of Gender: The New Man in Disney/Pixar," *Journal of Popular Film and Television* 36.1 (2008): 2-8.

[10] *Frozen*, dir. Chris Buck and Jennifer Lee, Walt Disney Studios, 2013; *Maleficent*, dir. Robert Stromberg, Walt Disney Studios, 2014. In *Frozen*, the bait-and-switch has two levels: (1) the love-at-first-sight romance between Princess Anna and Prince Hans is upended when Hans is revealed to be a villain; (2) the audience is led to expect that Hans or Kristoff will bring the true love that saves Anna, but she is saved by her own love for her sister. Similarly, In *Maleficent*, a revisionist retelling of *Sleeping Beauty*, the kiss of true love that saves Aurora is not Prince Phillip's, but Maleficent's.

[11] *The Princess and the Frog*, dir. Ron Clements and John Musker, Walt Disney Studios, 2009. As many viewers and critics have remarked, it's unfortunate that she spends the majority of the film as a frog.

[12]Bridget Whelan, "Power to the Princess: Disney and the Creation of the 20th Century Princess Narrative," *Interdisciplinary Humanities* 29 (2012): 21-34.

[13]It should be noted, however, that the story of Disney's most recent (as of this writing) "princess" has no romantic arc. *Moana* (dir. Ron Clements and John Musker, Walt Disney Studios, 2016), is the daughter of a Polynesian tribal chieftain. The question of whether she is actually a princess is made an in-joke in the script.

[14]Orenstein, *Cinderella Ate My Daughter*, p. 20, emphasis in original.

[15]Karen E. Wohlwend, "Damsels in Discourse: Girls Consuming and Producing Identity Texts Through Disney Princess Play," *Reading Research Quarterly* 44 (2009): 57-83.

[16]Lawrence C. Rubin, "Are Superhero Stories Good for Us? Reflections from Clinical Practice," in Rosenberg, *Our Superheroes, Ourselves*, chapter 3. It should be noted that Superman was also his mother's favorite.

[17]G. Frank Lawlis, "Story as Personal Myth," in *Healing Stories: The Use of Narrative in Counseling and Psychotherapy*, ed. Stanley Krippner, Michael Bova, and Leslie Gray (Charlottesville: Puente Publications, 2007), p. 182.

[18]Lawlis, "Story as Personal Myth," p. 178.

[19]For example, the Walt Disney Company reportedly has plans to widen the market for its products in China and Southeast Asia. See "How Disney Plans to Conquer Asia," at http://www.thedisneymoviereview.com/how-disney-plans-to-conquer-asia/.

[20]Eric and Leslie Ludy, *When God Writes Your Love Story*, rev. ed. (Colorado Springs: Multnomah, 2009), pp. 2-3.

[21]Donna Freitas, *Sex & the Soul: Juggling Sexuality, Spirituality, Romance, and Religion on America's College Campuses* (New York: Oxford, 2008).

[22]Freitas, *Sex & the Soul*, p. 129.

[23]Freitas, *Sex & the Soul*, p. 132.

[24]Freitas, *Sex & the Soul*, p. 215.

[25]Freitas, *Sex & the Soul*, p. 81-82.

[26]See, e.g., Cameron Lee, *Marriage PATH: Peacemaking at Home for Christian Couples* (Pasadena: Fuller Institute for Relationship Education, 2015), pp. 46-53.

[27]In fact, feminist scholar Phyllis Trible considers this to be one of the many misogynist "texts of terror" in Scripture. See Trible, *Texts of Terror* (Philadelphia: Fortress, 1984).

[28]Freitas, *Sex & the Soul*, p. 76.

[29]Freitas, *Sex & the Soul*, p. 92.

[30]Kerry Cronin, "Intimacy: It's Complicated," *C21 Resources* (Spring 2014), pp. 3, 5. Emphasis in original.

[31]As noted in chapter 3, the screenplay and novel were both written by William Goldman. As a successful screenwriter, he obviously knew the plot conventions well enough to parody them effectively throughout the film. That includes the lyrics of the song, "Storybook Love," written and sung by Willy DeVille for the closing credits: "My love is like a storybook story / But it's as real as the feelings I feel." I take the clunky quality of the lyrics as part of the parody.

[32]See Stephen Crites, "The Narrative Quality of Experience," in *Why Narrative? Readings in Narrative Theology*, ed. Stanley Hauerwas and L. Gregory Jones, reprint ed. (Eugene: Wipf and Stock, 1997), pp. 65-88.

[33]Arthur W. Frank, *Letting Stories Breathe: A Socio-Narratology* (Chicago: University of Chicago Press, 2010), Kindle location 228. Emphasis in original.

[34]Robert Sternberg, *Love is a Story: A New Theory of Relationships* (New York: Oxford, 1998), p. x. This is similar to Robert Solomon's use of dramatic metaphor in *Love: Emotion, Myth and Metaphor*, as described near the end of chapter 2 of this book.

[35]*Guys and Dolls*, dir. Joseph L. Mankiewicz, Metro-Goldwyn-Mayer, 1955; *The Music Man*, dir. Morton DaCosta, Warner Bros., 1962. For an example from the westerns, see *Open Range* (dir. Kevin Costner, Touchstone, 2003), or even Best Picture winner *Unforgiven* (dir. Clint Eastwood, Warner Bros., 1992), in which the woman's role is an important part of the film's backstory.

[36]See Sternberg, *Love is a Story*, for a typology of the romantic stories that may shape couples' expectations.

[37]See, e.g., Dan McAdams, *The Stories We Live By: Personal Myths and the Making of the Self* (New York: Guilford, 1993), chapter 2. This is similar to the idea of *internal working models* in what is known as *attachment theory*. For an example of the influence of the relationship between parents on adolescent expectations of love and romance, see Sara J. Steinberg, Joanne Davila, and Frank Fincham, "Adolescent Marital Expectations and Romantic Experiences: Associations with Perceptions About Parental Conflict and Adolescent Attachment Security," *Journal of Youth and Adolescence* 35 (2006): 333-348. They found that the more adolescent girls saw their parents fight, the more likely they were to have problems in their current dating relationships, and to expect divorce in their own future.

[38]Alasdair MacIntyre, *After Virtue*, 2nd ed. (Notre Dame: University of Notre Dame, 1984), p. 216.

[39]*A Monster Calls*, dir. J. A. Bayona, Focus Features, 2016. The line is spoken by a man explaining his failed marriage to his son, as the boy's mother dies of cancer. The story makes a point of subverting traditional fairy tale expectations, in favor of telling more honest stories that deal with the reality of ambiguity and suffering.

[40]As I suggest elsewhere, from a narrative perspective, faith means "indwelling the story." See Cameron Lee, *Beyond Family Values: A Call to Christian Virtue* (Downers Grove: InterVarsity, 1998), chapter 7.

[41]See Acts 16:7; Rom 8:9; Phil 1:19. Although Paul rarely refers directly to the "Spirit of Christ," he speaks often of Christ being "in" believers.

[42]*Roman Holiday*, dir. William Wyler, Paramount Pictures, 1953. For this, her first major role, Hepburn won the Oscar for Best Actress.

[43]Frederick Buechner, *Telling the Truth: The Gospel as Tragedy, Comedy, and Fairy Tale* (New York: HarperCollins, 1977).

Chapter 5: A Father's Embrace

[1]See, e.g., James Barr, "Abba Isn't 'Daddy,'" *The Journal of Theological Studies* 39 (1988): 28-47. One of Barr's key points is that, whatever the origins of the Aramaic word *Abba*, by the time of Jesus adults and children alike used it to address their fathers. This suggests that the English word "Daddy," which has an element of childish dependence, isn't quite equivalent. It should be noted that the gospels only mention Jesus using the word once, as he prayed in Gethsemane (Mark 14:36); far more frequent is the Greek word *pater*—the typical word for "father"—as in the Lord's Prayer (Matt 6:9). There are only two other instances of *Abba* in the New Testament, both in Paul's letters (Rom 8:15; Gal 4:6). Moreover, in no case is *Abba* used by itself; it is always combined with *pater*. Having said all this, however, there can be no doubt as to the intimacy of Jesus' relationship with the Father, especially as seen in the gospel of John, and both Jesus and Paul invite us to call upon God in the same way Jesus did.

[2]Michael Reeves, *Delighting in the Trinity* (Downers Grove: IVP Academic, 2012), p. 23. Emphasis in original.

[3]To complete the Trinitarian picture: the apostle Paul identifies love and joy as part of the fruit of a life lived in obedience to the Holy Spirit (Gal 5:22).

[4]C. S. Lewis, *The Problem of Pain* (New York: MacMillan, 1962). This is known as the question of "theodicy," a term originally coined in French, from a combination of Greek words meaning "God" and "justice." Theodicy is the interrogation of God's supposed justice on the basis of the experience of suffering and evil.

[5]In *The Uncontrolling Love of God*, Oord proposes yet another option. God does not *choose* to let evil exist, nor is he powerless against it. Rather, God relates to humanity and the world in an uncontrolling, non-coercive way because self-emptying love is his nature. In other words, God doesn't prevent evil not because he can't, but because he would have to act against his nature to do so. This open-theology solution to the problem of pain rescues God's love from the accusation of cruelty or disinterest, but at the price of the certainty of our hope in the victory of God.

[6]This list is adapted from Walter Brueggemann, *The Psalms and the Life of Faith*, ed. Patrick D. Miller (Minneapolis: Fortress, 1995), p. 105.

[7]Walter Brueggemann, *The Message of the Psalms: A Theological Commentary* (Minneapolis: Augsburg, 1984), pp. 80-81.

[8]Robert Farrar Capon, *The Third Peacock: The Problem of God and Evil*, rev. ed. (San Francisco: Harper & Row, 1986), p. 82.

[9]As Reeves states in the opening lines of his argument for the centrality of the Christian doctrine of the Trinity, "God is love *because* God is a Trinity." See Reeves, *Delighting in the Trinity*, p. 9 (emphasis in original).

[10]Capon, *The Third Peacock*, p. 22.

[11]See, for example, Caroline J. Simon, *The Disciplined Heart: Love, Destiny, and Imagination* (Grand Rapids: Eerdmans, 1987).

[12]Here, I am drawing upon the distinction between "mundane" and "sacred" stories in Stephen Crites, "The Narrative Quality of Experience," *Journal of the American Academy of Religion* 39 (1971): 291-311.

[13]The exact nature of the confrontation is unknown. Rather than inflame the situation further, Paul withdrew to Ephesus wrote a tearful and severe letter (cf. 2 Cor 2:3-4, 9) demanding their repentance and obedience. The majority repented, and the man at the center of the controversy was disciplined (2 Cor 2:5-8). Paul writes 2 Corinthians after this to express his confidence in those who have turned around, but also to deal with remaining pockets of resistance before he visits the city a third time. He must also deal with new challenges from visitors who set themselves up as rival apostles.

[14]Emphasis added. The NIV renders Paul's words a bit more literally—"as servants of God we commend ourselves in every way: in great endurance; in troubles, hardships and distresses..." In other words, though Paul lists "great endurance" as if it were merely the first entry in the list, the CEB renders it as the key idea: that the commendation of Paul's ministry is found in how God enables him to endure the suffering he then describes.

[15]As F. F. Bruce has said, "Paul...knew the love of Christ to be the all-compelling power in life. Where love is the compelling power, there is no sense of strain or conflict or bondage in doing what is right: the man or woman who is compelled by Jesus' love and empowered by his Spirit does the will of God from the heart." See Bruce, *Paul: Apostle of the Heart Set Free* (Grand Rapids: Eerdmans, 1977), p. 21.

[16]As David G. Horrell has written: "Pauline thought cannot be conveyed as a series of propositions to be believed but only as a story that is 'lived,' retold, and embodied in the practices of the community that celebrates that story." Horrell, "Paul's Narratives or Narrative Substructure? The Significance of 'Paul's Story,'" in *Narrative Dynamics in Paul: A Critical Assessment*, ed. Bruce W. Longenecker (Louisville: Westminster John Knox, 2002), p. 170.

[17]In the retelling, I am relying heavily on the work of Kenneth Bailey, a New Testament scholar who is deeply familiar with the languages and culture of the Middle East. See Bailey, *Finding the Lost: The Lost Cultural Keys to Luke 15* (St. Louis: Concordia, 1992), especially chapters 3 and 4.

[18]Bailey, *Finding the Lost*, Kindle location 1940.

[19]The verb *splagchnizomai* is related to the noun *splagchna*, which refers to the innards or guts. In English, the word gives rise to anatomical references to the "splanchnic nerves."

[20]The parable of the Prodigal Son is the third of three stories Jesus tells about God's attitude and behavior toward the lost (Luke 15:3-10). The parables of the Lost Sheep and the Lost Coin both convey the same message: God diligently seeks the lost, and throws a party when the lost are found. We will return to these parables in chapter 11 of this book.

[21]We should probably not think of this as the older brother being out in some enormous back yard. The field was not in the same place as the house, and he would have to walk some distance to get home.

[22]Bailey notes a number of problems in the older son's complaint: (1) he neglects to address his father respectfully as "Father"; (2) he ignores that the father had already divided the estate (Luke 15:12); (3) he implies that if he were to celebrate, he'd rather do that with friends than family; (4) he accuses his brother of things he could know nothing about, since he was not home when the boy returned. Surely, Bailey observes, if the older brother had known about the prodigal feeding a Gentile's pigs, this would have been part of the slander. See *Finding the Lost*, chapter 4.

[23]Bailey, *Finding the Lost*, Kindle location 3198. Emphasis in original.

[24]Borrowing from Rabbi Harold S. Kushner's bestselling book on theodicy, *When Bad Things Happen to Good People* (New York: Random House, 1978).

Chapter 6: Taking the High Road

[1]The specific passages cited do not include everything Paul has to say on each matter, and should be read in context. We can't be certain, of course, exactly what the problems were. For the most part, however, there is broad scholarly consensus over the outline of the issues the congregation faced.

[2]Speaking in tongues, or glossolalia, is a form of spontaneous, ecstatic speech or prayer in an unrecognizable language. Those who speak in tongues report that they are not in conscious control of what they are saying, but are speaking under the control of the Holy Spirit.

[3]Corinth is in modern-day Greece, Ephesus is in modern-day Turkey, and the two cities are separated by the Aegean Sea. The sea voyage between them was a dangerous one, but the alternative was to take the much longer land route around the Aegean through the northern part of Greece.

[4]Indeed, it's because of passages like these that the church has held to a doctrine of the Trinity, even though the word "trinity" appears nowhere in Scripture. It would be an exaggeration to say that Paul has a well-developed doctrine in this regard, but

he seems to suggest that the church's unity in diversity reflects and embodies something similar in the Godhead.

[5]See, for example, Israel Galindo, *The Hidden Lives of Congregations: Discerning Church Dynamics* (Herndon: The Alban Institute, 2004), especially chapter 5. Galindo's suggests that congregations want to grow numerically, but don't recognize how their life together will change if they do.

[6]The technical term for this structure is *chiasm* or *chiasmus*, named after the X-shaped form of the Greek letter *chi*. In a chiasm, "words, clauses or themes are laid out and then repeated but in inverted order." See Matthew S. DeMoss, *Pocket Dictionary for the Study of New Testament Greek* (Downers Grove: InterVarsity Press, 2001), p. 29. The structure emphasizes the words or themes at the center of the chiasm (or in my visual metaphor, at the top of the pyramid). In reading 1 Corinthians 13 chiastically, I am echoing the exposition of Kenneth E. Bailey, *Paul through Mediterranean Eyes: Cultural Studies in 1 Corinthians* (Downers Grove: InterVarsity Press, 2011). Not all New Testament scholars, however, agree that the chapter should be read this way, e.g., Hans Conzelmann, *1 Corinthians: A Commentary on the First Epistle to the Corinthians*, trans. James W. Leitch (Philadelphia: Fortress, 1975).

[7]There is some question here of whether verse 3 should read "hand over my own body to be burned" instead, suggesting that Paul's final example is the extreme of martyrdom by fire. This is because the verbs for "that I may boast" and "that I may burn" are almost identical, differing only by one letter. Scholars today judge the manuscripts with the former reading to be more reliable. But Paul's basic point is the same either way: even extremes of physical sacrifice for religious reasons are worth nothing without love.

[8]This is essentially Kenneth Bailey's argument, *Paul through Mediterranean Eyes*, pp. 380-381. Note also that although the CEB translates "child" in 13:11 and "babies" in 3:1, Paul uses the same Greek word in both places (*nepios*).

[9]The phrase "childish things" in verse 11 sounds pejorative in English—but a more literal translation would be "the things of the child." There is, unfortunately, no good English equivalent for this more neutral phrase.

[10]Corinth was known throughout the empire for producing some of the finest polished brass mirrors in antiquity. Note that the CEB translates Paul as saying that we see "a reflection in a mirror," whereas a more literal translation would be "we see through a mirror in a riddle (enigma)." Paul's exact meaning is itself a riddle, but in context, seems to be one more way of contrasting what is imperfect and indirect with what is perfect and direct.

[11]Thus, Gordon Fee takes Paul's metaphor of the mirror to emphasize not the distortion of our vision of God but its indirectness and therefore its incompleteness. "In our own culture the comparable metaphor would be the difference between seeing a photograph and seeing someone in person. As good as a picture is, it is

simply not the real thing." Fee, *The First Epistle to the Corinthians* (Grand Rapids: Eerdmans, 1987), p. 648.

[12]Tom Wright, *Paul for Everyone: 1 Corinthians* (London: SPCK, 2004), pp. 176-177. Not everyone agrees, however, on the extent to which differences in spiritual gifts were causing a problem in the church. See, e.g., Fee, *The First Epistle to the Corinthians*, p. 615.

[13]Bailey, *Paul Through Mediterranean Eyes,* p. 357. Part of Bailey's argument runs as follows. The Greek word is *huperbolen.* Whenever Paul uses the word (and he is the only writer in the New Testament to do so), it intensifies some other word, just as the adverbs "extremely" or "exceedingly" modify other words and cannot stand by themselves. Literally, Paul seems to be saying, "an extremely way," which would be nonsensical. But Bailey finds precedent in other Greek literature for translating *huperbolen* as "mountain pass."

[14]Conzelmann, *1 Corinthians*, p. 217.

[15]Wright, *Paul for Everyone: 1 Corinthians*, p. 159.

[16]See, again, Psalm 1, which paradigmatically introduces "the way of the righteous" and the "way of the wicked" (vs. 6); the contrast between these characterizes much of the so-called wisdom literature of the Old Testament.

[17]See Cameron Lee, *Unexpected Blessing: Living the Countercultural Reality of the Beatitudes* (Downers Grove: InterVarsity Press, 2004).

Chapter 7: Remember God's Patience and Kindness

[1]Kent Nerburn, *Make Me an Instrument of Your Peace: Living in the Spirit of the Prayer of Saint Francis* (San Francisco: HarperSanFrancisco, 1999), p. 57. Various unattributed versions of the story have circulated around the Internet since its publication.

[2]Nerburn, *Make Me an Instrument of Your Peace*, p. 58.

[3]Nerburn, *Make Me an Instrument of Your Peace*, p. 61.

[4]E.g., Phil Ryken writes that Paul is not describing "a feeling we have in our hearts" but "something that we do—love as an action, not an affection." See Ryken, *Loving the Way Jesus Loves*, Kindle location 447. Many other examples can be found in Elliott, *Faithful Feelings*, especially pp. 154-159.

[5]Dallas Willard, "Getting Love Right." Paper presented at the American Association of Christian Counselors Conference, Nashville, TN, September 2007. Kindle location 106-111. Emphasis in original. Similarly, drawing upon Augustine, ethicist Oliver O'Donovan states that love is "an attitudinal disposition which gives rise to various actions without being wholly accounted for by any of them. ...Love, whatever actions it gives rise to, is contemplative in itself, rejoicing in the fact that its object is there,

not wanting to do anything 'with' it." See Oliver O'Donovan, *Common Objects of Love* (Grand Rapids: Eerdmans, 2002), Kindle location 145-148.

[6]Literally, "ten thousand talents." A talent was a measure of weight, not currency, so the actual debt is difficult to judge without knowing what coinage Jesus may have had in mind. The CEB estimates this as "wages for sixty million days," while the New Revised Standard Version (hereinafter, NRSV) estimates "more than fifteen years' wages" for a day laborer. We are not told how the servant came by such a large debt.

[7]In Joel 2:13 (quoted earlier), the phrase "very patient" is rendered "slow to anger" in the KJV. The corresponding verb is *makrothumeo*, a combination of *makros* (long) and *thumos* (temper, anger). Thus, in the KJV, the word is translated different ways in different contexts: "slow to anger" in Joel, "have patience" in the parable in Matthew 18, and "suffereth long" in Paul's love chapter (1 Cor 13:4).

[8]The verb *splagchnizomai* derives from the word for "bowels" or "innards," and is usually translated as a reaction of pity or compassion (see chapter 5, n. 19).

[9]Here, Jesus describes the amount as one hundred *denarii*. A *denarius* was a Roman coin typically paid for a day of manual labor. If we go by the CEB's estimate of the two debts, then, the ratio was 600,000:1.

[10]The words are not exactly the same. The first servant's plea translates from the Greek as, "Have patience with me, and *everything* I will pay back to you." The second servant's plea leaves out the word "everything." On the one hand, this may be nothing more than stylistic variation. On the other hand, the difference in wording may have to do with the difference in size of the two debts. Given the enormity of the first servant's debt, the promise to pay back everything may be a brash but unrealistic attempt to convince the king that he has matters under control.

[11]Lee, *Unexpected Blessing*, pp. 120-123.

[12]It is also possible to translate Jesus' response as "seventy times seven." But as we'll see in chapter 10, Jesus is not correcting Peter's number, but trying to startle him away from counting offenses.

[13]A similar interpretation could apply to Jesus' teaching in Matthew 6:14-15, immediately following the Lord's Prayer: "If you forgive others their sins, your heavenly Father will also forgive you. But if you don't forgive others, neither will your Father forgive your sins." The prayer is not merely an act of piety, but a daily reminder of our dependence upon God's mercy and our calling to extend that mercy to others.

[14]In the Greek, *chrēstotēs*. The citations from the Psalms that follow are from the Septuagint, from which Paul often quoted.

[15]See also Ps 65:11 and 85:12.

[16]The words translated in Rom 2:4 as "generosity" and "kindness"—*chrēstos* and *chrēstotēs*—are actually closely related words (see note 11 above). Here, the New International Version (hereinafter, NIV) and the NRSV render both as "kindness." I

suspect that the CEB elected to translate them differently in order to convey the word "kindness" as a more general, overarching idea. The word translated as "tolerance" (*anochē*) suggests the act of holding something back; in context, it suggests God holding back judgment and wrath (cf. Eph 2:3), and is thus a synonym for patience. The two words "patience" and "kindness" therefore sum up nicely the qualities Paul lists.

[17]E.g., as argued by Douglas J. Moo, *The Epistle to the Romans* (Grand Rapids: Eerdmans, 1996). There is clearly tension between Jewish and Gentile believers in the letter as a whole. The question is whether these verses in particular apply to the whole congregation or to the Jewish contingent specifically.

[18]John Chrysostom, *The Love Chapter*, p. 34. Emphasis in original.

[19]The saying is attributed to Bill McGlashen.

Chapter 8: Repent of Your Rivalries

[1]As quoted by Samantha M. Shapiro, "The Lives They Lived: Abigail Van Buren," *New York Times Magazine* 21 Dec 2013, paragraph 3. www.nytimes.com/news/the-lives-they-lived/2013/12/21/abigail-van-buren/.

[2]See, e.g., Beverly Beyette, "Columnists' Daughters Carry on the Feud," *Los Angeles Times* 28 June 2002. http://articles.latimes.com/2002/jun/28/news/lv-landerfeud28.

[3]Adele Faber and Elaine Mazlish, *Siblings without Rivalry* (New York: Avon, 1987).

[4]For other examples, see David E. Garland and Diana R. Garland, *Flawed Families of the Bible: How God's Grace Works through Imperfect Relationships* (Grand Rapids: Brazos, 2007).

[5]The CEB and NRSV both translate the description of the garment in Gen 37:3 as a "long" robe. In the Septuagint, the Greek translation of the Hebrew renders it as "many-colored." Whatever the nature of the robe itself, the Bible portrays it as an obvious mark of favoritism.

[6]E.g., Maria Miceli and Cristiano Castelfranchi, "The Envious Mind," *Cognition and Emotion* 21 (2007): 449-479.

[7]See, e.g., Michael Kingham and Harvey Gordon, "Aspects of morbid jealousy," *Advances in Psychiatric Treatment* 10 (2004): 207-215. Morbid jealousy is often accompanied by some form of mental illness. Indeed, it merits its own psychiatric diagnosis: "delusional disorder, jealous type." See American Psychiatric Association, *Diagnostic and Statistical Manual of Mental Disorders: DSM-5,* 5th ed. (Arlington: American Psychiatric Press, 2013).

[8]E.g., Niels van de Ven, "Envy and Admiration: Emotion and Motivation Following Upward Social Comparison," *Cognition and Emotion* 31 (2017): 193-200.

[9]As reported by the digital marketing site Zephoria.com. See https://zephoria.com/top-15-valuable-facebook-statistics/.

[10]E.g., Daniel Boorstin, *The Americans: The Democratic Experience* (New York: Vintage, 1974), chapter 42.

[11]Hui-Tzu Grace Chou and Nicholas Edge, "'They Are Happier and Having Better Lives than I Am': The Impact of Using Facebook on Perceptions of Others' Lives," *Cyberpsychology, Behavior, and Social Networking* 15 (2012): 117-121.

[12]See, e.g., Helmut Appel, Alexander L. Gerlach, and Jan Crusius, "The Interplay of Facebook Use, Social Comparison, Envy, and Depression," *Current Opinion in Psychology* 9 (2016): 44-49. The authors rightly caution that the causal links need to be more firmly established.

[13]The beginning of what is known as *social comparison theory* is attributed to psychologist Leon Festinger, "A Theory of Social Comparison Processes," *Human Relations* 7 (1954): 117-140.

[14]Festinger, "A Theory of Social Comparison Processes," pp. 117-118.

[15]Judith B. White, Ellen J. Langer, Leeat Yariv, and John C. Welch IV, "Frequent Social Comparisons and Destructive Emotions and Behaviors: The Dark Side of Social Comparisons," *Journal of Adult Development* 13 (2006): 36-44.

[16]On the matter of whether the other's good fortune is deserved, see Niels van de Ven, Marcel Zeelenberg, and Rik Pieters, "Appraisal Patterns of Envy and Related Emotions," *Motivation and Emotion* 36 (2012): 195-204. For a study of the role of the perception of control on the development of envy, see Maria Testa and Brenda Major, "The Impact of Social Comparisons After Failure: The Moderating Effects of Perceived Control," *Basic and Applied Social Psychology* 11 (1990): 205-218. As Testa and Major and others note, one can cope with the feelings of inferiority through *downward* social comparison, i.e., by seeing ourselves as more fortunate than someone else.

[17]The CEB and the NASB, for example, translate Paul as referring to "jealousy." The NRSV and NIV, however, translate the same word as "envy."

[18]The noun is *zelos*; the verb is *zeloō*.

[19]Various translations of the text render the verb differently. The CEB says, "Use your ambition to try to get the greater gifts," while the NRSV and NIV translate Paul as commanding the Corinthians to "strive for" or "eagerly desire" the greater gifts, respectively. But in no case is Paul translated as saying, "Be jealous for the greater gifts."

[20]The verb is *phusioō*, from the noun *phusa*, a bellows. When said out loud, the word *phusa* makes a sound like someone blowing air into a balloon.

[21]The verb translated as "brag" in 1 Corinthians 13:4—*perpereuomai*—is a rare one, appearing in that verse and nowhere else in the New Testament. The noun form refers to a braggart or show-off. Paul speaks of boasting often (e.g., 1 Cor 4:7, already cited), especially in 2 Corinthians; the word is *kauchaomai*, which refers to boasting or glorying. The fact that Paul would use the latter word so often suggests that

boasting must have been a significant problem. But as with the matter of rightly or wrongly directed zeal, Paul suggests that there are good and bad ways to boast.

[22]Russell P. Spittler, *The Corinthian Correspondence* (Springfield: Gospel Publishing House, 1976), p. 74.

Chapter 9: Look Out for Number Two

[1]Karen Ehman, *Listen, Love, Repeat: Other-Centered Living in a Self-Centered World* (Grand Rapids: Zondervan, 2016), pp. 49-50.

[2]David Kinnaman and Gabe Lyons, *unChristian: What a New Generation Really Thinks About Christianity* (Grand Rapids: Baker, 2007).

[3]David Kinnaman and Aly Hawkins, *You Lost Me* (Grand Rapids: Baker, 2011).

[4]Barrie's novel was first published in 1911, under the title *Peter and Wendy*. Today, it is generally reprinted under the more recognizable title of *Peter Pan*. Of the numerous film adaptations, probably the most iconic is still Disney's 1953 animated classic (*Peter Pan*, dir. Clyde Geronimi, Wilfred Jackson, Hamilton Luske, RKO Radio Pictures, 1953).

[5]*Hook*, dir. Steven Spielberg, TriStar, 1991.

[6]The verb translated as "to be rude" in 1 Corinthians 7:36 and 13:5 and is *aschēmoneō*, which is related to the word *schēma*, or "form." The adjective in 12:23 is *aschēmon*. In 12:24, Paul uses the opposite adjective, *euschēmon* (roughly, of good or proper form), to refer to the parts of the body that *are* presentable.

[7]John Chrysostom translates 1 Corinthians 13:5 as "love does not behave shamefully." See *The Love Chapter*, p. 37.

[8]That is one possible implication of what Paul writes in 1 Corinthians 6:12-20. "Food is for the stomach and the stomach is for food" may have been a slogan used by some in the church to argue that sex was a purely natural appetite and biological function, like eating. The argument, apparently, was combined with a rather libertine notion of Christian "freedom" and used to justify sexual immorality.

[9]The metaphor would have had special significance for Jews, to whom yeast was already a symbol of sin and corruption. Once a year, in obedience to God, they cleaned their homes of every trace of yeast in preparation for the Passover and the Feast of Unleavened Bread (e.g., Exod 13:7; Deut 16:3-4).

[10]Cameron Lee and Jack Balswick, *Life in a Glass House: The Minister's Family in its Unique Social Context* (Grand Rapids: Zondervan, 1989), pp. 48-53.

[11]It is possible that the person referred to in this passage is also the incestuous church member of 1 Corinthians 5.

[12]It is not entirely clear to what Paul is referring. He may have been thinking about a Jewish hope based on Daniel 7:22. See also Revelation 20:4.

[13]Mary Ann Glendon, *Rights Talk: The Impoverishment of Political Discourse* (New York: Free Press, 1991).

[14]See, e.g., Lee, *Beyond Family Values*, chapter 4.

[15]A more literal translation would be that love doesn't "seek its own things." The NRSV and NIV render Paul's phrase as "does not insist on its own way" and "is not self-seeking," respectively.

[16]For an example of the first position, see Wright, *Paul for Everyone: 1 Corinthians*, p. 136. For an example of the second, see Fee, *The First Epistle to the Corinthians*, pp. 483-484. Fee argues that Paul uses a specifically pagan word—*hierothyton*—to refer to the meat, and thus means us to understand that the speaker was not a Christian.

Chapter 10: Get Off the Merry-Go-Round

[1]The word is *paroxunō*.

[2]See, e.g., Acts 15:39, where the noun form is used to describe the argument between Paul and Barnabas. While the CEB translates that the argument became "intense," the NRSV and NIV both refer to a "sharp" disagreement.

[3]The verb *logizomai* means to reckon or consider.

[4]Paul's complete phrase is *ou logizetai to kakon*. The word *kakon* is a neuter, singular pronominal adjective; it means "bad" in a more general sense, though it sometimes takes on the stronger meaning of "evil" (for which the word *ponēros* is frequently used instead). Rendering *logizetai* in its more general sense, the KJV translates Paul as saying that love "thinketh no evil," meaning that love "doesn't think bad/evil thoughts." Contemporary translations, however, opt for the more specific meaning of keeping an account of the wrongs one has suffered personally. More simply, therefore, the NRSV simply translates that love "is not...resentful."

[5]Stephanie Van Goozen and Nico H. Frijda, "Emotion Words Used in Six European Countries," *European Journal of Social Psychology* 23 (1993): 89-95.

[6]*Inside Out*, dir. Pete Docter, Walt Disney Studios, 2015. In part, the story is based on the work of Paul Ekman, who argues for a limited set of basic emotions with universally recognizable facial signals (e.g., people the world over know an angry face when they see one) and distinctive physiological signatures. See, e.g., Paul Ekman, "Basic Emotions," in *Handbook of Cognition and Emotion*, ed. Tim Dalgleish and Mick J. Power (New York: Wiley, 1999), pp. 45-60. The idea of discrete basic emotions is still somewhat controversial.

[7]Paul Ekman, "What Scientists Who Study Emotion Agree About," *Perspectives on Psychological Science* 11 (2016): 31-34.

[8]Roy F. Baumeister, Ellen Bratslavsky, Catrin Finkenauer, and Kathleen D. Vohs, "Bad is Stronger than Good," *Review of General Psychology* 5 (2001): 323-370.

[9]The phenomenon is known as the "hedonic treadmill," a term originating with Philip Brickman and Donald T. Campbell, "Hedonic Relativism and Planning the Good Society," in *Adaptation Level Theory: A Symposium*, ed. Mortimer H. Appley (New York: Academic Press, 1971), pp. 287-302.

[10]Baumeister, et al., "Bad is Stronger than Good," p. 326.

[11]The story is told in the preface to Norman E. Rosenthal, *The Emotional Revolution* (New York: Citadel, 2002). And yes, the attackers were eventually caught.

[12]Ron and Sonja are a fictional couple.

[13]Fredrickson, *Positivity,* p. 164.

[14]Marriage researcher John Gottman calls this *negative sentiment override,* a state in which people become hypervigilant and hypersensitive. See John M. Gottman, *The Marriage Clinic: A Scientifically-Based Marital Therapy* (New York: Norton, 1999), pp. 164-165.

[15]Ronald Potter-Efron, *Healing the Angry Brain* (Oakland: New Harbinger, 2012), p. 134.

[16]The general idea of a relational merry-go-round has been variously described, e.g., the "Protest Polka" and "Demon Dialogues" in Johnson's *Hold Me Tight*, and the "vicious cycle" of Andrew Christensen and Neil S. Jacobson, *Reconcilable Differences* (New York: Guilford, 2000), pp. 114-118.

[17]For couples, see Terry Hargrave and Shawn Stoever, *5 Days to a New Marriage* (Amarillo: The Hideaway Foundation, 2011), chapter 1. For therapists, see Terry D. Hargrave and Franz Pfitzer, *Restoration Therapy* (New York: Routledge, 2011), chapter 7.

[18]For a review of the research, see Fredrickson, *Positivity*, chapter 7. In his research, John Gottman finds that the "magic ratio" of positivity to negativity in stable marriages is 5:1. See, e.g., John Gottman, *Why Marriages Succeed or Fail* (New York: Simon & Schuster, 1994), pp. 56-61.

[19]Fredrickson, *Positivity*, pp. 165-166.

[20]As mentioned in chapter 2, this is the basic idea behind Fredrickson's broaden-and-build theory.

[21]Gottman, *Why Marriages Succeed or Fail*, pp. 59-61.

[22]Laura B. Luchies, Jennifer Wieselquist, Caryl E. Rusbult, Madoka Kumashiro, Paul W. Eastwick, Michael K. Coolsen, and Eli J. Finkel, "Trust and Biased Memory of Transgressions in Romantic Relationships," *Journal of Personality and Social Psychology* 104 (2013): 673-694.

[23]John M. Gottman, *The Science of Trust* (New York: Norton, 2011), p. 339, emphasis in original.

[24]Leon Morris, *The First and Second Epistle to the Thessalonians*, rev. ed. (Grand Rapids: Eerdmans, 1991), p. 171.

[25]Robert A. Emmons, *Thanks! How Practicing Gratitude Can Make You Happier* (Boston: Houghton Mifflin, 2007), p. 46.

[26]Emmons, *Thanks!*, p. 203.

[27]Emmons, *Thanks!*, pp. 189-191.

[28]Emmons, *Thanks!*, pp. 191-192.

[29]Corrie ten Boom, *The Hiding Place*, 35th anniversary ed. (Grand Rapids: Chosen, 2006), p. 227.

[30]Ten Boom, *The Hiding Place*, pp. 247-248.

[31]Corrie ten Boom, "Guideposts Classics: Corrie ten Boom on Forgiveness," originally published November 1972. See https://www.guideposts.org/better-living/positive-living/guideposts-classics-corrie-ten-boom-on-forgiveness?nopaging=1.

[32]Ten Boom, "Corrie ten Boom on Forgiveness." A similar story appears in Corrie ten Boom, *Tramp for the Lord* (New York: Jove, 1974), pp. 179-180, in which she is the one giving the advice to a young Flemish woman concerned about lust and temptation.

Chapter 11: Celebrate the Gospel

[1]The word is *chairō*.

[2]The two cities are known respectively as Syrian Antioch and Pisidian Antioch.

[3]The word is *adikia*. See, for example, Romans 1:29-32 for a sweeping list of sins headed by *adikia* (which the CEB translates again as "injustice").

[4]Bailey, *Paul Through Mediterranean Eyes*, p. 374.

[5]David A. DaSilva, *An Introduction to the New Testament: Contexts, Methods, and Ministry Formation* (Downers Grove: InterVarsity, 2004), p. 556.

[6]"Injustice" and "wickedness" are both translations of *adikia*, the same word used in 1 Corinthians 13:6.

[7]It should be noted that the word translated here as "happy with" is not the same one found in 1 Corinthians 13:6; *eudokeō* means "to be pleased with" rather than "to rejoice." The point, however, is in the contrast between truth and injustice, between the gospel and unrighteousness.

[8]The second verb is *synchairō*, which adds the prefix "*syn-*" or "with" to the original verb.

[9]Only in the first parable is it actually said that the person who finds "rejoices," and the verbs *chairō* and *synchairō* are missing altogether from the third parable. The linked themes of joy and communal celebration, however, are clear throughout.

[10]The dining area was known as the *triclinium*, so named for the arrangement of the three couches on which people would recline to eat. That room might accommodate

at most a dozen people, including the host's family and the most prestigious of the guests. Everyone else would have to gather in the *atrium* or entrance hall.

[11]The institution of slavery was crucial to the Roman Empire and thus a widely accepted practice. Many were highly educated captives taken in Roman conquests, and served important functions in the household, such as the training and education of Roman children.

[12]O'Donovan, *Common Objects of Love*, Kindle location 194. Emphasis in original.

[13]Again, to quote O'Donovan: "Loving *things*, not loving *one another*. ...The love that founds the community is not reciprocal, but turned outward upon an object" (*Common Objects of Love*, Kindle location 216-217). That is not to say, of course, that relationship seminars are unhelpful or unnecessary. But in O'Donovan's view, the mutuality of love within the community must be a secondary outgrowth of a shared primary love for the gospel.

[14]Barna Group, "New Marriage and Divorce Statistics Released," March 31, 2008, https://www.barna.com/research/new-marriage-and-divorce-statistics-released/#. Note that there are different ways to calculate divorce rates. Barna's method in this study is to conduct a telephone survey of a large random sample of adults, ask who has been married and who has been divorced, and report the percentage of those who have been married and divorced by demographic group. The results indicated that 33% of American adults who have been married have also been divorced. The rates for "born-again Christians," "non-born again Christians," and "Evangelical Christians" were 32%, 33%, and 26% respectively. Respondents are not asked to self-identify as "born-again," etc., but are classified by their answers to questions of personal and doctrinal belief.

[15]See, e.g., Bradley R. E. Wright, *Christians are Hate-Filled Hypocrites...and Other Lies You've Been Told* (Bloomington: Bethany House, 2010), chapter 6. It should also be noted, however, that the divorce rate that Wright reports for religiously affiliated people, on the basis of the General Social Survey, is hardly cause for celebration: 42% as opposed to 50% for the unaffiliated, and 46% for Evangelicals. Cohabitation and divorce rates among Evangelicals have been rising in recent decades.

Chapter 12: Love Story

[1]The phrase is uttered by the character of Mrs. White, played by the late comic actress Madeline Kahn in *Clue* (dir. Jonathan Lynn, Paramount Pictures, 1985), based on the classic board game. Controversially, in 2014, pop icon Cher posted a variation of the saying on her Facebook page, substituting the word "men" for "husbands."

[2]This is John Gottman's notion of "perpetual problems." What matters for the stability of the marriage is not the fact that a couple disagrees, but the emotional quality of their disagreement. Gottman, *The Marriage Clinic*, pp. 96-104.

[3]Caryl Rusbult and her colleagues, for example, have studied the relationship of

forgiveness and commitment. Commitment is described as having three parts: the intent to persist in a relationship, emotional attachment, and a long-term orientation in understanding. They discovered that the mere intent to persist was the part of commitment that was most strongly related to people's willingness to forgive in the face of the betrayal of relationship norms. See Eli J. Finkel, Caryl E. Rusbult, Madoka Kumashiro, and Peggy A. Hannon, "Dealing with Betrayal in Close Relationships: Does Commitment Promote Forgiveness?" *Journal of Personality and Social Psychology* 82 (2002): 956-974.

[4]Transliterated, the phrase is "...*panta stegei, panta pisteuei, panta elpizei, panta hupomenei.*" The NIV tries to preserve Paul's brevity and staccato rhythm: "always protects, always trusts, always hopes, always perseveres." Note that *panta,* which means "all things," is technically the object of the verb in all four cases, as in the CEB's "puts up with all things," etc. But as Gordon Fee notes, the "rhetorical repetition...comes very close to an adverbial use ('in everything,' or 'always')" (Fee, *The First Epistle to the Corinthians*, p. 639). Hence the NIV's use of the adverb "always," as a way of saying "*in* all things."

[5]The CEB and Eugene Peterson's *The Message* have the more colloquial "puts up with"; the NRSV, New American Standard, and New King James have "bears"; the NIV reads "protects." Note that N. T. Wright also translates the verb *stego* as "bears." See Wright, *1 Corinthians*, p. 170.

[6]C. K. Barrett, *The First Epistle to the Corinthians* (New York: Harper & Row, 1968), p. 304.

[7]The noun is *stege.* See also Matthew 8:8 and Luke 7:6, in which the centurion declares that he doesn't deserve to have Jesus come under his roof, i.e., to have Jesus enter his house.

[8]Bailey, *Paul Through Mediterranean Eyes*, pp. 376-377. Though Bailey insists that we are not obligated to choose among the possibilities, some combination of covering and keeping confidences is the rendering he prefers.

[9]Some scholars, like Barrett (*The First Epistle to the Corinthians*, p. 304), shy away from this translation because it is too close in meaning and proximity to the fourth verb (see note 11 below), arguing that such repetition is unlikely. It is also possible, however, to argue that such repetition is used intentionally as a rhetorical device; Fee (*The First Epistle to the Corinthians*, p. 639), for example, suggests that the four verbs are arranged in a chiastic structure.

[10]See, e.g., 2 Corinthians 11:7-11. Paul doesn't want to "burden" the Corinthians with his needs, and is willing to receive financial support from the Macedonians to help make this possible. Whatever his reasons, in verse 11 he states clearly that he does this out of love.

[11]The verbs, respectively, are *pisteuo, elpizo,* and *hupomeno.* The corresponding nouns—"faith," "hope," and "endurance"—are *pistis, elpis,* and *hupomone.* While the verb *meno* means to "remain" or "abide," *hupomeno* is a stronger word that means to

"remain *under*," and thus can carry the sense of patiently enduring suffering without running away.

[12]John Stott, *Romans: God's Good News for the World* (Downers Grove: InterVarsity Press, 1994), p. 142.

[13]The verb is *excheō*, "to pour out": in both Acts 10:45 and Titus 3:6, it is the Spirit who is poured out upon believers.

[14]Gordon Neufeld and Gabor Maté, *Hold Onto Your Kids* (New York: Ballantine, 2014), Kindle location 2117. The book insists on the centrality of what is known as the *attachment* relationship, and argues that much of what ails the younger generation stems from being more attached to their peers than to their parents.

[15]The verb is *piptō*.

[16]The word here, in the Septuagint, is not *piptō*, but *ptōsis*.

[17]Bailey, *Paul Through Mediterranean Eyes*, pp. 379-380.

[18]*Love Story,* dir. Arthur Hiller, Paramount, 1970. As of this writing, the film ranks ninth on the American Film Institute's list of the 100 "greatest love stories." See "AFI's 100 Years...100 Passions," http://www.afi.com/100Years/ passions.aspx.

[19]The phrase ranks thirteenth on AFI's list of top 100 movie quotes. See "AFI's 100 Years...100 Movie Quotes," http://www.afi.com/100Years/quotes.aspx.

[20] *What's Up Doc?,* dir. Peter Bogdanovich, Warner Bros., 1972. With its main characters, the movie appears to pay loving tribute to the Katharine Hepburn/Cary Grant screwball classic, *Bringing up Baby* (dir. Howard Hawks, RKO, 1938). As of this writing, the two films rank 68th and 51st respectively on AFI's "100 Passions" list.

Made in the USA
San Bernardino, CA
04 May 2020

70218557R00146